BLACK PRESIDENTIAL POLITICS
IN AMERICA

SUNY SERIES IN AFRO-AMERICAN STUDIES
John Howard and Robert C. Smith, Editors

Ronald W. Walters

BLACK PRESIDENTIAL POLITICS IN AMERICA

A Strategic Approach

STATE UNIVERSITY OF NEW YORK PRESS

Published by
State University of New York Press

© 1988 Ronald W. Walters

For information, address State University of New York
Press, State University Plaza, Albany, N.Y., 12246

Library of Congress Cataloging-in-Publication Data

Walters, Ronald W.
      Black presidential politics in America.

      (SUNY series in Afro-American studies)
      Bibliography: p.
      Includes index.
      1. Afro-Americans--Suffrage--History. 2. Presidents--
United States--Election--History. I. Title. II. Series.
JK1924.W34   1987   324.6'2'08996073   86-30160
ISBN 0-88706-546-5
ISBN 0-88706-547-3 (pbk.)

10 9 8 7 6 5 4 3 2

To Pat
For her help in making these
experiences and the book realities.

Contents

Tables and Figures

Preface

This work represents the culmination of fourteen years of serious study and active involvement in presidential-level politics. Nevertheless, the necessity I have felt to write a political history of that period is only partially resolved in this brief account of such phenomena as the 1972 Gary convention, the National Black Political Assembly and its subsequent Black Independent Party formation, the Black Democratic Caucus and its various conventions, and the 1984 presidential campaign of Rev. Jesse Jackson. Rather, I have attempted to distill these experiences in an effort to understand the *essential strategy* with which the Black leadership has approached the task of obtaining favorable results for Black participation in presidential politics.

Surveying the record of participation in the process of presidential selection by Blacks, as a strategist, was an exhilarating experience, since so much of it covered important, though forgotten, events in the political landscape of the nineteenth and twentieth centuries. More recently, however, the overt concern with strategy began to crystalize with the emergence, in the early 1970s, of a substantial group of Black elected officials who were fresh with hope that they might foment great changes. Yet it was also sobering to have arrived at this era of heightened political gamesmanship in the 1980s provoked by new conservative ideologies, operatives, tactics and strategies with which the Black community now has to contend in the task of achieving its objectives.

In writing this book, I have had to confront the dual reality of my role as an activist and scholar, and often, in order to preserve the integrity of those roles, I have had to make a deliberate self-commitment either to be fully engaged as a partisan in the activity at hand, or to be basically a student of those events. Although I did, at times, select and maintain one role exclusively, I believe that just as the exposure to actual political events has helped to enrich my theoretical observations, my academic productivity was also useful in the technical roles I have played in various political settings. Thus, this work is not that of a "detached" scholar, but rather one of a committed scholar who also believes that truth is possible to attain from within a social phenomenon as well as from a distance.

For example, I was involved in the Gary convention of 1972 as a member of the Platform Committee, eventually helping to draft the "Agenda," indeed, helping to draft many national Black agendas up until 1984. In the 1974 Little Rock convention, I was invited to lead a workshop on electoral politics, and subsequently became active in the National Black Political Assembly (NBPA) as a member of its Political Council. In 1975, I drafted the '76 Presidential Strategy memorandum of the NBPA and participated as an observer in the 1976 Cincinnati convention. The NBPA politics culminated in 1980 with the development of the National Black Independent Political Party, and I served as chair of the Charter Commission which produced its first constitution. I took no further part in the organization after 1982.

With respect to the Democratic party, in 1973, I was a volunteer consultant to the Black Democratic Caucus in the construction of Article 10 of the Democratic party Charter, and I participated in the Charlotte (N.C.) convention of 1976 as a leader of the international affairs section, and in the Richmond conference of 1980 as an observer. I was a participant in the June 1983 Black leadership meeting in Chicago which approved the Black presidential strategy and was subsequently a member of Rev. Jackson's "exploratory committee."

At the same time, in 1976, as director of the Social Science Research Center, in the Institute of Urban Affairs and Research at Howard University, I initiated and directed a survey of Black delegates to the Democratic and Republican National Conventions (see Appendix) and "participant observation" at the 1976 and 1980 Democratic Conventions (staff also attended the Republican Conventions in those years). This research project continues to conduct presidential-election-year surveys of Black party convention delegates. Our study in 1976 was supported by a grant from the Ford

Foundation and additional support has been obtained from the Faculty Research Fund of the Office of the Vice President for Academic Affairs, and the Graduate School of Arts and Sciences at Howard University.

In January 1984, I accepted the position of Deputy Campaign Manager for Issues (and Political Strategy) in the presidential campaign of Rev. Jesse Jackson. This was a broad responsibility which entailed such tasks as preparing basic campaign policy positions, candidate briefings for televised debates and general issue positions, responding to the press and public requests for issue guidance, directing the campaign platform, rules and convention issue strategy, and other delegated tasks. Through this activity I had an unusual opportunity to develop insights into presidential election politics, and to assess the relative potentialities of dependent and independent politics within the Democratic party coalition. Thus, I reached critical conclusions regarding whether such a strategy — which I had previously written about in 1976 — enhanced Black power or the ability to achieve certain concrete political objectives.

The primary concern of this study with strategy distinguishes it from others in the field of Black politics. I have endeavored to analyze how effectively Black political leaders have implemented the theory of the "balance of power," as a belief about the potency of the Black vote which has occasionally realized its potential in national elections. It was discovered that electoral theory had guided Black participation in presidential elections since early in the nineteenth century, but it was also enlightening to discover the dichotomy between dependent and independent tactics and strategies and the tenacity with which independent positions proposed by progressive activists have historically been resisted by practical politicians. Although the concept of the "balance of power" has often materialized as a fact in national elections, to the extent that it has done so by chance, the content has amounted to more philosophy than strategy. Those who have attempted to consciously implement the philosophy have relied upon the uncertainties of voter registration and turnout in an effort for the Black vote to become the "margin of victory," putting Black leaders into a position to make policy claims upon a winning president, according to the extant pattern of party allegiance.

My attempt to understand the vulnerabilities implicit in the implementation of the "balance of power" concept stems, on the one hand, from an academic concern with strategies of Black politics in general, but on the other, from my assessment that there has been a diminishing yield in concrete gains from Black participation in presidential politics. Thus the critical moment for such a study is now, when the Democratic party coalition appears to be entering a watershed of history, attempting to readjust its liberal social welfare legacy of the New Deal to the more conservative political and economic trends of the 1980s and 1990s. In response, the constituent elements of the Democratic party coalition have sought to respond in ways which range from the attempt to preserve the objectives for which they originally entered the coalition, to accommodation to the new environment. Then, as many Black leaders view this problem, since their original objectives for entering the party coalition have not been fully satisfied, the shifting policy and political positions of the leadership risk serious intra-party conflict over new directions and possibly even a serious rupture of future relations.

This study has concluded that among the possible responses, Blacks should consider achieving greater organization of their political resources (votes, funds, mobilizational skills, issues, etc.) in an effort to acquire the flexibility and strength which increase their competitive position. This view challenges previous assumptions of political behavior by recognizing the arena *within* the coalition to be a legitimate theater for implementation of the "balance of power" concept. As such, the basis of organization within the party is challenged, since Blacks are encouraged to complement political integration strategies with autonomous organization. As a logical by-product, it also raises the question, "What if intra-party scenarios fail, are there logical and effective options for the exercise of strategy in inter-party scenarios?" The answer provided here is that antonomous political organization provides the flexibility to select voting or non-voting options either inside or outside of the party coalition.

The case for organizing Black political resources does not rest entirely upon logic, but was patently evident in the 1984 campaign of Rev. Jesse Jackson for the Democratic nomination for president. This campaign created a considerable opportunity to bridge the gap between philosophy and strategy by illustrating what could be achieved within a party through legitimizing the instrument of a presidential campaign. I have argued that the racial differences within American society which have created a "Black politics" demand that the Jackson campaign cannot be viewed in traditional terms. In this sense, the first unique factor of this campaign was its organizing role in the development of political resources and in directing them toward a given objective. The second critical factor was that this organized resource facilitated the creation of enhanced bargaining scenarios at each stage of the presidential selection process, which I have referred to as the "three-ballot scenario" of the primaries, the convention, and the general election. The third factor was the existence of the potential for acquiring favorable returns from political participation, a potential that was only partially realized.

The writer, therefore, has not attempted more than a brief summation of the Jackson campaign in an effort to extract from it the essential elements for developing the intellectual criteria for understanding it and other such dynamics. These criteria, as they have emerged from this study, presuppose an understanding of the demographic configuration of the Black vote, the dynamics of Black electoral elite intra-party interaction, the basis of Black political mobilization, the limits of coalition politics, as well as the institutional factors involved in any election campaign. Thus, the distinction between this study and others which seek to evaluate the Jackson campaign's impact upon the larger political scene through the perspectives of traditional political institutions and actors, is the difference between addresssing phenomenological considerations and exploring the *systematic* potential of a strategy designed to enhance group goals.

This examination has, therefore, been concerned with clarifying the distinction between dependent and independent strategies and the functional advantages of each. Dependence upon membership within a major party coalition has generally provided the context for the implementation of the "balance of power" theory. However, this study illustrates that such tactics and strategies are implicated in the low yield from political participation at the national level. This is especially serious since, as an historically subordinated minority group, the investment of Blacks in national elections has been generally designed to achieve tangible policy results which assume the existence of a linkage between participation, public policy commitment and administrative policy execution. Perhaps, in the current period with the apparent conservative ideological realignment producing such deleterious consequences for the Black community, scholars, politicians and other leaders will be tempted to re-evaluate the electoral strategies utilized by Blacks and other minority groups in America which assume that dependence is the way to achieve political power.

While it is standard, in the production of a work such as this, to say that although others have contributed to it the writer bears sole responsibility for the results, it is also true that there is a sense of collective responsibility for this product, such that I have only a vague sense of the distinction. In a sense, history has helped write this book, and thus, I would like to share a few of the names of those whom I view as somewhat culpable, either directly or indirectly. They have helped me to answer the question, "What is this politics for, especially to a people situated as we are in the American social order?". In the early stages of the writing and active involvement, I would like to thank Chuck Stone, Ron Daniels, William Strickland, James Turner, and Imamu Baraka for helping me to understand the logic and ultimate grassroots utility of national elections; Mayor Richard Hatcher whose leadership has been a model for Democratic party activists; Frank Cowan who helped me to understand the inner-workings of the Democratic party; Congressmen Walter Fauntroy and Charles Diggs for inviting me to serve the larger Black community in various capacities; and Congressman John Conyers for involving me in his 1970s "Skyline Dialogs" on presidential election year politics; and a special thanks to Rev. Jesse Jackson for being himself, for daring to take on the burdens he has assumed, and for providing a political scientist with the rare opportunity to place his hands on the process of presidential politics. In 1985, I was awarded a Fellowship from the Rockefeller Foundation which enabled me to take a Fall semester leave from Howard and complete the balance of the writing of this manuscript. I greatly appreciate the responsiveness of Bruce Williams, Assistant Director of Equal Opportunity at Rockefeller in facilitating my attempt to make the best use of the Fellowship. My association with the Princeton University Afro-American Studies Program, arranged by its Director, Professor Howard Taylor, that Fall gave me access to a fine research library and much-needed time away from Washington, DC.

I owe a boundless debt of gratitude to Dr. Robert Smith, Professor of Political Science at Howard University, an accomplished and prolific colleague, who encouraged me to include this book in the Black Politics series of which he is co-editor at SUNY Press, with Professor John Howard of SUNY Purchase, and who, together with the anonymous reviewers, raised many questions in the editing process which helped to make this a better work. Michelle Martin, former editor at SUNY, assumed well the initial responsibility of sheparding the rough manuscript through the press. The many opportunities to evaluate political trends with friends and colleagues such as Professors C. Vernon Gray, William Nelson, Ron Bailey, Harold Cruse and Ernest Wilson, Jr. have been extremely helpful. I would also like to note the persistence and professionalism of Dr. Diane Brown in accomplishing the many research tasks associated with the Howard University Black Delegate Survey, and the enthusiasm of graduate students Jerry Ravenell and Brenda Brittain and others in the early stages. Also, as I review this work, it is apparent that had the Joint Center for Political Studies not existed, there would have been even more significant gaps in the information available to produce such a study. The information they have developed through the years has been of considerable value to practitioners, strategists and students of Black politics. Over the years some of the articles cited in this work were published in *The Black Scholar*, a popular journal of Black studies. For providing me with an early opportunity to develop aspects of the theory of independent-leverage and for its sheer existence, the publication has meant a great deal to me and to many other Black scholars as well. Then, my department has an outstanding collection of faculty in the Black Politics field, and I thank my colleagues and students for providing me with the sounding board to test many of these concepts. Finally, I have dedicated this work to my wife Pat, who also lived in her own way, many of the experiences to which I have referred, and who suffered my theoretical formulations, encouraged me to keep writing, and who read and helped to edit the final drafts. I will always be grateful for her dedication.

Chapter 1

The Evolution of Black
Electoral Theory

INTRODUCTION

One important aspect among the several activities I collectively consider to be "presidential politics" is the process of selecting the individual and, by extension, the political party, which comes to hold national office and, thus, will play a vital role in shaping public policy for the nation. Although the presidential election itself is decisive, other stages of the process such as the party primaries, the party conventions, and state and local politics, all play an important role, and thus, belong in the definition of "presidential selection."[1]

Therefore, we seek to examine the ways in which Blacks participate in the various phases of the process of presidential selection, based upon the assumption that the Black presence has provoked dynamic and yet enigmatic social interactions in this area as in other aspects of American life. In fact, the Black presence has often been decisive in determining the outcome of presidential elections. Nevertheless, the occasional salience of the Black vote leads one to ask two vital questions: Has the strategic role of the Black vote served to secure Black public policy interests and goals as the political participation of other cohesive groups has done? This, in turn, leads to the attendant question of whether or not Blacks (and other non-white minorities), who have occupied a different place in the social structure than other groups within a racially stratified social system, and who, consequently, have different goals, are able to utilize political participation in the same manner as the composite of these groups—the white majority.

These theoretical questions compel us to note that much of what has survived as political philosophy is devoted to an analysis of the "good society" and the democratic principles of order upon which it is based. One such principle is that in a society which pretends to employ democratic practices, the vote of a citizen contributes to the establishment of *legitimate* decisions by the adherence of other citizens to those decisions through their voluntary "consent," even though some may not have originally voted in favor of them. Some philosophers have rationalized this result by arguing that in the mythical "state of nature" the a priori consent of an individual to government adds to the collective expression of the "general will," a legitimizing force that is reflected in the authority given to a majority vote. This is the derivation of the principle that the majority rules. Consent to this principle involves the ultimate subordination of private judgment to public judgment, but as Tussman has said:

> If, then, the agreement which constitutes a body politic in-
> volves the subordination of private judgment to public judg-
> ment, and if the public judgment is directed at the public in-
> terest there is also a significant subordination of private
> interest.[2]

Hobbes, for example, believed it necessary that the general will should be established by such a voluntary act even though it often worked to the detriment of the individual who was part of a minority in a losing vote rather than in the majority. In this way, he argued, an individual developed an obligation to society and ulti-mately to its governmental apparatus, the state. This was reciprocal, in the sense that, as he gave up absolute freedoms through acquiring social membership, he also gained the protection of society through the rights protected by the state.

One assumes, then, that it is the function of government to pro-tect the individual from decisions which have a deleterious effect upon one's interests because that person has assented to recognize the majority will (ignoring for the moment the process through which assent is derived) as the legitimate expression of the general will. It becomes, then, the basis of the social contract that, as Rosseau has said, all of the characteristics of the general will come to reside in the will of the majority.[3]

William Bluhm suggests an interpretation by which we understand the harmony implicit in this arrangement: "In other words community is so strong that the opposition between majority and minority can be understood as a mere technical disagreement as to how best to serve the common end which all desire, not as a clash of interest."[4] However, since we know many disagreements to be, in fact, disputes over interests, what happens to the "strength of society," to the legitimacy of majority decisions and ultimately to the general will under such circumstances?

I submit that the general will in America is flawed, not only at this moment in history, but that it has always been flawed by the inability of a significant segment of society to "consent" on a fair and voluntary basis. As is well known, slavery mitigated the voluntary inclusion of Blacks into society, and continuing injustices have robbed the substance of consent of its full measure of impact and meaning. Thus, if the dictum is accurate that "governments derive their *just* powers from the consent of the governed" in a democratic system, since the role of Blacks in society has always involved an imperfect process of consent, there has concomitantly remained a question regarding the degree to which decisions of authoritative entities in any given case were just. The social turmoil caused by the fact that because of white subordination Blacks have been substantially trapped outside of the process of consent by their role and status is theoretically addressed by Rosseau, who felt that the thing which made the member of a minority on the losing side of a vote accept the will of the majority as legitimate was the pre-conditioned existence of an equalitarian basis of society. The clear presumption of this pre-condition was that there was no *permanent* minority.

The cost of social (permanent racial minority) status based upon an imperfect social contract for Blacks is that rarely has it been possible to participate in crucial decisions such as the selection of national leadership in a manner which reflects the "interests" of Blacks (interests defined here as both racial preference and race-related issue preference) through what is called "sincere" or "straightforward" voting.[5] Since even though Blacks constitute nearly 15% of the American population, they are largely reduced to "strategic voting" for candidates who may often not represent their interests. This is not a problem peculiar to Blacks only, but given the depths of their historic alienation from society based on their near-permanent minority status it is considered here to be a more profound problem. Indeed, the source of the profundity of such alienation may be understood by the fact that, because of their subordinate status, Blacks have often been part of a winning coalition in a presidential election, and even then, have not had their policy interests satisfied by subsequent presidential actions.

This situation, largely unexamined in its objective form, has probably contributed historically as much as any other factor to depressing Black political participation along with the more well-known patterns of exclusion. Studies have focused on responses derived from questions regarding "trust in government" by Blacks and whites in an effort to identify the comparative rates of alienation which contribute to lower or higher levels of political efficacy and political participation. But few have contrasted these scores with responses to the level of "trust in the process by which government is selected" in order to measure the relative depth of commitment to the general will and the process by which it is legitimized.

These questions might all rest comfortably in the realm of theory were it not for the evidence that there are real costs (to society) associated with an imperfect social contract. For example, the failure of Blacks and other minorities to have regular access to an effective vehicle of legitimate decision-making exacerbates the differential in status and in perspective between Blacks and whites to the point of serious social cleavage. This has been illustrated by a series of recent elections, beginning in 1968, ending with the racial differences in the vote in the 1984 presidential elections where, the "objective minority" on the losing side of the vote also has largely included the Black racial minority. In 1984, the result was that 65% of whites voted for Ronald Reagan while 85% of Blacks voted for Walter Mondale. The first period of such a phenomenon began, however, in 1877 when both white Republicans and Democrats turned their backs on the recently emancipated class of Black slaves. Likewise, this second period appears to be following a similar course of events, reflecting a wide disparity between Blacks and whites over presidential pre-ference.

Nevertheless, since the white majority is in control of the major political institutions and of the decisions which move them to per-form, then I agree with T. H. Green who, writing on Rosseau, says:

> It is a fault of the state if this conception (of a common good maintained by law) fails to make him (the individual) a loyal subject, if not an intelligent patriot. It is a sign that the state is not a true state; that it is not fulfilling its primary function

of maintaining law equally in the interest of all, but is being
administered in the interest of classes; whence it follows that
the obedience which, if not rendered willingly, the state com-
pels the citizen to render, is not one that he feels any spontan-
eous interest in rendering, because it does not present itself
to him as the condition of the maintenance of those rights
and interests, common to himself with his neighbors, which
he understands.[6]

Government, of course has a responsibility to provide the leadership
necessary for the establishment of the equalitarian character of society through which the "classes" come to feel that since they are *occasionally* the minority, the decisions of the majority are legitimate. If
government abdicates such responsibility, then a climate of group
conflict is substituted for one of social harmony and the perception of
the necessity of social change by the minority becomes more intense.
Thus, in circumstances where a social (racial) minority such as
Blacks is consistently part of the (objective) losing minority, the
political strategies of the minority should become as competitive as
possible in order to influence vital decisions affecting their status.

In any case, what we derive from the foregoing discussion is a
frame of reference which allows us to view the politics of society from
the perspective of the minority, raising both questions of the correct
description of its political situation and clarifying its strategies. This
perspective questions whether or not it may be possible for Blacks to
satisfy their interests by formulating strategies which have the
capacity to intervene more effectively in the process by which the official majority concensus (or the general will) is established. I will go
on to summarize the historical situations in which Blacks have
resorted to "strategic voting" to influence the general will in the process of presidential selection.

The Evolution of Black Electoral Theory

Not long after the founding of the nation, free Blacks and their
white allies sought the establishment of civil rights and, more
urgently, the abolition of slavery as their primary agenda. The question of whether to turn to institutionalized "politics" was settled by
the use of both strategies of "moral suasion" and electoral politics
toward these ends. Nevertheless, it is striking that many of the questions concerning the strategic use of the vote that began in this era
have persisted to this very day, such as whether to support the two

major parties or a third party. This consideration was all the more critical since the Black vote was not large. Blacks, having been disenfranchised in sixteen states by 1840, voted only in such Northeastern states as Maine, New Hampshire, Vermont, Massachusetts, and with property qualifications in Rhode Island and New York.[7] Even in these states racial intimidation meant that Black turnout at the polls was low.

In 1840, the question was raised regarding whether or not Blacks should support the Liberty party, composed of abolitionists and their supporters. The practical politicans within the Black community took various points of view such as; by supporting one of the major parties Blacks could become the "balance of power" between them, thus gaining respect in matters of policy; that even though this posture would have Blacks vote for "the lesser of two evils . . . [it would] . . . prevent a greater evil"; that the moral virtue of the abolitionists' cause could be preserved better through supporting the status quo than through a politics which threatened it; and, finally, that since the Liberty party was bound to be in the minority, a vote for it would be to "throw ones vote away."[8] This inclusive position was also supported by those who found the option of third party voting to be against their struggle to legitimize the right to vote at all. Most of those who supported this view, consequently, voted for the Whig party.

On the other hand, those who championed the Liberty party, such as Henry Highland Garnett and John Mercer Langston, counseled others to support it out of "principle," in order to establish an anti-slavery standard for the nation. For example, at the 1843 National Negro Convention it was argued both that the anti-slavery cause was hurt by the strategy of voting for either of the major parties (since both were committed to slavery) or by not voting at all. Thus, the only correct alternative became support of the Liberty party. Nevertheless, most Blacks had gravitated to the more populist Free Soil party in 1848, with an odd mixture of those from other parties who supported the Wilmot Proviso and who, consequently, considered slavery legal where it existed, but opposed its expansion to the new territories.

The Liberty party had attracted 7,069 votes in 1840 and 63,000 in 1844, but Blacks were partially seduced to join the Free Soilers because it had attracted some of the abolitionists, and its increased political potential amounted to 261,000 votes in 1848.[9] This same practical logic of coalition politics had led Blacks and their supporters to support the Republican party by 1856 when the Free Soil effort failed, but it also yielded the ambiguous political consequences expressed by Frederick Douglass: ". . . it was possible to be both 'antislavery' and anti-Negro, to proclaim both free soil and white supremacy. 'Opposing slavery and hating its victims has come to be a very common form of abolitionism'."[10]

With the instrument of politics yielding uncertain and often contradictory results to those desired, there appeared no course left to abolitionists in 1860 save the increasing resort to force as the highest form of politics to achieve their ends. In the post–Civil War years, Blacks would have somewhat greater success, yet the returns from the balance of power strategy were still inconsistent. In an extremely useful and exemplary collection of documents, Professor Charles Hamilton sought to portray the range of electoral strategies which Blacks had formulated with respect to elections in the period 1912–1948. He accurately prefaces these documents with the following observation:

> This has been a dilemma throughout the Black experience:
> . . . on the one hand, to advocate political involvement in
> institutions deliberately designed to disappoint and therefore
> lead possibly to alienation and withdrawal on the part of
> Blacks; on the other hand, to counsel non-participation and
> non-cooperation with no acceptable alternative and therefore
> lead possibly to a vacuum and alienation. From Reconstruc-
> tion on, this has been the unenviable role of black leaders —
> i.e., to chart a course that avoids these results and at the
> same time to engage in political action calculated to bring
> about some meaningful benefits.[11]

Although Hamilton suggests that this situation has been the histor-ical setting for the challenges of Black electoral leadership, at no time were there more challenges than those presented by what Howard University Professor Rayford Logan has called "The Nadir," or that period at the turn of the century when the negative consensus on Black progress was reflected in the attitudes and activities of both major political parties.

Indeed, a considerable body of Black political theory developed in the crucible created by the Republican party's rejection of respon-sibility for the political fortunes of Blacks after the Hayes-Tilden Bargain of 1877 and the Democratic party's rapacious conquest to restore their hegemony over Black lives in the South. As an example, by 1901, all of the Black members of Congress had been eliminated through the resurrection of white power in the South, as the northern Republicans acquiesced in the political disenfranchisement of Blacks through the new constitutions promulgated by southern legislatures and implemented by economic and political intimidation, physical violence and the terrorism of the Ku Klux Klan.

The most salient reason for the use of political terrorism and military tactics by the white South was that Blacks were a barrier to the restoration of its power. As such, they had to be eliminated from voting since they held "the balance of power" in national elections, even as an appendage of the Republican party. This may be illustrated by the fact that in the process of reconstructing the southern governments after the Civil War, the Freedmen's Bureau assisted Blacks in their registration and voting, such that a series of elections in the South in 1867 concerning whether or not there should be state constitutional conventions found over 700,000 Blacks registered to vote.[12] In addition, when one surveys in Table 1.1 the margins by which several presidential elections in this period were won, it becomes clear that the Black vote was strategic.

That the total electorate went from roughly four million in the 1860s swiftly to six million in the 1870s is testimony to the presence of the Black vote. But as we see in Table 1.1, the margins of Republican victories narrowed considerably when the Democratic party slowly regained its competitive position. This culminated in the Democratic victory of 1884. Then, as Blacks were steadily

Table 1.1 Winning Margin of Votes for Major Party Candidates, 1864-1900.

Year	Margin	Party
1864	414,299	Republican
1868	309,380	Republican
1872	763,664	Republican
1876	251,746	Republican
1880	9,457	Republican
1884	23,737	Democrat
1888	95,096	Republican
1892	365,516	Democrat
1896	597,012	Republican
1900	861,668	Republican

Source: Composed from "Historical Review of Presidential Candidates from 1788 to 1968," Congressional Quarterly, Washington, D. C., January, 1969, pp. 14-16.

eliminated from the electoral process, the margins of victory widened between the two major parties, even making occasional Democratic party victories possible. Indeed, the largest margin was registered in 1900, when Blacks were all but eliminated from the process, and by Dr. W. E. B. DuBois' calculations, Black voters fell from nearly one million in 1892 to 400,000 by 1904.[13] In any case, the balance of power role for the Black vote is evident from the election of 1868 until it is eliminated from participation.[14]

The elimination of the Black balance of power was achieved by enacting the new southern constitutions which skirted the language of blatant racial prohibitions to Black voting, but which did include strictly enforced mechanics, such as literacy clauses, and property qualifications. The effectiveness of this "coup d'etat," as Van Deusen has called it, saw Black voter registration in Mississippi, for example, decrease from 147,000 to 8,615 at the turn of the century; Louisiana went from 127,000 to 7,000 and Alabama went from 130,000 to 5,000.[15]

The fertile mind of Dr. DuBois wondered at "The Possibility of Democracy in America," noting the stark fact of both Black and white voter exclusion in the statistic, and showing that the South was electing a number of representatives comparable to the five other regions of the country — with three-times fewer votes. These missing votes, the census of 1920 clearly showed, were those of Blacks who had been locked out of the process, causing DuBois to suggest that democracy was thus prevented from being realized because, "the theory of democracy . . . does depend upon the widest possible consultation with the mass of citizens on the theory that only in this way can you consult ultimate authority and ultimate sovereignty."[16]

Equally important, despite their exclusion, Blacks gave every indication that they were determined to continue to utilize presidential politics as an instrument of race advancement and thus faced the complex question of how, under the circumstances, to make the greatest impact with their votes. To have fully utilized the opportunity for all (available) eligible Blacks to vote would not have had the desired strategic impact because of the massive disenfranchisement; moreover, they saw that the major parties were not responsive to their public policy concerns. The issue became how to utilize whatever ballot power they possessed to compel presidential candidates to make *binding* commitments to their cause. Professor Hamilton correctly infers above that despite the urgings by some Black leaders that unconventional strategies should be adopted, the Black voter continued to hew to the line of practicality. The question raised by this study is whether the unsuccessful attempts of these leaders to break the habit of practicality, as it was perceived at that time, and to establish more daring strategies was related to the failure of Blacks to extract what might be regarded as effective (binding) political commitments.

One of the first questions Black leaders faced was the character of their position toward the Republican party in the post–1877 period. The natural inclination of most Blacks was to continue to vote Republican and hope to weather the storm of neglect. Others, however, felt that a discipline inherent in providing political support to a party is that when it betrays the interests of the group, that support should be withdrawn and the party, thereby, punished. Accordingly, by the early 1900s there had developed among some Black leaders (notably among what would become the Niagara Movement group of 1905), an anti-Republican sentiment. However, Black leaders with this tendency were effectively cancelled out by the more moderate leadership of Booker T. Washington and his associates, who still counseled Blacks to vote for Republican candidates. The pages of *The Colored American Magazine* in 1904 carried articles by Robert Terrell (soon to be appointed the first Black Federal District Court Judge) praising Roosevelt and an equally negative article damning the Democrats.[17]

Bishop Alexander Walters, for instance, who led the National Independent Political League, spoke strongly against the candidacy of Theodore Roosevelt, who was running on the Republican ticket in 1904. An associate of Washington's wrote to him of a July meeting at which Bishop Walters spoke out against Roosevelt, and how only his intervention prevented Walters and his associates from passing a negative resolution against Roosevelt.[18] Washington himself performed what has now come to be one of the ritual exercises of Black political influence, suggesting to Roosevelt those aspects of "the Negro problem" which were to be included in his speech accepting the Republican party's presidential nomination. Without describing further the close personal relationship which existed between Roosevelt and Washington, suffice it to say that Washington continued to be an influential force in maintaining Black allegiance to the Republican party until his death in 1915.

The election of 1912, however, found Niagara members such as DuBois and William Monroe Trotter, editor of the Boston Guardian, making in-roads in developing Black support for the presidential candidacy of Democrat Woodrow Wilson in 1912, against

Republican William Howard Taft.[19] The Black press was the scene of intellectual battle for Black Republicans who urged Blacks to vote neither for the progressive Bull Moose party (whose candidate was Theodore Roosevelt), because of its absence of a program for Blacks, nor the Democratic candidate, on the grounds of his generally sordid past relationship to Blacks including the lack of Democratic appointments.[20]

The result was that the Black vote largely split between Taft and Roosevelt, yet in several northern cities, as Douglas Strange points out, Wilson drew a substantial Democratic vote.[21] Precise returns from election districts in cities such as New York, Pittsburgh, Chicago, and Philadelphia substantiate DuBois' estimate that 100,000 of Wilson's six million votes were from Blacks — roughly 5–7% of the total Black vote. However, Trotter and other members of the Black press welcomed the Wilson victory, largely on the strength of the following pre-election pledge: "I want to assure them [Blacks] that should I become President of the United States they may count upon me for absolute fair dealing, for everything by which I could assist in advancing the interests of their race in the United States."[22] But, of course, Wilson's victory would be regretted by the Niagara group as, once elected, he promptly expanded racial segregation in federal employment. Wilson's victory was to be repeated in 1916, albeit this time with no measurable flirtation by Blacks as they learned very early that the size of Wilson's Black vote was not salient enough to compel him to make effective (binding) commitments.

In 1924, James Weldon Johnson in a seminal article painfully characterized the Black vote as a "political nonentity" because:

> The Negro demands less by his ballot, not only in actual
> results but even in mere respect for himself as a voter than
> any of all the groups that go to make up the American
> citizenry; although some of these groups are far smaller in
> numbers and even weaker economically.[23]

Johnson sketched out the reason that a stronger Republican party in the South was not of interest to the whites who held the patronage, if it meant extending the vote to Blacks. They were well satisfied that the larger Democratic party forces had eliminated Blacks from serious competition for both Democrats and Republicans. Johnson, however, considered it "pathetic" that Blacks themselves had ironically assisted the two parties in the "annulment of the power they hold in their hands":

> It is possible because practically every Negro vote is labeled, sealed, delivered and packed away long before election. How can the Negro expect any worth-while consideration for his vote as long as the politicians are always reasonably sure as to how it will be cast?[24]

Suggesting that Blacks were at the "Fourth of July" stage of political strategy—using sentiment as a basis for voting rather than logic— Johnson felt that the only way the "Gentlemen's Agreement" would be "smashed" was to destroy the *certainty* of the Black vote.

> He [the Negro] must keep politicians uncertain as to how he will vote; serving notice that the way his vote will be cast depends upon certain pledges and performances. In a word, he must put a higher price on his vote:the price of recognition as a full-fledged citizen, the price of recognition as a participator in the administraton of the affairs of his government.[25]

But rather than follow this strategy, Johnson noted, that Blacks had fallen into the practicality of settling for "the lesser of two evils" in exercising their choice among the available candidates for president. He suggested, "there are other ways out; there are other parties besides the two major parties," but the sentiment that was necessary for the exercise of such a daring choice was one of more political independence. Even though one observer of the 1920 elections for president noted that both party platforms had forsaken Blacks, and that Blacks, therefore, were "free of entangling alliances," they still gave most of their votes to the winning Republican candidate Warren Harding.[26]

The 1924 presidential election was truly a confusing affair with three major candidates in Coolidge (Republican), Davis (Democrat) and LaFollette (Progressive). A. Phillip Randolph addressed this question with a stunningly analytical primer of basic political science which not only put the three major contenders into some perspective with regard to their attitudes toward the Negro, but went further to draw out the economic interests behind each political force. This was important, since there was some confusion between DuBois and

Randolph, with the former suggesting that LaFollette, for example, had attacked the Klan, and the latter saying that the Progressive convention had dodged the Klan issue. Nevertheless, Dubois had no disagreement with Randolph's view that "the Negro was a man without a party," largely because of the significant influence of the Klan in national politics at that time.[27]

The NAACP made its first presidential endorsement by public-ly supporting LaFollette, and Randolph concurred, in what ap-peared to be sound theoretical terms.[28] First, he felt that because of the sheer number of parties in the race a strategic situation had been created which Blacks might effectively exploit to "secure more sub-stantial concessions in the form of constructive legislation (sic) in-crease."[29] Second, that as a general principle Blacks should split their votes, and, thirdly, repeating Johnson's logic, more could be achieved if it were generally understood "that the Negro is no longer a *sure thing* politically . . . and that (he) is beginning to think in terms of political, economic and social reforms for the benefit of not only himself as a race, but for the nation as a whole."[30]

The NAACP activists and others such as Bishop John Hurst of the AME Church, of course, would agree with this, but in a sym-posium in the *Crisis*, it is interesting to observe the strong weight of practical opinion among the variety of rationales for Black leaders giving support to each of the major and some of the minor can-didates. The practical people (attorneys, politicians, government ap-pointees, etc.) played heavily on the conventional arguments such as: "We tried dividing our vote with Wilson, but the door of political hope was very quickly closed in our faces after he was elected"; and, "Third Parties heretofore have met with small success, falling of their own weight"; and, "vote for men rather than party".[31] Needless to say, the Black vote was split, with the largest part of it going to Coolidge. Although LaFollette did not win, he gained a respectable showing of four million total votes, though not enough for it to be said that the LaFollette vote was the balance of power between the two major parties. For the Black vote to have been strategic, such a claim would have been necessary. Thus, even though the practical politicians appear to have been right about the fortunes of third par-ties, it is noteworthy that their accuracy profited so little for the Black masses who supported one of the major parties.

With the defeat of LaFollette, the fortunes of progressive politics waned such that by 1928 the main battle for the presidency was again between the Democrats and Republicans, fielding Al

Smith and Herbert Hoover respectively. This campaign took place in a tense atmosphere with racist pronouncements issuing forth from all of the major contestants. Thus, Black leaders representing all political tendencies came together and issued a statement "[accusing] the political leaders of this campaign of permitting without protest, public and repeated assertions on the platform, in the press, and by word of mouth, that color and race constitute in themselves an imputation of guilt and crime."[32] Noting that neither white politicians nor religious groups had made any counter assertions, the undersigned list of distinguished Black leaders called for a repudiation of these racist tactics.

Despite this highly negative environment, the practical politicians kept to their political loyalties, as the now-traditional *Crisis* symposium, "How Shall We Vote?" reveals. For instance, John Hawkins, head of the Republican Colored Voters Division, urged support for Hoover on the grounds of his humanity, since he came to the aid of Mississippi flood victims; Ferdinand Q. Morton, Civil Service Commissioner of New York City, urged a vote for Smith on the strength of his record as governor of New York, saying that "the intelligent Colored American realizes that the Negro problem, so-called, is no longer a national issue," and that local battles were more important. DuBois cast his vote for Socialist Norman Thomas, since Thomas was for "the laboring classes" and because his platform "dared to mention Negro disenfranchisement as a prime cause of reaction, fraud and privilege . . . ."[33]

Ironically this very negative political environment, no doubt, was also instrumental in keeping alive the political strategy of third party voting, since DuBois proceeded, in his own *Crisis* byline, "Postscript," to denounce both parties, citing a litany of insult and neglect. But after eliminating these parties and asking rhetorically, "If the Negro does not vote for Smith or Hoover, what should he do?" he rationalized his vote for Thomas on the grounds of "moral protest."[34] DuBois' position was obviously symptomatic of the fact that, as one observer put it, "Politically speaking, the Black man was like a caged bird."[35] This time, although Thomas polled nearly 900,000 votes, Hoover won by a landslide in the electoral college, obviously, again, with the bulk of the Black vote.

The election of 1932 was important in ending both the nation-wide depression and the exclusion of Blacks from national government administration. It also marked the beginning of the end of "the Nadir," by dramatically signaling the initial shift of the Black voter to the Democratic party in national elections. Hoover came out of the Great Depression badly scarred by mismanagement and with little program for national advancement. Yet, true to form, Rev. Hawkins, chair of the Republican Voters Division, again urged Blacks not to forget the Democrats' connection with slavery and "Jim Crow," or that Hoover piloted the "ship of state through severest storms," suggesting that "the issue was between parties, not individuals." His colleague, J. S. Coague, holder of the traditional Negro patronage job of Recorder of Deeds of the District of Columbia, offered other reasons, such as Hoover's establishment of a six-hour day, five-day work week.[36]

In any case, there was considerable dissatisfaction with Hoover and, alarmed over signals which indicated a sizeable defection of Blacks from his campaign, Hoover hosted a meeting at the White House of two hundred Black leaders. However, a black journalist, Lester Walton, noted that amid all of the oratory, "not a note of protest was uttered either at the White House or at the [preliminary Black planning meeting at the] Masonic Temple against Mr. Hoover's three years of apathy and unfriendliness."[37] Remembering the Democratic administration of Grover Cleveland in 1892, Walton argued that as a Democratic governor of New York State, Roosevelt also had established a record of making Black appointments and made possible the election of two judges at high salaries. Hoover, he went on, had insisted upon the appointment of racist Judge Parker (who opposed the right of Blacks to vote) to the Supreme Court and continued the discrimination against Black applicants to the civil service.

Thus, having connected the White House meeting to his appeal for Roosevelt, Walton was able to make a powerful theoretical point: he said that the meeting served to "point out to thinking Negroes just why the race occupies so lowly a status in the realm of politics," and credibly suggested that "it is to the best interests of the race to divide its vote and not regard politics as a sentimental attachment."[38] It appeared to be necessary for those wishing Blacks to vote for a Democratic or Socialist candidate for president to appeal not only to their sense of value in terms of the tangible reward of appointments or other such favors, but to strategic principles such as logic, or the necessity to divide their vote as a good principle of politics.

Again, the Black community was split, as traditional Black newspapers such as the *Chicago Defender* defended the vote for Hoover, based not on any strategic principles, but hewing closely to the traditional line of past merit. It is worth noting that many of the Black newspapers were kept tied to the Republican party by its practice of giving them political ads and government printing contracts, which meant that these financially strapped operations could hardly alienate their patrons during election time with appeals to alternative strategies. On the other hand, there was building a significant breakthrough, as Rev. Reverdy Ransom, Bishop of the AME church in Nashville, Tennessee, gave evidence of a new rationale for supporting the Democratic party which would describe many elections to come.

> The capitalistic system which prevails in the country dom-
> inates both of the major parties, but the Democratic party
> is closer to the great body of common people, than is the
> Republican. The day is near at hand when something more
> politically radical than the most extreme radicalism of pro-
> gressive Republicans will sweep the country in a great social
> upheaval. [39]

While explaining that the direction of this progressive "upheaval" was not yet focused on Black support for the Socialist party program, he suggested that Roosevelt represented a plausible change from the conditions of the past. In addition, DuBois delivered a stinging indictment of Hoover from a comprehensive vantage point, showing that from direct insult and indirect actions, to the negative impact of his foreign policy, the brief "which Americans of Negro descent have against Herbert Hoover is long, and to my mind unanswerable." [40]

Although it is not clear from the available sources who DuBois favored for president in 1932, it is certain that it was either Norman Thomas or Roosevelt, the more progressive of the available candidates. DuBois requested an article on Roosevelt from the distinguished Chicago attorney and Democratic party regional official Earl B. Dickerson, but Dickerson was reluctant to openly urge Blacks to vote for the untested Roosevelt, rather he favored Norman Thomas, saying he would probably vote for Roosevelt as a practical personal choice. This would also have been the likely decision of many of the Duboisian progressives.

Nevertheless, it is clear that DuBois looked upon this transformation as the maturing fruit of the effort of the progressives to put the Black vote into a position where it might become the subject of serious competition by the major parties. DuBois says of his compatriots at the NAACP that their political efforts were abortive, probably because they could not initially believe in the possibility that the "Gentlemen's Agreement" could so weld the white interests of the North and South together that they might make an effective unified program out of the disenfranchisement of Blacks, largely ignoring their political impact and their policy needs.

> We found that our political efforts were abortive for reasons which, while possible, did not seem to us probable. We had calculated that increased independence in the Negro vote would bring a bid for the Negro vote from opposing parties; but it did not until many years later. Indeed, it was not until the re-election of the second Roosevelt in 1936 that the Negro vote in the North came to be eagerly contended for by the two major parties.[41]

In 1932, this process had begun as the Black vote went for Roosevelt in a range extending from 20.7% in Chicago's predominately Black Third Ward to 70.8% in Kansas City's largely Black Fourth Ward.

Myrdal says that the Republicans had been hurt by the performance of Hoover, since many of the northern cites were controlled by the Republican party before 1930, and by the fact that in places such as Chicago, "the party felt sure of the Negro vote and hardly made an attempt to solicit it or favor it."[42] Furthermore, the Republicans had not calculated the effect of Black migration on voting outcomes in such cities, as between 1910 and 1930 the Black population of Michigan went from 17,115 to 169,453; Illinois from 109,049 to 328,927; Indiana from 60,320 to 111,982; and Ohio from 111,452 to 309,304. This led one observer to suggest: "[In these states] where the balance of power has been close between Democrats and Republicans, the Negro has asserted a political influence."[43] As DuBois indicated, all of this would have a significant political impact after 1933, and certainly by 1936, when Republican competition for the Black vote became spirited. Nevertheless, it was too little and too late, as the Democrats registered solid majorities of the Black vote based on the performance of Roosevelt's relief programs in his first term.

Table 1.2 Percent of Major Party Vote for Roosevelt, 1932, 1936, 1940, in Each Ward Having More Than Half Its Population Negro, Selected Cities.*

	Baltimore			Chicago		Columbus			Detroit		Kansas City, Kans.	Kansas City, Mo.	New Haven	Pittsburgh	Wilmington
Ward	5	14	17	2	3	6	7	3	5	7	2	4	29	5	6
1932	46.4	49.2	43.0	25.4	20.7	27.9	23.2	46.0	50.2	53.9	41.5	70.8	38.9	53.3	28.3
1936	64.2	54.6	46.9	47.9	50.1	47.7	46.6	71.4	75.0	79.0	61.3	79.4	61.0	76.6	40.1
1940	72.1	60.7	59.6	51.2	54.2	50.7	57.1	75.3	79.2	80.0	59.6	66.5	58.7	77.1	41.5

*The cities selected are all those with over 100,000 population, containing wards having 50 percent or more of their population Negro, where Negroes were allowed to vote unhampered or almost unhampered, and where ward lines were not changed over the period 1932–40. The only exception is Philadelphia, which refused to supply information. The data in this table were collected for this study by Shirley Star.

Source: Gunnar Myrdal, *An American Dilemma,* Vol. 1 ((New York: Harper & Row, 1944, p. 424, Table 1.

THE BLACK ELECTORAL SYSTEM:
DEPENDENT- AND INDEPENDENT-LEVERAGE

Dependent-Leverage

The most obvious fact which arises from this brief description of Black electoral politics in the period between the Roosevelts is that it did constitute a distinct sub-system of political behavior with many critical aspects and determinants. Within that system it is possible to identify two major tendencies in the theory of Black electoral behavior. The first might be called the system of "dependent-leverage" which was characterized by the dependence of the Black community upon the Republican party to continue its benevolent immediate post–Civil War policies that resulted in the emancipation of slaves and in the Reconstruction regime. As the power of whites confronted the powerlessness of Blacks, in the arena of public policy competition, Blacks attempted the practical strategy of locating that faction of the white community with the most advanced attitude toward them and the best political prospects for governing. Their assent to be directed by these political leaders was simultaneously an acknowledgement of their powerlessness and, thus, they granted a certain legitimacy to this paternalistic relationship. This paternalism initially demanded loyalty to the Republican party based on the sentiment of past favors, dictating the two-fold logic that by being part of a strong party institution Blacks were often able to protect their own interests. Secondly, that this was true enough in certain cases made the act of voting for Republican presidential candidates appear the most practical thing to do. For some, it was also personally rewarding since, for example, by 1872 Blacks were discovered to have been given fifty-eight federal appointments of some significance, including some diplomatic posts.[44]

Black participation in the Republican party, then, was distinctly a function of the control of the Black vote for Republican candidates. An office known as the "Negro Bureau" of the party was set up with faithful Black leadership, essentially the white Republican power structure's political surrogate operation in the Black community. As such, it appealed for votes based upon the usual rationales, and dispensed temporary favors to national and local Black leaders, potential voters and Black institutions such as the press, church, fraternal associations, educational organizations and, of course, Black businesses.[45] Attention was duly paid to the resulting party platforms, but as we have seen from the complaints of DuBois and others, the weakness of the Republican platforms in this period did not dissuade Blacks from voting for Republican candidates. So, the content of the platform as an expression of the current attitude of the party toward Blacks was obviously not controlling.

This led to the charge that the rationale for the use of the Black vote was not strategic but that it was traumatized by sentiment. Furthermore, dependency overpowered strategy in that the Black vote was often not responsible to political conditions — such as the presence of progressive candidates in the contest for the presidency — especially in view of the desultory Republican attitude and actions against them. In the place of actual public policy benefits, such as legislation against lynching or promoting various civil rights measures, the Black community often accepted the symbolic appointment of a few Black politicians and occasional humanitarian gestures by the president. At other times, the Black vote, having no strong substantive rationale for staying with the Republicans, was often deployed on the weakest strategy of voting for "the lesser of two evils."

Independent-Leverage

What appears to be a novel finding in our discussion was the existence of a strongly argued theory of Black electoral behavior which countered dependence with "independent-leverage" strategies. A rather small band of Black leaders, centered in the NAACP, but extending to others such as Trotter in Boston and Dickerson in Chicago, carried on a veritable battle for the mind of the Black voter by appealing to logic over sentiment, boldness over loyalty, and independence over paternalism. To be sure, they were facilitated in this quest by the fact that most of them were in the North and in territory dominated by Democratic party politics. Therefore, a resort to more independent strategies was not unnatural to them, as it would have been were they totally within the hostile environment of the South as was Booker T. Washington, their arch enemy. Blacks in New York, for instance, reacting to the Hayes bargain, were led by T. Thomas Fortune, editor of the New York Age, to vote Democrat in rather large numbers as early as the Cleveland election of 1892, and later, as we have seen, in the 1912 election of Woodrow Wilson. But to the extent that this more liberal atmosphere was conducive to the conception of more flexible strategies, progressive Black leaders were unable to compete for the main body of Black votes which was located in the South. While the 1920 census counted only one million Blacks in the North, nearly six million were in the South, though most of them were disenfranchised.

The progressives were further hampered by the conservative national mood which would not support ultra-liberal candidates. Not considering it wise to field their own candidate in most elections, they had to choose among the available compliment of candidates. This often gave them scant choices to employ a strategy of flexibility, so that, aside from the occasional progressive (liberal) Republican, the most desirable candidates in the race were often Socialist.

In the 1920, 1924, and 1928 races, however, the most palatable choices for progressive Blacks were the Progressive and Socialist party candidates. The recent Marxist revolution in Russia had frightened European and American capitalists and, as was noted by A. Philip Randolph and Bishop Ransom alike, capitalism was at the basis of both the Democratic and Republican parties. Thus, if there was a strongly negative attitude toward socialism among whites, dependent blacks would also manifest such antipathy. Although the advice to vote for Socialist candidates was reached after cold analysis of the content of all party platforms, the fact that Socialist platforms were generally more favorable to Blacks was not overwhelmingly persuasive as a basis for support.[46]

The lack of an acceptable choice of candidates, both theoretically and practically, limited the political flexibility of Blacks. Indeed, the choice was often stark. For example, DuBois said of the candidates in the 1924 election:

> Any black man who votes for the present Republican Party out of gratitude . . . is born a fool. Equally no Negro Democrat can for a moment forget that his party depends primarily on the lynching, mobbing, disfranchising South. Toward any Third Party advocates the intelligent Negro must be receptive . . . [47]

Discrediting Black allegiance to the Republican party was not entirely the result of the New Deal program, but also a result of the attack upon the party's legitimacy as well as the resulting groundwork laid for Democratic voting by the Black progressive leadership. In addition, while criticism of the Democratic party by Black Republicans was expected, it should be noted such criticism also came from Black progressive Democrats such as T. Thomas Fortune of New York, who quipped as early as 1889: "When the Democratic Party ceases to be a party of unmitigated cussedness the discussion of the question of a division of voters in the South will be in order."[48]

It is interesting, therefore, that in the incipient stages of the transition of the Black vote from Republican to Democrat, there was no conception that this would be a permanent alliance. The Black vote was seen to have indeed become independent. In fact, the January 1944 issue of *Crisis* carried a "Declaration by Negro voters," signed by, among others, Mary McLeod Bethune and A. Philip Randolph, which urged Black political independence as the key to fairer treatment in both national parties.[49] Then, as late as 1940, Ralph Bunche suggested that certain theoretical precepts had come to be accepted as the basis for the transition. To begin with, he says that:

> In the present presidential campaign, it appears that the Negro vote will assume larger significance than ever because of the great importance now attached to the *independent* (my emphasis) vote, which is expected to swing the election. The Republicans, who have now awakened to the realization that they can no longer depend upon the traditional allegiance of the Black voters, have taken unusual steps to attract the Negro electorate. The Democrats are likewise beginning to employ measures to hold the newly won Negro support . . .[50]

As a result of what Bunche calls "beginning to wield the stick of political power," he suggests the Black vote could be more effective in the political bargaining for goods and services: ". . . it does seem evident that the black vote can be and is traded for improved facilities and services wherever the Negro votes in any significant numbers."[51]

This theory, Bunche confirms, is that of the "Balance of Power," which began, as we have seen, in the early nineteenth century. It became institutionalized by the turn of the century when pamphlets of the United Color Democracy, founded in 1898 and later known as the National Independent Political League, suggested that a transition to voting for Democratic candidates could mean that the Black vote could wield the "balance of power" between the two major parties.[52]

It should be quickly noted that the recognition of this status of the Black vote was not confined to Blacks, but that whites also early understood this fact. It became the basis of their ruthless suppression of Black political power and the origin of the "solid South." For example, Henry Grady, a Virginia legislator, noted in the late 1880s that by dividing politically, the South was destroying the integrity of its social defense, and that, "this alien influence [the Negro] that holds the balance of power . . . must be bought by race privileges as such."[53]

Though Bunche did not feel philosophically that the Black community should vote as a bloc, he observed that "the Negro vote assumes its greatest importance when it is voted as a single bloc and is able to hold the balance of power between opposing factions or parties."[54] Suggesting that this had been the case in some local municipal elections, he noted that claims had recently been made for the application of this theory to the national elections. He cautioned that the case had been made on the basis of the total Black population figures, not the effective Black voting population turnout.

In 1948, Parker Moon, NAACP press secretary (and later editor of *Crisis*) also argued that the Black vote, which "was in the vest pocket of no Party" and had grown to 3.5 million, could become the balance of power in that election. It was his view that "The Negro's political influence in national elections derives not so much from its numerical strength as from its strategic diffusion in the balance-of-power and marginal states whose electoral votes are generally considered vital to the winning candidate."[55] That Moon's analysis of the effect of the Black vote indicated that a Democrat might be the recipient of its balancing influence was a bold assumption in view of J. Errol Miller's findings that in the election of 1946, Blacks in the numerically populous wards in Philadelphia and St. Louis were again voting Republican, leading spotty trends found in other areas. Miller's data show the rising political participation of Blacks through increased registration rates (Philadelphia, 74.7% and St. Louis, 71.5%), and through the build-up of Black majorities and significant proportions of Blacks in an increasing number of city voting districts (Philadelphia, 11, St. Louis, 5).[56]

Refining the "balance of power" theory to mean the cumulative role of the Black vote in providing the winning margin of victory in key states, Moon cited eight states where the Black vote exceeded the number needed to shift the state from the Democrat to the Republican column.[57] Given its balancing role, he thought: "This vote is more decisive in presidential elections than that of the solid South."[58] There is evidence that the importance of this vote was beginning to be acknowledged. In 1940 the Democratic party mentioned Blacks favorably in its platform for the first time. In addition to Roosevelt's inclusion of Blacks in the New Deal program, Harry Truman led the way to Democratic party positions on fair employment and civil rights principles which laid the groundwork for the laws which would come later. The Black role was, thus, virtually secured by the Democratic convention of 1948.

In words which were reminiscent of the older NAACP cadre, but also seemed to define the new coalition, Moon suggested that "an alert, independent, and aggressive Negro electorate in collaboration with organized labor and other progressive forces may be an important factor in determining the political complexion of the Congress."[59] He was, no doubt, also suggesting the general impact which the new coalition between the Congress of Industrial Organization (CIO-Political Action Committee) and Blacks was having on improving Black voter turnout and even beginning to elect some Blacks to office in local campaigns. In 1948, CIO support helped to boost the Black vote for Truman to 70%, proving Moon correct by providing the winning margin of victory.[60] Such a coalition would not only be politically potent in presidential elections as was proven in 1944 and 1948, but as Moon suggested, it would challenge the value of the southern vote within the Democratic party and help to lay the basis for the rise of a winning coalition in the 1960s.

CONCLUSION

In this light, it is apparent that the atmosphere which sharpened the necessity for strategic thinking on their part was the frustrating search for political influence because of the fact that both major political parties had abandoned any commitment to Black progress. Part of the frustration in this search was the obvious fact that the vote was a political resource which if used, as Myrdal says, in an "opportunistic" fashion might even become a strategic resource. The difference between a political resource and a strategic one is that we conceive of the latter as involving a higher order of politics, the kind of politics which implies the successful management of Black political resources in a way that yields maximum real dividends.

In the period discussed, it was evident that the Black political resource of voter support had suffered serious exploitation, such that it was utilized basically for the benefit of white politicians and their Black surrogates without yielding maximum dividends. It is, then, obvious that the goal of Black political leadership was to seek to achieve a strategic value in the use of the vote as a resource in electoral participation. A healthy debate existed among black leaders concerning what actions were the most strategic in the sense that they would protect Black interests in a general sense.

It may be observed that those who followed the theory of dependence were sincerely seeking leverage for group objectives within the major political institutions, but by doing so became captive of the politics and ideologies of those institutions, even when they pointedly did not serve the broad interests of the Black community. One would, therefore, have to suggest that political action from the "captive" position yielded only minimal strategic benefits since the actors attached themselves to a host institution such as a party where there was the inevitable lack of control of the political parameters and, thus, far less flexibility of action.

On the other hand, those who have favored independent-leverage challenged the tendency of some practical politicians to place the party institutions before the fundamental interests of their constituency. The challenge was in an effort to have them consider the *objective* basis of political action more thoroughly. The attempt to attract Black voters away from single-minded dependence upon and allegiance to the Republican party began shortly after the Hayes bargain of 1877 and was only successful beginning in 1932. This occurred not so much as a result of the logic of progressive politicians, but largely from the practical sense of timing of the Black voter. It is, therefore, impossible to dismiss the practical logic which causes people to adopt a moderate course of action in achieving their own interests, since the character of the times also occasionally causes them to rise above the traditional responses to problems and employ different strategies. However, as we have seen, practicality may also be a serious impediment to exploring alternative strategies.

The challenge to develop independent leverage was led by a band of intellectual activists centered in some NAACP progressives and augmented by others. There was a fundamental division of opinion between this group and practical politicans who most often held positions of patronage — a rather small but highly influential group since they were given great visibility, access and resources by the white power structure. It appears, because of the structure of patronage, that the practical politicians were more individually motivated while the progressives were more concerned with the acquisition of broad policy which would affect the well-being of all Blacks.

The strategic rationale of the progressives was that voting for candidates who placed the issues of Black progress squarely into their campaigns or party platforms, even though they were not favored to win, would demonstrate that the Black vote was disciplined to support such candidates. Thus, the major party candidates would have strong incentives to support such issues in exchange for Black votes. DuBois' observation that both parties had ignored the Black vote was testimony to the effectiveness of the "Gentlemen's Agreement," having disenfranchised most Blacks in the South by 1900. The crippling effect of this exclusion from the political system upon the power of the Black vote, constituting (by Bunche's estimation) 250,000 in the South and two million in the North by 1932, was that it could only have been the "balance of power" in 1916, where the difference between the candidates was 583,000 votes, or in 1908, where it was 1.2 million. Otherwise, as we have indicated, the voting power of Blacks was most effective in the immediate post–Civil War elections.

Given the intriguing possibilities that the theory of electoral independence apparently still is an attractive basis for Black political participation in presidential elections, I will examine more current political dynamics in an effort to assess the possibilities for translating independent strategies into instruments of Black progress.

Chapter 2

The Balance of Power and Dependent-Leverage

INTRODUCTION

It has now become apparent that the euphoric pronouncements of the political "independence" of the Black vote in the 1930s and 1940s was somewhat premature, in that it has since settled comfortably into a reverse pattern of Democratic party dependency, rather than becoming a true "swing" vote. How could it be otherwise when the interests of Blacks historically have not swung very often from party to party, rather the parties themselves have over time manifested periods of ideological stability in their orientation toward national issues and specifically Black progress, a fact which has helped to shape the basis of Black party allegiance. The other factors which have helped shape Black party allegiance besides the structural stability of the two-party choice itself, have been the stability of the character of the items on the agenda of Black progress, and the continuing dominance of practical Black political leadership. The combined impact of these factors has enhanced the practice of dependent-leverage: the attempt by Blacks (or any other such group) to achieve political influence by both seeking institutional integration into the party's administrative and political structure, and by seeking to become a "balance of power" factor in the voting coalition through contributing dependable and substantial electoral support to party candidates. It is expected, then, that the party will satisfy their political and policy objectives once it accedes to government.

The function of the Black vote as a balance of power has essentially worked against Republican candidates since 1936. This has increased since 1960, as Blacks have been a secure part of the Democratic party coalition, even to the extent that the labor/Black vote replaced the South as the dominant aspect of the party coalition. Given the fact that only the elections of 1960, 1968, and 1976 have been regarded as clear examples of the most recent impact of the national Black vote exercising the "balance of power." I will explore these elections in an attempt to understand the implications of the use of such a strategy.

The Making of a Voting Coalition

The Eisenhower victories in 1952 and 1956 were important in keeping alive the illusion that the Black vote was inclined toward independence, since it had split, giving Democratic Presidential Candidate Stevenson only 50% in both races.[1] By 1960, fresh from the Montgomery Bus Boycott victory and the formation of the Southern Christian Leadership Conference, Martin Luther King, Jr. went to the Democratic convention to indicate strong concern for the civil rights content of its platform. In addition, he teamed with other leaders such as NAACP head Roy Wilkins and Congressman Adam Clayton Powell (D-NY) to hold a mass meeting at the site of the convention to hear the candidates address issues of concern to Blacks. The man most favored by Blacks was Hubert Humphrey, primarily for his role at the 1948 convention in bringing the issue of their rights to the forefront of the party's attention. Humphrey, however, was not a candidate that year, and although John F. Kennedy was not received politely by those assembled at the conference, his astuteness after the convention in focusing upon King as the symbol of his positive interest in the exploding Civil Rights Movement, won him 70% of the Black vote.

Of course, the details of Kennedy's dramatic role in helping to get King released from Reidsville State Prison in Georgia and its political effects are well known. More important, it helped to solidify the New Deal realignment pattern of political behavior with the result that Blacks have given substantial majorities of their vote to Democratic presidential candidates for the past quarter of a century.[2]

The strategy of utilizing the Black vote as an instrument of the new movement for civil rights was best explained by Martin Luther King, Jr. and Bayard Rustin. In 1963, King argued in his book, *Why*

Table 2.1 Pivotal National Elections: Black Role, 1960–1984 (%).

Year	Preference	Vote Split	Vote Outcome	Turnout Rate	Role
1960	Kennedy	49.7–49.5	Kennedy	70%	Pivotal
1964	Johnson	61.1–38.5	Johnson	94%	N-Pivotal
1968	Humphrey	43.4–43.3	Nixon	85%	Pivotal
1972	McGovern	60.7–37.5	Nixon	89%	N-Pivotal
1976	Carter	51.0–49.0	Carter	92%	Pivotal
1980	Carter	55.3–44.7	Reagan	90%	N-Pivotal
1984	Mondale	59.1–40.8	Reagan	88%	N-Pivotal

Sources: CBS/New York Times Exit Poll, November, 1984; *Gallup Opinion Index*, 1960–1980.

We Can't Wait, that a "new stage in civil rights had been reached" which called for a "new policy" which could be achieved only by Blacks moving closer to the "inner arena of political decision, from which they had been distant." He felt that in this new stage the movement was:

> . . . strong enough to form alliances, to make commitments in exchange for pledges, and if the pledges are unredeemed, it remains powerful enough to walk out without being shattered or weakened.[3]

One of the great problems of Black political participation, King wrote, was that Blacks had seldom had "adequate choices" and that this was related to the low regard Blacks had for the potential of electoral politics, including the fact that it had not attracted the "best elements" of the Black community in leadership capacities. Most important, he believed that it was time for Blacks to abandon what he called "abstract political neutrality" and risk entering an alliance for greater political gain, bearing in mind that "alliance does not mean reliance, our independence will remain inviolate."[4] King's statement gives evidence of the fact that in the early 1960s some Black leaders were still using the assumptions of the politics of the 1940s and 1950s which held that the Black vote was independent, a view which was even more credible to those in the politics of the Civil Rights Movement which had developed, essentially, from an independent base outside the institutionalized system of elections and public policy. King then gives us the demographic argument for the possible exercise of Black voter influence:

> The Negro potential for political power is now substantial.
> Negroes are strategically situated in large cities, especially in
> the North but also in the South, and these cities in turn are
> decisive in state elections. These same states are the key in a
> Presidential race, and frequently determine the nomination.
> This unique factor gives Negroes enormous leverage in the
> balance of power.[5]

King further suggested that the effort was potentially successful
because the value and disciplined habits of the Civil Rights Movement were amenable to actions tailored to electoral mobilization.
Still in his arguments is the unmistakable call for a transition in the
movement's focus. This call for transition was even more obvious in
an article, "From Protest to Politics" published two years later by
Bayard Rustin, a close associate of King.

Rustin suggested that Blacks were making "a conscious bid for
political power and in that effort a tactical shift is being effected."[6]
Although Rustin's definition of "politics" (actions within the framework of political institutions) is overly narrow, since the Civil Rights
Movement was a thoroughly political phenomenon, nevertheless, he
was perceptive in his view that the Civil Rights Movement was in
transition to a fully developed *social movement*— a conceptualization
which has been greatly under-utilized by most writers on this
period. The great implication of this, Rustin felt, was to join a "coalition of progressive forces which becomes the *effective* political majority in the United States."[7] Moreover, agreeing with King that the
Negro "swing vote" was crucial in the urban areas as the "source of
the Negro's independent political power," he went on to make the
critically important observation that in order to effectively and inde-
pendently use this power, the leadership of the Black vote had to be
wrested from the political machines. Rustin held that the effect of
successfully building a "majority liberal consensus" was to achieve
the revolutionary goals of restructuring the Democratic party and
thereby restructuring the nation. Thus, Rustin agreed with King
that an alliance strategy was called for, and that it should express
itself in electoral support for a Democratic party candidate for president in exchange for public policy rewards, and that it should be
achieved from a base of independent control of the political
machines at the local level.

A real opportunity to achieve the goal of restructuring the
Democratic party lay, ironically, in the death of President John

Kennedy, which created the national sentiment for his unfinished agenda and swept Lyndon Johnson into power in the 1964 landslide. The role that Black leaders had begun to play in Democratic party politics that year solidified their role as a vital member of the coalition and was nowhere more evident than at the convention.

The Mississippi Freedom Democratic Party (MFDP) had risen to challenge the exlusion of Blacks from electoral politics, and a delegation of MFDP, Student Non-violent Coordinating Committee (SNCC), and Congress of Racial Equality (CORE) workers from the South, led by Fannie Lou Hammer, attempted to take the seats of the lily-white Mississippi delegation. President Johnson's key advisers saw, in the Black protests that were occurring, a threat to his nomination if the southern delegations were alienated. These protesters would also test the loyalty of Black political and civil rights leaders to Johnson. For example, James Forman's striking account described the attempt of Martin Luther King, Jr., Roy Wilkins, James Farmer, Bayard Rustin, Congressman Charles Diggs, Jr. (D-MI) and others to negotiate with the MFDP a compromise giving them two symbolic seats within the Mississippi delegation. When the MFDP refused, the Johnson forces turned to ruthless pressure to abort the challenge.[8]

The second aspect of the Black leaders' cooperation with Johnson was agreeing to a moratorium on civil rights protest demonstrations, a pledge which was in conformity with the previous strategy outlined by Rustin and King.[9] Black leaders perceived the stakes to be exceedingly high: the prospect of the election of Barry Goldwater, a conservative Republican from Arizona, and the fact that the largest package of civil rights legislation in modern times was working its way through the Congress, as was an intensely sought one billion dollar anti-poverty program.[10] Consequently, in 1964, Blacks rewarded Johnson with a turnout that has not since been exceeded, and although the black vote was not decisive in his victory, its performance and subsequent policy rewards profoundly signaled the temporary success of the strategy adopted.

By 1968, the national mood was one which made this a critical year for the utilization of the vote to effect national public policy, as a pervasive pattern of alienation overtook electoral strategy. This pattern is reflected in the depression in Black voter turnout in the North and West, down from the previous election from 72% to 65%, even as it was rising in the South (44%–52%) under the strong pressures created by the Voting Rights Act of 1965. However, factors such as dissatisfaction with the Vietnam War, the rise of a Black Nationalist Movement, the death of Martin Luther King, Jr. and Robert Kennedy, appeared to mark a loss of faith by the electorate in institutional solutions, as both the national and the Black voter turnout went down by one percent from 1964 to 1968, then plunging by 5% between 1968 and 1972.

Scammon and Wattenberg have pointed out, however, that "had nonwhites outside the South come to the polls in 1968 as they had in 1964, Hubert Humphrey would have received a greater popular vote than Nixon."[11] We consider the Black vote to have been "pivotal" in this sense because the balancing function of this vote (or any other vote) is an objective property, not to be accorded only when the Black vote is the "winning margin of victory." The fact that it occasionally can be the losing margin of victory should give it a double-edge in the consideration of strategies, since part of the power of any balancing entity should be its ability to penalize as well as support. Perhaps one reason why the 1968 election has not been regarded as an expression of the power of the Black vote is that the low turnout implied a boycott of the Democratic candidate by Blacks, a negative sanction in the eyes of party leaders and strategists — black and white. That a boycott of some considerable proportions did, indeed, occur should be understood in its strategic terms, one of the implications of which is that it would have had much greater political value if it had been perceived to have been a *deliberate act*, rather than mere happenstance.

With a stronger and more self-assertive Black Power mood in the late 1960s an electoral strategy could be re-fashioned that adopted an even more independent stance, dictating that Blacks should "reward their friends and punish their enemies." Indeed, one observer suggested within the context of the presidential campaign of 1972:

> While there would be many strategies and counter-strategies
> and some falling off from these new attitudes as the
> primaries heated up and each presidential candidate vied for
> black support, one thing was evident to most black people,
> the old unquestioning powerless dependence on presidential
> and white liberal political leadership was gone.[12]

This mood and the movement which accompanied it were responsible for several political dynamics in the watershed year of 1972, such as the National Black Political Convention, the presidential bid of Congresswoman Shirley Chisholm, (D-NY) the rise of Black elected officials, the creation of the Black Political Assembly, and others. Here I would isolate one aspect of the 1972 political convention for brief comment, because it combined the continuing strategy of electoral politics with the new assertive mood.

The National Black Political Convention was held in Gary, Indiana in the spring of 1972, in an effort to prepare the Black community to participate in the presidential politics of that year with maximum effect. Despite its shortcomings, what emerged was a critical assumption — that its platform, the National Black Political Agenda, would be the yardstick against which the candidacies of *both* Democratic and Republican presidential candidates would be measured in exchange for Black support. The implementing strategy held that explicit bargaining would occur with both major party candidates over their support of the agenda. Whichever agreed to support its contents, Blacks would support that candidacy. Thus, if the person supported by Blacks won, the contents of the agenda would constitute some of the key policies of a victorious president toward the Black community.

This strategy was not totally new in the history of Black politics. There were, however, new elements, such as the degree of mass involvement in a Black political convention, the use of this convention as a mobilizing instrument for explicit political bargaining with the white power structure, and the outcome of the bargaining as the basis of political choice.

The fact that the election of 1976 is regarded as one wherein the Black vote constituted the "balance of power" provided an important test of the previously established frame of reference for Black electoral participation. It was not evident that the year began for Blacks with any strategy, save stopping George Wallace in the Florida Primary on March 9, since Jimmy Carter had tried to develop support among northern Black politicians and had been rebuffed. The real sentiment of most Black leaders was with Senator Hubert Humphrey (D-Minn) who, again, was not an announced candidate. Morris Udall had inherited the McGovern mantle and Sargent Shriver, a member of the Kennedy family, was running as well. The short-term strategy was successful, as Carter won with 35% of the vote to 31% for Wallace, and, although Carter swept the Black vote winning 70%, the turnout was lower than the previous presidential primary due to the existence of a conservative field for both Democrats and Republicans.[13]

Nevertheless, soon after Florida it became evident that what had begun as a short-term reponse to Wallace had developed into a firm commitment on the part of at least some southern Black politicians, such as Andrew Young and the King family, who were from Carter's home state of Georgia. Julian Bond, Georgia state senator from Atlanta, however, backing northern liberal Morris Udall, reflected the continuing ambiguity of most Black leaders and voters by considering Carter too conservative, suggesting suspicion of someone who could capture both 70% of the Black vote and 50% of the anti-Black vote simultaneously.[14]

In the end, it was politics as usual which brought many of the seasoned politicians, who had previously wavered, into the Carter camp. Carter went into the Democratic convention without much opposition, but still without unified Black support. After the convention, however, many of the key holdouts were attracted to the Carter campaign by the opportunity to assume the traditional role as broker of the voter registration and "get-out-the-vote" funds in the various states.[15] As the funds began to flow and a team of highly visible Black supporters mounted a traveling voter registration drive, Black interest in the campaign apparently picked up with the result that Blacks overwhelmingly (94%) supported Carter during the general election against Gerald Ford.[16] In fact, Eddie Williams, president of the Joint Center for Political Studies, said that the Black vote was a decisive factor in the outcome of the election, and added:

> This is the first time in history that the black vote has played such a major role in the nomination of a presidential candidate and in the election of a president. The size and strategic impact of the black vote give clear evidence of the black community's determination to use the political process to achieve its goals and to participate fully in shaping the nation's policies and programs.[17]

Williams perhaps overstates the point, especially in view of other elections we have surveyed and since the total black voter turnout was lower in 1976 than it had been since the passage of the Voting Rights Act. Nevertheless, the Joint Center for Political Studies had surveyed five hundred heavily black wards and precincts in twenty-three states, and found that the black vote provided Carter with the winning margin of victory in seven states having a total of 117 electoral votes while Carter's margin of such votes was only fifty-six.[18]

Shortly after Carter's victory, Williams was the first to lead a chorus of Black leaders asking "What can blacks reasonably expect from the new president?" It was, he suggested, the time for a "transition from promise to performance that is on the minds of Black Americans."[19] He went on to say that the new administration possessed the opportunity "to open up the lily-white world of policy formulation" to black participation, and that "that is what blacks meant during the arduous days of the primaries and the campaign when they said to Carter and to other politicians 'count us in or we will count you out.'"[20] Under the editorial heading "A Debt That Must Be Paid," *Ebony* magazine also said that "President Carter's debt to Black people must be paid and the first installments should come soon. As a downpayment on that debt Carter's priority should lie in jobs for the poor and the black."[21] The chorus of views confirming this debt rose, as the editors of *Time* magazine said, "To say that the President-elect is in debt to Blacks is to put it mildly."[22] Black journalist, J. K. Obatala also suggested that Carter had a debt beyond middle-class appointments, to the "physical existence of citizens" in their quest for employment.[23] Also, Vernon Jordan, the then-powerful head of the National Urban League, said that black people had a "strong claim on Carter . . . that he should not be allowed to forget."[24]

Perhaps only Chuck Stone's dissent from the notion of "accrued debt" was accurate, as he suggested that Black leaders' expectations might prove "over-inflated" since, despite the electoral showing by blacks, their issues were lowest on Carter's list of priorities, because of his need to re-position his politics to attract white voters in light of his thin margin of victory.[25] Stuart Eizenstat, Carter's campaign issue adviser, confirmed Stone's view that the economy was "far and away the number one priority," and it became clearer that the view of other key economic advisers was that Carter was really a "balanced budget moderate," a fact which would establish a conflict in economic priorities with groups such as Blacks.[26]

In late 1977, Vernon Jordan openly criticized President Carter for not having paid his debt to Blacks by the establishment of any new programs. Carter eventually made more Black senior level appointments than any other President; however, many of Carter's rewards to Blacks were considered symbolic. He signed, then promptly ignored, what was widely regarded as "a watered-down" version of the Humphrey-Hawkins Bill and, though in 1978 he created the job-training Comprehensive Employment and Training

Act, he also issued an FY 1980 budget that severely cut this program.[27] By 1980, disaffection with Carter's public policy performance was so generalized among Blacks that there was a significant
split among both the leadership and ordinary voters between Carter
and his primary challenger, Senator Edward Kennedy.

The reasons for the striking difference between political promise and policy performance in the Carter case is intriguing, and,
perhaps, related to the fact that Black leaders have continued to
manifest much faith in the strategy of making policy claims based
primarily on the "balance of power" function of the Black vote. We
suggest that the strategy has occasionally worked because of the
demography of the Black vote, and its continuity has been assured
because it has the allegiance of a "new class" of practical politicians.

DEMOGRAPHICS

In looking at the statistical keys to the "balance of power" function of the Black vote in presidential elections, we will provide a simple analysis which illustrates the basis of its impact within the states.
For example, if we consider the two national elections since 1960 in
which the Black vote has played a critical role in the Democratic candidate's victory, we find the pattern illustrated below:

Table 2.2 Electoral Votes for Selected States 1960 and 1976.

NORTH

State	1960 Electoral Vote	1960 % VAP Black	State	1976 Electoral Vote	1976 % VAP Black
New York	45	8.0	New York	41	12.6
Pennsylvania	32	7.0	Pennsylvania	27	8.2
Illinois	27	9.2	Illinois	26 (R)	12.4
Michigan	20	8.7	Michigan	21 (R)	11.3
New Jersey	16	7.7	New Jersey	17 (R)	10.8
	120		Ohio (new)	25	8.9
				157	

SOUTH

Alabama	5	25.9	Alabama	9	22.0
Arkansas	8	18.2	Arkansas	6	14.4
Georgia	12	24.4	Georgia	12	23.7
Louisiana	10	28.2	Louisiana	10	26.4
Mississippi	8	35.5	Mississippi	7	30.5

Table 2.2 Electoral Votes for Selected States 1960 and 1976. (cont'd)

SOUTH

	1960			1976	
State	Electoral Vote	% VAP Black	State	Electoral Vote	% VAP Black
North Carolina	14	20.7	North Carolina	13	18.8
South Carolina	8	29.1	South Carolina	8	26.1
Texas	24	11.4	Texas	26	11.6
	89		Tennessee (new)	10	13.8
			Florida (new)	17	10.6
				118	

BORDER

Maryland	9	15.2	Maryland	10	18.3
Missouri	13	8.1	Missouri	12	9.3
	22			22	

Total: Democrat - 303   Total: Democrat - 297
         Republican - 219   Republican - 240

Source: Census of Population 1960, Bureau of the Census, Department of Commerce, Washington, D. C., Statistical Abstract, 1966. Guide to Black Politics 1976, Part II Republican National Convention, Joint Center for Political Studies, August 1976, Washington, D. C., p. 55–56.

Examining the profile of Kennedy's 1960 victory, we find that the Black vote had an impact on a grouping of five northern industrial states, eight southern states and two border states. Altogether, they contributed 209 out of 303 electoral votes won by Kennedy, or about 70% of the total necessary for his victory. The northern states contained an average of 8% of the Black voting-age population, and the southern states had 24%, although the average northern popular vote and consequently the average electoral vote of such states was much higher than others. Nevertheless, with the exception of California at this time, these thirteen northern and southern states compromised the largest Black voting-age populations with the most significant impact upon the close presidential contest of 1960 which split 49.7% to 49.5% for Kennedy.

By 1976, the most striking change was that three of the original industrial states — Illinois, Michigan and New Jersey — voted Republican, and while in 1960 they accounted for 53% of the electoral votes in the northern group, this loss was not offset in 1976 with the addition of Ohio's twenty-five votes. At the same time, Tennessee and Florida were new additions to the Democratic totals, increasing the share of the Democratic winning margin which may be accounted for by the votes of southern states. The fact that southern states contain such a high percentage of the Black voting-age population (VAP) (but a lower turnout than northern Blacks) gives southern Blacks greater potential regional influence overall in an election year.

Table 2.3 Regional Black Registration and Turnout in Presidential Elections, 1964–1984 (%).

	1964	1968	1972	1976	1980	1984
Democratic						
Voting	94	85	89	92	94	90
Registration	60	66	65	59	60	66
North & West	69	72	67	61	61	67
South	53	62	64	56	59	66
Total Vote	6,056	6,290	7,032	7,273	8,287	10,300
Turnout	59	58	52	49	51	56
North & West	72	65	57	52	53	59
South	44	52	48	46	48	53

Source: "Voting and Registration in the Election of November 1980," Bureau of the Census, U. S. Department of Commerce, April 1982, Government Printing Office, Washington, D. C., p. 2; "Voting and Registration in the Election of November 1984," Advance Report, January 1985, p. 1.

This table shows that in 1968, for example, the regional gap of 13% in voter turnout between the Northwest and South had narrowed by more than half to 6% by 1984, and registration rates by 1984 are almost comparably equal. This increase in the southern Black voter turnout which was stimulated, no doubt, by the reversal of all other Black electoral behavior in 1980, portends greater regional influence for the southern Black vote. The two-party nature of the South has resulted in slender margins to Republican senators, governors and presidential candidates, and the recent southern primary movement for 1984 has created new opportunities for the collective manifestation of its voting strength.

What should be kept in mind about these regional figures is that up until 1980 they were based on a deterioration in the proportion of all Blacks voting but there were, nonetheless, steady increases in the raw vote totals. Thus, even though Black voter registration and turnout dropped effectively between 1968 and 1980, the total number of Blacks who actually voted increased by about 2.2 million because of population increases. Beginning in 1980, as is illustrated in Table 2.3, the national pattern has improved markedly for Black registration and voting in both regions.

Even before 1980, however, regional trends were important in determining the effect of key states and assessing the critical role of the Black vote. For example, if one averages the Democratic victories over this period — 1960, 1964, and 1976, the following profile of support emerges:

Table 2.4 Democratic Voting and Black Voting Age Population (VAP) in Selected States, 1970, (%).

NORTH

State	Democratic Voting Percent	Percent Black VAP 1970
Illinois	52.5	11.1
Michigan	54.6	10.3
New Jersey	54.5	9.3
New York	57.7	10.7
Pennsylvania	55.5	7.8
Average	54.9	9.8

SOUTH

Alabama	47.5	22.9
Arkansas	57.1	15.3
Georgia	58.2	22.7
Louisiana	48.4	26.6
Mississippi	50.1	31.4
North Carolina	54.4	9.3
South Carolina	49.5	26.2
Texas	54.9	11.3
Tennessee	52.8	13.8
Florida	50.3	12.5
Average	52.3	19.2

BORDER

Maryland	57.3	16.0
Missouri	55.1	8.9
Average	56.2	12.4

Source: See Table 2.2.

The northern region manifested slightly higher loyalty to the Democratic party in these selected elections than the South, with a higher average vote of 54.9% to 52.3%, but the two border states were even higher with a 56.2% rating. Nevertheless, the fact that the highest region of Democratic voting also has a lower Black voting-age population, should be interpreted as a critical balance of power effect upon large groups of electoral votes, because of the effect of the concentrated urban Black vote on the electoral college outcomes in those states. Already one sees, then, the effect of the defection of southern states such as Alabama, Louisiana, South Carolina and the spotty Democratic voting records of Mississippi and Florida. This, together with the loss of key northern industrial states by 1976, such as Michigan, Illinois and New Jersey, meant the loss of states with a 22% average Black voting-age population.

Table 2.5 gives a clearer view of the impact of the Black vote in these states in 1976.

From Table 2.5, it is possible to observe that in the grouping of states which formed the 1960s winning Democratic coalition, those states with large Black populations were, in fact, shrinking since, in 1976, Illinois, Michigan, and New Jersey were in the Republican

Table 2.5 Margin of Victory (MOV) of the Democratic Vote Compared to the Margin of Victory of the Black Vote, 1976.

State	Total Vote	% Dem	Carter Black Vote	%	MOV
Alabama	1,183	55.7	182.5	15	13.1
Arkansas	651	65	62.7	10	30.1
Florida	2,583	51.9	261.8	10	5.3
Georgia	1,467	67.0	262.0	18	33.7
Illinois	4,719	48.1 (R)	352.5	7	-2.0
Louisiana	1,278	51.7	264.6	21	5.7
Maryland	1,440	52.8	149.8	10	6.1
Michigan	3,654	46.4 (R)	208.1	6	-5.4
Missouri	1,954	51.1	125.7	6	3.6
New Jersey	3,014	47.9 (R)	187.0	6	-2.2
Mississippi	769	49.6	122.8	16	1.9
New York	6,534	51.9	610.0	9	4.4
North Carolina	1,679	55.2	204.8	12	11.0
Ohio	4,112	48.9	243.2	6	0.2
Pennsylvania	4,621	50.4	256.8	6	2.7
South Carolina	803	56.2	166.9	20	13.1
Texas	4,072	51.1	259.2	6	3.1
Tennessee	1,476	55.9	138.9	9	13.0
Averages		53.15		11	6.9

Source: Election Research Center, Washington, D. C., 1976; "Voting and Registration in the Election of November 1976," Total Votes by State, Bureau of the Census, Department of Commerce, March 1978, pp. 41–43; "The Black Vote: Election '76," Joint Center For Political Studies, August 1977, p. 10. (R) — Republican.

column. Thus, in all states the Black vote became more critical to Carter's margin of victory (the proportion of the margin to the total two-party vote) by contributing on an average of 11% of his vote, which was much larger than his average margin of 7.4%. With the three northern industrial states indicated voting Republican, the impact of the Black balance of power increases by reducing the average margin to 6.9%, making Carter more heavily dependent upon the South as a region, and upon the Black vote in the South to provide his margin of victory. Then, there is an obvious correlation in the data between low percentages of the Black vote in such states as Missouri, Ohio, Pennsylvania and Texas and Carter's low margins of victory in those states. The central point, however, is that if one subtracts the 6.9% average Black voting-age population from the average Democratic vote in the states, the Democratic vote goes to 46%, a margin too low to win any presidential election.

As suggested above, what causes this impact of the Black vote is its concentration in certain cities, such that it is no accident that the fifteen highest ranking states in Black population are included in the table listing, and that the largest Black percentage of the state Democratic votes are in the South. Indeed, the only cities which appear in the listing of the top thirty-five high Black population cities which are not represented by states in the table listing are Gary, Indianapolis, Milwaukee, and Boston. Table 2.6 illustrates the group of states with the fastest growing Black population between the 1970 and 1980 census:

Table 2.6 Largest Percent Black Voting Age Population Increase by States, 1970–1980 (one percent or more), (%).

State	% Black VAP 1970	% Black VAP 1980	Increase
California	6.2	7.3	1.1
Illinois	11.1	12.8	1.7
Maryland	16.0	20.1	4.1
Missouri	8.9	10.8	1.9
New Jersey	9.3	11.4	2.1
New York	10.7	12.8	2.1
Ohio	8.4	9.4	1.1
South Carolina	26.2	27.7	1.5
Georgia	22.7	23.9	1.2

Source: Selected from Table 3 "Black Voting Age Population Projections for November 1980 by State and Region," in "Black Politics in 1980: A Guide to the Republican National Convention," Joint Center for Political Studies, Washington, D.C., 1980, p. 39. U.S. Census of Population 1980, Bureau of the Census, U.S. Department of Commerce, 1981.

The nine states listed above have had the largest inter-censual increases in Black VAP, and nearly 80% of this group are northern, western or border states. This would appear to indicate that these states will enhance the national ability of Blacks to contribute to the margin of victory for candidates of either party or, under any other circumstances, to become a political factor in their own right. Since five of the above states are northern and two are border states, but only two are in the South, and given the trend toward reversal of southern Black outmigration, this northern and southern population balance indicates that there will remain a 15–20 state base where the Black vote will likely continue to be a factor in national elections.

THE NEW MOVEMENT

A crisis of general political strategy developed in the Black community in the early 1970s as a result of the intersection of two powerful movements. The first was the Black Nationalist/Pan-Africanist Movement which had all but taken the place of the former Civil Rights Movement by the end of the 1960s, and which emphasized pro-Black, politically independent strategies in various arenas of action. While the leaders of this movement were alienated from establishment politics such as elections, they nonetheless saw the opportunity to further legitimize their own national leadership role by co-sponsoring with elected officials a Black Politicial Convention in 1972.

At the same time, in the early 1970s, there arose a body of Black elected officials, (BEOs) largely as a result of the increased use of the vote in the Black community, made possible both by the Voting Rights Act of 1965 and the ambitions of northern Black politicians who understood the mass mobilization potential of the new Black-oriented movement. For these new politicians the 1972 Black Political Convention also served as a legitimizing tool which symbolized their arrival as national leaders, although many of this group followed the older strategies of political dependence for one reason or another. In any case, they were generally more wedded to electoral strategies than others because of their role as elected officials, and their interest in Democratic party affairs enhanced the involvement of Blacks in local and national politics. There developed, then, a "structural" dimension to the support of dependent strategy which, as we have suggested, might help to explain its survival, especially in the face of equally strong pressures for independent politics.

The Electoral Movement

The modern period in the utilization of electoral politics as a strategy for social change began in the early 1960s. It approached "movement" proportions in the early 1970s as a consequence of the successful production of Black elected officials through the mobilization of Black voters. Table 2.7 shows the dramatic proportions of that movement.

The rapid increase in the number of BEOs in the early 1970s gave evidence of the arrival of a significant group of new political leaders with attachments to electoral politics, such as to constitute a new "class." The BEOs constituted a significant "class" first with respect to the sheer size of the group in comparison to their past number. They would go on to institutionalize their offices and profession on a national basis, to routinize their personal relationships and professional approaches, and there would arise a new focal point in many communities for policy and political action.

The impact of this new political class was felt most immediately by the presence of Black mayors at the local level. Chuck Stone characterized 1967 as the "year of the Black Mayor" when Carl Stokes of Cleveland and Richard Hatcher of Gary became the first of the elected "Black Power" mayors of large northern industrial cities and Walter Washington was appointed mayor of Washington, D.C. Currently one-half of the top twenty cities of highest Black voting-age population have Black mayors. In those cities with Black mayors there is an impact of city votes on the state elections, a fact which has traditionally made cities such as Chicago, with an elected Black mayor in 1983, coveted by the national Democratic party.

Table 2.7 Annual Rates of Increase of Black Elected Officials (%).

Year	Percent
1970	19
1971	26
1972	22
1973	15
1983	2
1984	6

Source: National Roster of Black Elected Officials, 1974 and 1984. Joint Center for Political Studies, Washington, D.C., 1975 and 1985.

In fact, there has occurred a city-suburban/rural split in state voting in many areas. Whereas the urban areas of Chicago, Detroit and Newark now have effective voting majorities producing Black mayors, the electoral vote of those states, influenced by sprawling white-controlled suburbs and rural areas, frequently now contain many Republican voters. Nevertheless, the political control of such cities is important because they also tend to influence state legislature, county and congressional elections as well. Thus, if a mayor has effective political control over an urban base, he or she is often able to exercise some influence over these other political jurisdictions as well.

This reality has been the source of the influence exercised in national politics by mayors such as Coleman Young of Detroit, a key functionary of Jimmy Carter in the presidential campaign of 1980. Perhaps none of the other mayors have risen to the level of Richard Hatcher of Gary, Indiana in national politics who has enjoyed access to Democratic presidents and presidential candidates by virtue of his leadership role in national Black organizations such as TransAfrica and Operation PUSH, policy organizations such as the National League of Cities, National Conference of Black Mayors, and party offices such as the Black Democratic Caucus, the Democratic party, and chair of the Jackson campaign of 1984. From these various vantage points, for over two decades, he has been one of the central participants in both the campaign and policy politics of the Black community.

Just as important, this class of Black elected officials has performed the normal activity of institutionalizing their function by forming broad associations. Statewide political organizations have developed in several states involving Black elected officials and laypersons. At the national level, the pattern is impressive: the Black Legislative Clearinghouse was organized in 1969; the National Black Caucus of Local Elected Officials was organized in 1970 within the National League of Cities and the U. S. Conference of Mayors; the Judicial Council of the National Bar Association was formed in 1971; the National Association of Black County Officials was organized in 1975; the National Caucus of Black School Board Members was formed in 1971; the Southern Conference of Black Mayors was created in 1972; and the Congressional Black Caucus was formed officially in 1970.[28]

The Congressional Black Caucus

One product of this urban Black electoral base that is critical to presidential politics is the election of Blacks to Congress. It is perhaps at this level that Blacks have had the most direct impact upon national politics. Although their local vote for president is affected by the indirect impact of the Electoral College and is often diluted in the direct vote for United States Senator, it often has great impact where congressional districts are substantially within the urban area.

The recent presence of Blacks in the Congress dates from 1928 when Oscar DePriest of the Second District, Illinois (Chicago) won election, the first Black elected since 1901. By 1965 there were five, and then the number accelerated with the increased pace of the vote.

Although all except one of these members were Democrats,' the numbers also reflect the presence of the popular Republican Senator Edward Brooke from Massachusetts who, in his two terms from 1967 to 1978, was the only Black to serve in that body since 1881. Although he never functioned as a formal member of the Congressional Black Caucus, (CBC) an organization of Black members of the House of Representatives all of whom happened to be Democrats, there were frequent consultations on important legislative issues such as full employment and busing, both supported by Brooke.

Considering that Brooke's party controlled the White House during most of his tenure in the Senate, his presence was extraor-

Table 2.8 Annual Number of Black Members of Congress.

Year	Number
1970	10
1971	14
1973	16
1974	17
1975	18
1977	17
1981	18
1983	21
1985	20
1987	23

Source: National Roster of Black Elected Officials 1984, Joint Center for Political Studies, Washington, D. C., 1985.

dinarily valuable in having access to Republican presidents. His views were regarded as more liberal than the presidents', though somewhat more conservative than those of the Black Caucus members in the House. For example, he tended to have a tough-on-crime stance in the Senate, supporting measures such as the infamous "no-knock" bill. He supported Republican presidents by voting against cuts in the military budget, for the use of defoliants in Vietnam and for Nixon's Philadelphia Plan of Black "set-asides" for minority businesses. However, he also supported liberal issues such as the 18-year-old vote and elimination of the military draft.[29]

Brooke also espoused the view that Blacks "hold the margin of winning votes on issues that have an effect upon our lives," and in his remarks at the Joint Center's Third Institute for Black Elected Officials in December 1975, he went on to suggest that Blacks should stand for all offices, including "the offices of Vice President and President of the United States."[30] Indeed, so popular had Brooke become by the 1976 elections that he was often mentioned as a candidate for vice president, and at the August convention, flyers were circulated and a hotel suite opened for this purpose. President Ford himself appeared to seriously consider this possibility in a meeting with Black delegates.[31] In the end, Brooke was one of those making a seconding speech from the podium of the convention in support of Ford's nomination.

It is extremely doubtful that Ford was serious about a Brooke candidacy. However, considering the closeness of the eventual vote between Ford and Carter, a Black vice president on the ticket may have provided him with a margin of victory—had he been able to hold on to his white support. The greater probability was that additional white votes would have defected to Carter in the South making such a Republican ticket even less likely to have won.

Finally, Brooke's position reflected the general Black Republican theory at the time:

> We must learn to deal with both political parties from a position of strength. For a long time now, Blacks have rallied to the Democratic party. But we cannot afford the luxury of supporting just one political party. The two party system is a reality of American life. Its continued viability of competing interests in our political system produces results. If we are to shape governmental priorities, our full, and effective, participation in both political parties is critical. Both parties

must be made to respond to our voices, our needs and our strength.[32]

What appears striking about this statement is that it could have been made by one of the "progressive" Black activists or Democrats before 1932. This may indicate that the espousal of theories of electoral independence changes within the Black community to reflect the minority-majority party allegiance position of the political leadership. The minimum position of Black Republican leaders, since the maturation of New Deal Black politics, appears to have been that Blacks should be active in *both* political parties, implying that allegiance to any party should be devalued as a political goal in itself, and that the Black vote should be flexible enough to swing between the two parties according to the momentary interests of Blacks.

In the House of Representatives, the development of the Congressional Black Caucus simultaneously brought with it the expectation that this group would provide national *political* leadership. In the period between 1970 and 1972, they sponsored several policy conferences on topics such as governmental lawlessness, Black education, and Africa, making clear in the environment of a conservative Republican administration that they intended to emphasize the question of presidential policy leadership.

The first strategy was to develop a comprehensive legislative agenda in opposition to the measures set out by the President in his State of the Union address, which was perceived by the group to be largely negative. Charles Diggs, Jr., first chair of the Caucus, presented a list of sixty-one recommendations to Nixon on March 25, 1971. Similarly, in January 1973, chairman Louis Stokes (D-OH) presented a voluminous list of recommendations to the House called "The True State of the Union Overview," in response to the President's remarks. This pattern was followed for the duration of the Ford administration, but largely abandoned during the Carter administration because of the perception of increased access to presidential policy formation.

Soon after the Caucus' initial meeting with President Ford, Charles Rangel (D-NY) the new chairman, reflected on its influence on presidential decision-making. As one result of the August 21, 1974 meeting, President Ford had promised to appoint Blacks to key White House positions. Rangel's public response to this was:

> If the Congressional Black Caucus is to make a meaningful
> contribution to the decisions of the Federal Government that
> affect our communities, there should be an institutionaliza-
> tion of communication between the executive branch and the
> Caucus symbolized by the meeting with President Ford. The
> best and most lasting way to achieve this goal is to have the
> type of executive agency appointees in this administration
> who will be sympathetic to the needs of the poor and minor-
> ities because of their ideological and philosophical com-
> mitment and, equally important, because of who they are.[33]

Despite the fact that the Caucus was giving Ford the benefit of the
doubt by expecting that he would make appointments that were
philosophically compatible, Rangel placed great value on having
White House staff to which the Caucus would have regular access. It
should be noted that in 1974 the Caucus was bidding for access to
the president traditionally through the White House staffer for
"Black Affairs," but as the institutional role of the Caucus has grown
to the point that its members have assumed the chair of five full Committees of the House and eight Subcommittees in 1985, policy access to
the president and key agency officials will become more routinized.

The question of the Caucus' political leadership, however, was
more difficult in this formative period. For example, individual
members of the group, such as Congressman Diggs, had played a
role in presidential politics since the days of Lyndon Johnson. More
recently, Congressman Walter Fauntroy (D-DC) provided legitimacy in the Black community for the largely unknown George
McGovern during his 1972 presidential campaign. Fauntroy, who
was chair of the Platform Committee of the National Black Political
Convention and a key actor in its formation, was also important in
getting McGovern to accept some of the issues contained in both the
National Black Convention's Agenda and the document developed
by the Caucus. There was also an attempt to get issues contained in
the latter document—the "Black Declaration of Independence and
the Black Bill of Rights"—accepted by the Platform Committee of
the Democratic party.

Ironically, it was the presidential candidacy of Congresswoman
Shirley Chisholm which caused the Caucus the most difficulty in
achieving a unified position on the question of presidential strategy.
As the strategy of running a Black politician for president was
discussed in 1972, it became apparent that other members of the
Caucus were also being mentioned as possible candidates. Chisholm's

candidacy neutralized the Caucus as a cohesive political force by posing the dilemma of challenging its members to support her candidacy or McGovern's, at least at the primary and convention stages. By 1976, Congressman Andrew Young (D-GA) played a role in legitimizing the campaign of Jimmy Carter similar to Fauntroy's actions in 1972. However, just as Gerald Ford was dropping hints about the possibility of Ed Brooke as his running mate in 1976, Carter countered at the July Democratic convention by initiating the suggestion that Congresswoman Barbara Jordan (D-TX) might qualify for such a role. Before Black delegates could begin a mobilization, she issued a statement declining to be considered, not only because of her illness and her satisfaction with Carter's eventual choice, but also, because, as a highly pragmatic politician, she doubted that the country was ready for a Black and a woman vice president.[34]

When one looks at the similar role played by Fauntroy and Young, it is tempting to suggest that their linkage to the Congressional Black Caucus was responsible for their access to major Democratic political leaders. However, the fact that they were both former staff members and associates of Dr. Martin Luther King, Jr., maintained close ties to the King family, and had attained legitimate and visible leadership roles within the Black community, *in addition to* their positions in the Congress, was probably most efficacious in convincing other Blacks to follow their leadership.

As other politicians have become key party activists, the influence of the King political legacy has waned, and the role of the Caucus has settled into a legislative mode, the Caucus has exercised political leadership as *one element* of a larger grouping of civil rights leaders and big city mayors. In fact, some of these leaders, such as Richard Hatcher, were among those initially calling for the Caucus "to change its focus," because it "could not be all things to all people."[35] This suggestion, subsequently taken seriously by the Caucus, led not only to a reformation of its style, but perhaps, at the outset of its development, signaled a level of leadership conflict that also indicated that the Caucus could not exercise autonomous leadership in national politics.

CONCLUSION

Some of the questions I raise by way of conclusion, then, are whether or not the occasional success of the balance of power strategy is made possible by deliberate skill of Black political leaders or whether the elements described above — the demographics, the accident of a new political movement, or other factors — may be decisive in its operation. This issue will be discussed in the chapter which follows, in the context of addressing the general question of the strategy of Black "political integration" into the party structure. It may be well to note that even a losing strategy may be compensated for by unexpected social or historical forces which stimulate a course of action in the voting population, as clearly indicated by the presence of Ronald Reagan in the 1980 election.

Although Carter's eventual nomination caused some disappointment among Black Democratic activists attending the Democratic National Convention, it would become evident by their behavior in the general election that they sensed a larger goal in defeating Ronald Reagan, despite predictions that turnout would be low because of the malaise provoked by Carter's candidacy. Indeed, observers such as Congresswoman Cardiss Collins (D-IL) noted a "sense of despair" given the candidacies of Carter and Reagan, both of whom most Blacks considered profoundly antithetical to their interests.[36] Reagan, for example, had encountered great difficulty in making even modestly successful appeals for the Black vote in 1980 at events as diverse as the National Urban League Convention and in a staged session on the streets of the South Bronx in New York City.

That Blacks had solidly opposed Reagan's candidacy was clear from the profile of Black voting in the primaries when, for example, in the Illinois Primary, George Bush won the Black vote against Reagan by 60% to 17%, and public opinion polls showed that Reagan rarely ever won more than 10% of the Black vote overall.[37] Nevertheless, predictions that the Black vote would be meager in the general election were credible because the trend had seen total Black turnout fall to 48.7% in 1976, the lowest level since 1960.

Confirmation that the strategic emphasis on voter turnout had been successful was discovered when the data revealed that Blacks had turned out in large numbers and had voted overwhelmingly for Carter. In the general election, the Black turnout rate was 50.5%, or 1.8% greater than 1976, reversing a downward trend that had been under way since 1968, and 85% of that vote went to Jimmy Carter.[38] However, given the disaffection among Blacks with Carter, Blacks were voting for the "lesser of two evils" and in this case, Ronald Reagan's status as the greater evil was perhaps a more powerful stimulus for Black turnout than Carter's record.

What this outcome suggests is that the perceptions of the voters regarding the nature of the election — in particular the character of the candidates and the extent to which they are perceived to be harmful to group interests — may itself be so compelling that other strategic decisions become secondary. This is another way of saying that the political environment itself is often decisive, since under normal circumstances the choice between two such candidates should logically have led to a continuation of the downward trend in Black voter turnout.

Chapter 3

The Strategy of Political Integration

INTRODUCTION

To politicians, scholars, and activists alike, cementing the role of Blacks within the Democratic party coalition required more than voting in order to become the "balance of power." It also required the development of a sustained institutional base of power within decision-making councils such as the party. In the words of Professor Charles Hamilton:

> My point is that electoral politics should point towards gaining and maintaining positions that ultimately can lead to more than sporadic office-holding. This means not only winning office, but gaining influence in large on-going 'office winning' structures, i.e. one of the major political parties.[1]

But while office-holding was one objective, Martin Luther King, Jr. and others held that exercising influence within the party councils was a key to obtaining the necessary power with which to attain other political and economic objectives.

> The new task of the liberation movement . . . is not merely to increase the Negro registration and vote; equally imperative is the development of a strong voice that is heard in the smoke-filled rooms where party debating and bargaining proceed. A Black face (that) is mute in party councils is not

political representation; the ability to be independent, assertive and respected when the final decisions are made is indis-
pensable for an authentic expression of power.[2]

Thus, we proceed beyond an analysis of registration and voting
strategies in this chapter in an effort to both describe and analyze the
political behavior of Blacks within the Democratic party as they have
attempted to establish a beach-head which could lead to sustained
power. This kind of political integration was a natural outgrowth of
the Civil Rights Movement which was substantially focused upon
the problems of securing and exercising citizenship rights. Thus, expanding the right to vote and the right to participate in all political
activities came under simultaneous challenge.

The task will be to understand whether or not such integration
has enhanced the ability of Blacks to participate in party affairs and
if so, has this, in turn, enhanced their ability to utilize the party institution as an instrument of the kind of "liberation" to which King
was referring. In doing so, we make the practical choice of being
concerned principally with the Democratic party as the party with
which Blacks have principally chosen to identify, and as the dominant political institution which stands as the subject of Black integration efforts. This, of course, is an example of the attempt to use the
strategy of "dependent-leverage" to maximize the rewards of electoral participation.

THE STRUGGLE FOR INCLUSION

Political integration would be extremely difficult to achieve as
long as Blacks were excluded from participation in the Democratic
party at the state and local levels. For, besides the role of the party in
making decisions with respect to crucial matters of state politics,
such decisions have also affected the participation of Blacks in presidential politics, in activities such as party presidential primaries,
convention delegate selection and as state representatives on the national party committee.

The 1964 challenge of the Mississippi Freedom Democratic
Party (MFDP) to the regular Mississippi delegation to the party convention was historically important. Though the challenge failed at
the time, it ultimately set the stage for other challenges and, thus,
some changes in delegate selection procedures. This point, driven
home under the glare of television lights at the 1964 and 1968 Democratic conventions, was initially noticed by James Forman in the

Black Caucus meeting at the 1964 convention when the MFDP rejected the Johnson compromise.

> There is, however, something in the resolution (compromise resolution from the Credentials Committee) which is only there because of the efforts to organize the Freedom Democratic Party, and what has happened here at Atlantic City, namely the section dealing with the composition of state parties and the call to be issued by the Democratic National Convention in 1968 to make sure that the Mississippi delegation is democratically elected.[3]

Forman was prophetic, as events unfolded in successive elections. In 1967, the party created a Special Committee on Equal Rights, headed by Governor Richard J. Hughes of New Jersey. The committee developed the "Six Basic Elements" of an open party including a non-discrimination standard for use by states in delegate selection. However, though a letter was sent to all state party chairs suggesting that unless their delegations were "broadly representative of the Democrats of that state" they might not be seated, the standards were far from vigorously applied.

In Georgia that year, party leaders loyal to the potential nomination of Hubert Humphrey, arranged to have a convention separate from the regular state convention that would expose the existing sentiments within the regular state delegation for either Governor Maddox or George Wallace. Accordingly, the convention was held in Macon, Georgia, and resulted in the nomination of Georgia State Representative Julian Bond as co-chairman but the actual leader.[4] For although the convention had been called by the Humphrey forces, Bond's nomination as leader signaled that the McCarthy forces which he represented were in clear control.

Bond, therefore, had a mandate to lead his delegation to the convention, and in doing so, he chronicled the exclusionary practices which led to the necessity for a separate delegation. In his statement before the Credentials Committee of the Democratic party convention, he set forth these exclusionary practices, including the method by which the all-white delegation was selected, stating that it was in direct violation of the official party Call to the Convention.[5] He went on to make an impressive case for other violations of party practice, but statements by Georgia State Representative Ben Brown, a Black Humphrey supporter, weakened the hard-line taken by Bond, leading the committee to offer an inevitable compromise. Again, reminiscent of 1964, the compromise was that the eventual Georgia delegation should be composed of 50% regulars and 50% challengers.

Bond drew the attention of the nation to the convention when he led his delegation on to the floor to challenge all the seats of the regulars. Although Bond's challenge was unsuccessful, the ensuing drama, an embarrassment for the party, led to another attempt at reforming the rules on delegate selection for the 1972 convention. It was all the more urgent inasmuch as, of the fifteen state delegations which were consequently challenged, seven were in the South and involved the issue of the under-representation of Blacks.[6]

As a result of the mandate of the 1968 convention, the final report contained language seeking to revise the delegate selection procedures to "assure the fullest possible participation and to make the Democratic party completely representative of grassroots sentiments," causing DNC chair, Senator Fred Harris, to appoint a Commission on Party Structure and Delegate Selection. This commission was headed by Senator George McGovern (D-SD), but when his presidential aspirations became clearer, he resigned and Congressman Don Fraser (D-CA) became chair. Among the findings of the commission's final report, "Mandate for Reform," was the fact that although Blacks comprised 11% of the population and 25% of the base of the Democratic party, they were only 5.5% of the delegates to the 1968 convention.[7] This was to be remedied by asking states to

> Seek as broad a base of support for the Party as possible by implementing the anti-discrimination standards adopted by the national committee; and overcome the effects of past discrimination by taking affirmative measures to encourage the representation of minority groups, young people and women in reasonable relationship to their presence in the population of the state.[8]

The language emphasized above in the report found its way into the Delegate Selection Rules (Article II) for the 1972 convention. These rules also contained a statement that prohibited the establishment of a system of quotas to meet the requirements of the above rules. The seemingly conflicting set of instructions to states was addressed by chairman Fraser in a letter of November 29, 1971 that attempted to clarify the situation. In doing so, he added the concept that a challenge to a state party's delegate composition on the grounds of insufficient minority representation, in itself constituted evidence of a violation of the guidelines, including those which required that an effective affirmative action program be implemented.[9] By the time of the 1972 convention, the then chairman of the party, Lawrence O'Brien, included in the Call to the convention, under "Party Responsibility," a resolution of the DNC of October 14, 1971 which stated that the party, in selecting delegates, undertook "to assure that voters in the State, regardless of race, color, creed or national origin, will have the opportunity to participate fully in party affairs, and to cast their election ballots for the Presidential and Vice Presidential nominees. . . ."[10] Furthermore, the Call contained a resolution of the DNC of February 19, 1971 which certified that each state party must undertake "to assure that all Democrats of the State will have meaningful and timely opportunities to participate fully in the election or selection of such delegates and alternates."[11]

When one puts these exhortations together with the de facto quota system which developed, the discouragement of the "unit rule," the appeal of the McGovern reform delegate program to his candidacy, and the virtual disenfranchisement of party regulars, what resulted was a convention to which the delegations were more representative of women, Blacks, youth, etc. than any Democratic party conventions had ever been. Black representation went from a mere 6.7% of the delegates in 1968 to nearly 15% of the delegates in 1972.[12] This represented more than a 100% increase in Black delegates within the four-year period, yet such progress still did not reflect the 25% Black share of the party voting base in the general elections. During the 1972 convention, however, resolutions were adopted which called for the establishment of two commissions, one on the development of a permanent charter, headed by Governor Terry Sanford (NC) and another on Party Structure and Delegate Selection, headed by the then Baltimore City Councilwoman, Barbara Mikulski.

The 116-member Delegate Selection Commission had a mandate, one part of which was monitoring the affirmative action efforts of the national and state Democratic parties "to achieve full participation of minorities, youth and women" in the delegate-selection process and in "all party affairs."[13] This commission, then, had a fundamental role to play in drafting a set of rules which would result in fairer electoral participation within the party by Blacks, women and other minority groups. These rules bore a direct relationship to the permanent charter, particularly in its section dealing with affirmative action. The Charter Commission's 160 members included fifteen Blacks and the Delegate Selection Commission included ten Blacks.[14] The Delegate Selection Commission (known as the Mikulski Commission) spent most of 1973 gathering information, and held its first meeting in September of that year. A drafting committee, which included commission vice chair, Mayor Richard Hatcher, was selected at the first meeting on September 21. At that meeting, the full committee heard a presentation from DNC chair, Richard Strauss, who repeated his call for "scrapping of the quota rules," saying that he would go to court if necessary to block any outcome that resembled fixed or mandatory allocation of delegate seats.[15]

The issue of methods assuring fair representation being far from settled within the commission, Patricia Roberts Harris, prominent Black attorney and chair of the Rules Committee, enunciated at this meeting the moderate principle that all presidential candidates should be required "to seek support from all groups in society" and should have a "reasonable number of members of minority groups" in each delegate slate.[16]

Something a bit "harder" than this, resembling guaranteed equal representation had been the wish of Mayor Richard Hatcher as he went into the drafting sessions in October, however, in the end, Strauss' view nullifying "hard quotas" was to prevail. One observer said that Hatcher "eventually acquiesced in the rejection of mandatory quotas as a way of bringing minorities into the delegate selection process."[17] The writer implied that Hatcher relented in order to get as "tough and enforceable" a program of affirmative action as possible that would have an impact on the structure and procedures of state Democratic parties.[18]

The important sections of the Delegate Selection rules on the question of Black participation consisted, first, of Section 16 of the Report, which called for an "open party" with the "Six Basic Elements" from the Hughes Committee having to do with such issues as the openness of meetings, the lack of loyalty tests, the publication of meeting times and places, broad registration and participation by all, and the like. Section 17 affirmed the basic principle of "Non-Discrimination," while the most important was Section 18 which dealt with "Affirmative Action." One immediate objective was achieved in Rule 18 (A,1) which called for representation of Blacks and minorities "by their presence as indicated in the Democratic electorate," as opposed to rules which based representation on the proportion of that state's population. The difference is obvious and critical, since the percentage of Blacks in the *Democratic electorate* (or among voting Democrats) is much higher than in a neutral State electorate. Thus, there was the attempt to bring Black numerical influence in the convention in line with their voting influence. Finally, the most important section was:

> Performance under an approved affirmative action plan and composition of the convention delegation shall be considered relevant evidence in the challenge of any state delegation, but composition alone shall not constitute prima facie evidence of discrimination, nor shall it shift the burden of proof to the challenged party. If a State Party has adopted and implemented an approved Affirmative Action Program, the Party shall not be subject to challenge based solely on delegation composition or primary results.[19]

This language shifted the burden from the state party to the challenger to prove discrimination on the basis of the lack of Blacks and other under-represented groups in the delegation, and also focused on the adoption of an acceptable Affirmative Action Plan.

Therefore, what constituted an "acceptable Affirmative Action Plan," and a fair delegate selection process began to be the subjects of much political confusion. The rules, however, attempted to clarify this in Section 19, by setting up the Compliance Review Commission (CRC) to administer the party affirmative action requirements and to review delegate selection plans for the 1976 convention. This issue was finally settled by drafting "model Affirmative Action Plans" to include in the Appendix to the Commission Report, which was officially adopted at a meeting of the DNC on March 1, 1974.

By December 1973, the Charter Commission had its third meeting in Atlanta, Georgia and produced a first draft of the document. The draft contained an Article IX on the principle of "Non-Discrimination," reaffirmed the "open party" concept by adopting the Six Basic Elements, and followed the formula of the Delegate Selection Commission in proposing the establishment of a "Compliance Review Committee to monitor and enforce these provisions of the Charter."[20]

Since it was becoming clear that the CRC was critical to the monitoring process of both major party functions, its leadership, racial composition, and role became the subjects of intense intra-party bickering.[21] In any case, the Charter Commission met in mid-March for its fourth meeting, and developed the all-important Article 10 on "Full Participation," incorporating many of the elements recently adopted in the Mikulski Rules.

The position of Black politicians following the Charter Commission deliberations at this time was that they had made major concessions in an effort to achieve compromises, starting with the quid-pro-quo of eliminating quota language for affirmative action, and that they were not disposed to make any further compromises. The task of representing these positions was accomplished by a faithful few, including Ben Brown, Barbara Morgan (Washington, D.C.) and Richard Hatcher. Since the attendance by Blacks at meetings was often spotty, this group led a major effort to consult with Black party activists and scholars concerning the concepts and language the proposed charter should include.[22] Congresswoman Yvonne Braithwaite Burke, (D-CA) vice chair of the Charter Commission, provided leadership at decisive points in the debate over Article 10.

Further compromises were sought from this group, however, because many regular party activists were unhappy with the adoption in the Charter of the language of the Mikulski Commission which said, in essence, that affirmative action would apply to "all party affairs." The most influential of those opposed to this concept as too broad an extension of the participation mandate were Joseph Crangle, former New York State party chair; Harvey Thiemann, Pennsylvania State chair; and Don Fowler, South Carolina State party chair.[23]

Consequently, Thomas Foley of Seattle, offered an amendment to Article 10 which had the effect of prohibiting "mandatory" quotas by striking the word "mandatory" and deleting that section of the convention delegation goals which said, "as indicated by their presence in the Democratic electorate." This amendment was part of a strategy to go to the Kansas City Mid-Term Convention in 1974 which would approve the charter with *two versions* of Article 10 of equal weight for the delegates to vote on, perhaps even defeating the affirmative action language favored by Blacks as it applied to both commission reports. But journalist Michael Malbin says of this maneuver:

The blacks' counter-strategy was to offer a third affirmative
action proposal, more to their liking than the draft language.
They thought that if they could send the draft language to
the mini-convention as the centrist alternative, they would be
able to get what they wanted all along, the draft language
without changes.[24]

This amendment, offered by Congresswoman Burke, added
language which changed the sense of Article 10 to read that equal
participation was to be ensured, countering Foley's approach by
adding the language, "in reasonable relationship to their presence in
the Democratic Electorate." This tactic was buttressed by the threat
of Willie Brown (Black State Assemblyman from California) to walk
out of the Charter Commission meeting in Kansas City, immediately preceeding the convention, if the Foley amendment passed.
Rather than supporting the Foley amendment, however, the
regulars on the commission voted (69–53) to send *four* proposals on
Article 10 to the Kansas City convention.

Willie Brown, however, made good his threat to walk out of the
Charter Commission meeting in Kansas City, and the fact that the
commission did not select any of the four proposals, stimulated
many interpretations of Brown's motives for doing so. Some thought
by playing the role of "militant Black leader" he might enhance his
leverage to lead the California delegation, but Brown himself said
that his walkout was related to the attempt of the regulars to
reinstate the "unit rule" as a symbol of all they had attempted to do to
"gut" the charter. In any case, the emergence of the slogan "Ten or
Walk" and the fact that his walkout was joined by other Black and
white members of the commission, supported the Black strategy
designed to have a strong version of Article 10 adopted. In this
sense, one might agree with Ben Brown that the tactic was effective
because it deprived the meeting of a quorum, and because it signaled
the fact that a base-line bargaining position had been reached beyond
which Blacks would not compromise.

Indeed, the fact that Blacks were becoming organized made
such sentiments a credible basis for intra-party conflict. Although a
Black Caucus had existed in 1972, in 1973 a more formal organization, the Black Democratic Caucus (BDC) was formed as an instrument to assist Blacks on both major commissions to coordinate
strategy. It was eventually comprised of those on the DNC as well
as any other commission appointees, and was led initially by local

Minnesota politician Earl Craig. On September 28, 1974, in Washington, D.C., a two-hour meeting of thirty-five Black Democrats was convened to "alert the Democratic party to the risks involved in any attempt to erode the affirmative action section of the proposed new Democratic Charter."[25] Speaking for those assembled, the newly created Steering Committee of prominent Black party activists said:

> If the Democratic leadership continues to bow to pressure from those who limit black, women, youth and other minority participation in Party Affairs, and if the Party leadership continues to insist on further compromises on Party Affirmative Action provisions, *we have no alternative but to reassess our involvement in and support of the Democratic party* (my emphasis).[26]

This statement, read by Mayor Coleman Young of Detroit, stated, "We see no need for further compromise," and delivered a warning that there would be trouble at the Mid-Term Conference if Blacks were forced to compromise further. Strauss and other party leaders responded by saying they would attempt to find some solution to the potential impasse.

The BDC, however, did not rely on Strauss' promises, but initiated a lobbying effort among Democrats to mobilize for the potential Kanses City show-down. Personal contacts were made and a memorandum was sent out on November 11 to potential delegates, spelling out the preferred position. It indicated that of the affirmative action language developed by the two commissions — Article 10 and Rule 18 — the BDC preferred the Mikulski Commission's Rule 18, saying, "The major difference in Article 10 and Rule 18 is that the former does not refer specifically to minorities, women and youth as primary targets of affirmative action."[27] Both did, however, have the key sections dealing with participation in "all party affairs," that such participation should be "as indicated by the presence (of Blacks and other minorities) in the Democratic electorate," and that the goal of the party should not be accomplished by the imposition of "mandatory" quotas. The memo ended with a plea for delegates to support the position taken by the Black leadership at Kansas City. One fortuitous show of support, in this regard, was the statement issued by the Democratic Governors Conference meeting November 18 at Hilton Head, South Carolina affirming their preference for the Mikulski language.

The Kansas City Mid-Term Conference began on December 5, 1974, and although early estimates of Black delegates attending were as low as 6%, final figures showed that they constituted 9.8% of the delegates.[28] Although this figure was lower than that in 1972 (14.6%), it was higher than the 1968 figure of 6.7%. The concern expressed about the decrease between 1972 and 1974 was registered because the new delegate selection rules proposed for 1976 were actually used as a guideline for the Kansas City Convention. Nevertheless, the fact that this was an "off-year" convention was also taken into consideration in assessing how the new rules might work in 1976.

The first meeting of the Black Democratic Caucus (chaired permanently by Willie Brown) at the convention, was held Thursday evening December 5, and as it aired the views of the newly arrived delegates regarding the principles at stake, it became clear that sentiment for a walkout was building. The next morning the meeting reconvened, and as if to pre-empt a serious move toward a walkout, the leadership of the Caucus went on the offensive, attempting to move the discussion back to tactics short of this drastic step. Basil Patterson asked how many delegates had the freedom to walkout and how far the BDC was prepared to go.[29] The head of the New York delegation said he would walk, followed by a labor union leader, who also questioned who would be left to counter reactionary measures within the party. The mayor of a southern city said that he would have some difficulty walking out because, after nearly one hundred years, a Black person had become the leader of his delegation, and the walkout might well destroy any attempt to further build Black political strength in the state. Willie Brown said that the tactic of walking out was a political sanction meant to embarrass the party and asked for a formal show of hands on a motion of support for a walkout. The hands raised were a clear majority of those in the room.[30] Thus fortified by the resolve of the delegates, the discussion was refocused on Article 10. It was decided that there would be no further compromises, and that a negotiating committee and "whip system" would be set up to get Article 10 passed without the offensive language.

Performance under an approved affirmative action plan and composition of the convention delegation shall be considered relevant evidence in the challenge of any state delegation. But composition alone shall not constitute prima facie evidence of discrimination, nor shall it shift the burden of proof to the challenged party.[31]

The leadership worked through Friday, December 6 to secure the support of the BDC language by the relevant minority caucuses, including women, who traded Black support for their "equal division" proposal to divide the convention delegates equally between women and men. Though this proposal had the effect of establishing a de facto 50% quota for women within the party, because their support was vital, Blacks agreed to the deal. Negotiations between Strauss and Blacks had become so extremely tense that at one point he was heard to say, "If the blacks want to walk, then tell them to get on their bicycles and go."[32]

On Saturday, as the conference was coming to a close, a pre-arranged break in the morning session was declared by Strauss to enable the caucuses to present the results of the bargaining. BDC leaders read the new language to the Black delegates.

If a state Party has adopted and implemented an approved *and monitored* affirmative action program, the Party shall not be subject to challenge based *solely* on delegate composition *or solely* on primary results.[33]

The trade-off appeared to be that the state party obligation to affirmative action was strengthened, while the point was softened somewhat so that challenges to a state's convention delegation could neither be based solely on the racial composition of the delegation nor on the results of primary delegate elections. This implied that additional due process violations of the state party would have to be proved as well, and the onus would be on the state party so challenged. After Mayor Coleman Young explained that the Steering Committee did, in fact, compromise but that it obtained as much as it could, the new language was put to a vote and passed by the BDC overwhelmingly.

On the floor of the convention, meanwhile, Strauss had lined up an impressive array of speakers on the compromise language, fearing that if the vote did not go well, the party would be split asunder. One key spokesman was Cecil Partee, Speaker of the House of the Illinois State Legislature and a Black lieutenant of Mayor Richard J. Daley of Chicago. Daley had also threatened to walk out with George Meany's forces, if Article 10 was changed to favor Blacks. But the final compromise pleased Daley, thus Partee's speech was highly symbolic to all of the delegates.[34] Strauss and others such as Basil Patterson, Barbara Mikuski, Don Fowler and Yvonne Burke spoke to the convention, urging acceptance of the compromise in the name of party unity. The motion was accepted overwhelmingly by the delegates amid much cheering and relief that the central issue of the conference had been resolved.

Despite feelings among whites that the party had barely averted disaster and remained unified, and among Blacks that the Black Democratic Caucus had matured into a new force within party politics, there were questionable aspects to the "victory." Key concepts — such as what it meant to encourage equal participation in "all party affairs" — would be left to the bylaws to define, and as such would become the subject of continuing battles within the Rules Committee over definition and implementation.

Richard Hatcher waged a determined battle within the CRC to have two concepts adopted. The first was the concept of "goals and timetables" as the enforcing principles of affirmative action contained in Article 10 of the charter, and the second was that "all party affairs" meant beginning at the lowest levels and proceeding up through the highest levels of activity in a given state. These concepts were not contained in the bylaws pursuant to the charter, passed by the DNC on October 14, 1975. Nevertheless, during the 153-member Rules Committee meeting (twenty-two blacks) on June 24, 1976, skillful planning by the Black Democratic Caucus reversed this situation by working to have the concept of "goals and time-tables" included in the Majority Report to the convention.[35] The issue of defining "all party affairs" however, was relegated to Minority Report number 8 of the Rules Committee Report to the convention. Both issues were passed by the convention in accord with the wishes of the BDC and, thus, by the 1976 campaign key legal issues with respect to the political integration of Blacks into the party were settled.

Lillian Huff, Black Caucus chair (Washington, D. C.), David Dinkins (New York) and others appeared before the Rules Committee and made persuasive arguments that the principle of political integration followed by the BDC was to so structure the rules that Blacks would be able to achieve a role at the national and state levels commensurate with their voting influence in the party.[36] It would be interesting now to attempt to measure the degree of Black integration into the party after the promulgation of the rules, and the impact of this strategy on the process of presidential selection in 1976 and 1980 in the selection of the party nominee during the primary elections and in the bargaining during the conventions.

THE NATIONAL PARTY

The integration of Blacks into the national Democratic party in the early 1970s, as we have seen, was deemed insufficient by the rising tide of Black political leaders, inasmuch as they were considering a different standard of participation than the national party leadership. While the party leaders were attempting to make possible a level of participation as indicated by the presence of Blacks in the national and state populations, Blacks were seeking to participate according to their impact upon the party, as determined by their presence in the Democratic electorate. This conflict was joined in the battles within the Mikulski and Sanford Commissions and, as a result, the latter standard has been established. A secondary result has been that the percentage of Blacks on the various standing committees of the party has risen to the new standard, as shown in Table 3.1 in the 1972 and 1984 comparison of Black institutional participation within the party.

From the data in Table 3.1, it is easily seen that the increase in Black membership on key standing committees of the party was 7.7% percent in the period presented, and while recent membership on the large committees has averaged 20%, it has not yet approached the 25% level. Moreover, although the membership of these committees has increased overall, the percentage of Black members has increased more, and as the number of committees has expanded the Black membership on such committees has also expanded. For example, the National Committee created such additional committees

Table 3.1 Blacks on National Party Standing Committees, 1976 and 1984.

Standing Committee	1972	% Black	1984	% Black
National Committee	303	11.8	377	14
DNC Executive	25	12.0	40	17.5
Rules	150	7.3	159	21
Credentials	150	10.0	159	19
Platform	150	12.6	159	20.7
Averages		10.7		18.4

Source: Democratic National Committee data for 1972; and "Blacks and Democratic Politics," paper, Office of Black Affairs, Democratic National Committee, Washington, D. C., 1984.

as the Strategy Council, the Committee on State Participation, the Resolutions Committee, the Rules and By-Laws Committee, the National Education and Training Council, the Judicial Council and the ERA Advisory Committee, and thus, the Black membership has expanded by an additional ten members on these smaller bodies.

The result of having Black members at the committee level is that the inclusion of Blacks in the institutional base of the party has made it possible for Blacks to gain experience in acquiring political skills and participating in party decision-making. Then, as the strength of the Black Democratic Caucus grew, it provided added significance to the Office of Black Affairs as an administrative structure inside the DNC, even though its small budget has been a source of frustration for successive office directors.

One of the first persons to establish the modern Office of Black Affairs in 1960 was Louis Martin, journalist and savvy politician. In fact, it was Martin who operationalized the Kennedy-King affair, referred to earlier, that resulted in Kennedy being supported by the Black community in the 1960 election. He went on to have a longer tenure in the White House, as adviser to the president in the Kennedy/Johnson and Carter administrations, than any other Black person in history. Frank Cowan, Director of the Office of Black Affairs (1974–78), played a critical role within the national party organization during the formative period of the charter and the Black Democratic Caucus, and later became a key adviser to Jimmy Carter, traveling with the party nominee in the presidential campaign of 1976. Tony Harrison, Director of the Black Affairs Office in 1984, handled his duties with finesse, yet his era manifests the unique pressures on this office. The Black staff proliferation into the many campaigns in 1984 meant that the office was often caught between the incessant pressures of serving the needs of Rev. Jesse Jackson's presidential campaign, those of the front-running presidential candidate Walter Mondale, the Black components of other presidential campaigns, the interests of the party leadership, together with the Black Democratic Caucus members in the various states.[37]

As the party's Black political staff has expanded, many more of these operatives have been utilized in the presidential campaigns of the front-running candidates, such as the Carter campaigns of 1976 and 1980, but most especially in the Mondale-Ferraro campaign of 1984. Essentially, this new group of party functionaries has made the transition to the presidential campaign staffs (as is customary with other staff members) after strategic jobs on the staffs of the standing committees, as well as in other tasks areas such as policy, administration, management, political, finance and communications.

This manifestation of internal strength has enabled the Black party officers to be much more efficacious. For example, as a result of his work with the Carter campaign, Ben Brown was selected to be a vice chair of the Democratic National Committee, however, neither he nor his successor, Coleman Young, had as much support as vice chair Richard Hatcher (1980–84). Hatcher concentrated not only on maintaining the gains won by the BDC in the charter and delegate selection fights, but he also extended and monitored affirmative action as it applied to the party's contracting process.

> Minority economic participation in our convention (1984) was achieved through active and dogged oversight and aggressive affirmative outreach that has resulted in a participation of $1 million with minority construction firms and an additional sum exceeding $700,000 in the purchase of goods and services for this (1984) convention.[38]

The fact that Hatcher, party vice chair, was also chair of the Jesse Jackson campaign in 1984 probably meant that he had less direct personal contact with party nominee Walter Mondale, though it is arguable that he had less *political influence*. The question is which afforded him greater symbolic influence, his position as party vice chair, or his ties to the Jackson campaign.

The summary effect of the integration of Blacks into the party institution has resulted in better communication with key state actors, and a more pervasive racial integration of campaign staffs. At the leadership level, it has facilitated Black involvement in national political affairs. Nevertheless, the difference between the more open party institution and the more tightly controlled nominee's campaign apparatus often obscures the easy path to influence by those who are active in party affairs and those who seek to make the transition to being politically influential with the nominee.

In the final analysis, racism, lack of political influence and other tangible and intangible factors often limit real influence by Blacks both within the actual decision-making organs of the party institution and certainly within the presidential campaigns, even though Blacks may hold impressive titles in both areas. There is, perhaps, no better way to assess the relative salience of these factors as determinants of the general ability of Blacks to have decision-making influence within the party than to review them within the context of a presidential campaign — where the party reaches the height of its function. Accordingly, we will briefly review the role of Black party activists in the 1976 and 1980 Democratic party primaries and conventions in an effort to determine the effectiveness of this form of dependent-leverage.

THE PRIMARIES

1976

Clearly, the Black population was not enthusiastic as it supported Carter in the spring of 1976, given its turnout for him of 38.6% in Philadelphia during the Pennsylvania Primary, and 47.6% in Chicago during the Illinois Primary. Nevertheless, he was receiving overwhelming Black support in the South, in places such as the North Carolina Primary, where he received 90% of the vote in Durham defeating Wallace 533 to 3.[39] Carter appeared to be more distrusted among northern Blacks, and southern Blacks had to contend with both the absence of liberal candidates and the Wallace factor. These elements worked in both cases to drive turnout down to the lowest point it had been in recent history. In Boston, for example, where Carter received 42% of the vote, turnout was 30% for Black Democrats and 17% for Black Republicans; in Florida it was only 43% for Black Democrats, remaining at similar levels in other primaries with the exception of Illinois, where local races of anti-Daley Congressman Ralph Metcalfe and state attorney general candidate Cecil Partee, worked to boost turnout. Even where there were Black candidates, as in Michigan where Richard Austin, the secretary of state was running for a U.S. Senate nomination, the Black turnout in Detroit was only 27%.[40]

The low level of turnout caused Eddie Williams to attack the lethargy of Blacks:

> One of the most effective ways of making sure that our political candidates have the courage to protect the civil rights of us all is to be militant and aggressive at the ballot box. That's how to put civil rights back into the political picture.[41]

What is important about this statement is that it illustrates the obvious corollary to the "balance of power" thesis — maximum effort at Black voter turnout.

For the purpose of increasing the turnout, a new organization — Operation Big Vote — was created out of a coalition of forty-five Black civic organizations in August of 1976. It set specific goals to reduce the population of seven million unregistered Black voters, with local goals for the registration activities of member organizations. The relationship of registration to presidential strategy was explained in this manner: "With such potential clout at the polls and clearly holding the balance of power in any close presidential election, the outcome of this national election is threatened by the seven million unregistered Black voters."[42]

How, it might be asked, did Jimmy Carter eventually attract the support of the Black voter? Was it through Black leaders' strategy or through Carter's efforts? One would have to select the latter response, inasmuch as, late in the primary season, there was little Black leadership consensus on presidential strategy. For example, on the weekend of April 30, there was a conference of the Black Democratic Caucus held in Charlotte, North Carolina for the purpose of developing a consensus within the Black community regarding issues. However, as the various presidential candidates gave their speeches in turn, even though the Black surrogates of each had worked the delegates in attendance for support, it was clear that there had been no "winner." Coleman Young, for example, was often described as "Carter's chief surrogate" and his strong support of Carter in Detroit was instructive in that Carter's slim victory (44% to 43%) in the May Michigan Primary may also have been attributed to lack of Black voter enthusiasm.[43] Then, in the Ohio Primary on June 9, Carter was the only candidate to challenge the request of the Black Twenty-first Congressional District organization not to field delegate slates in the district, headed by Congressman Louis Stokes (D-OH). The Carter slate was soundly beaten, as 70% of the voters supported Congressman Louis Stokes' organization.

What gave Carter the sense that he could beat Stokes was attendant to the fact that it was largely his own effort which resulted in defining the Black presidential strategy. While some observers such as Andrew Young suggested that Carter was "appealing" to Blacks and at ease with them because his southern style was familiar to them (most of whom have southern roots), Carter himself suggested that northern liberals did not "understand Blacks' special needs," and that "those are my people . . . particularly Blacks."[44]

Other analysts, however, have suggested that Carter utilized his ties to the King family to get into the grassroots Black community through the network of churches represented by the Southern Christian Leadership Conference, thereby circumventing established Black leaders. Perhaps this was the key to former Congresswoman Yvonne Burke of California's view that Carter "goes into the black communities and he involves black people," and perhaps his southern origins made him a source of pride to southern Blacks as well as southern whites.[45] The contrary view was offered by Julian Bond who suggested that "Carter is getting the black vote by default, and it's wholly undeserved," a sentiment which appears to be in agreement with Congressman John Conyers (D-MI) who attributed "Carter's strength among black voters . . . to a failure of black leaders to lead; the politics of the moment overcomes being black."[46]

If Carter's detractors were correct, then the "politics of trust" may have been the key to the breakdown between politics and policy. It is unmistakable that Andrew Young, in supporting Carter and persuading others to do so, was following a strategy of trust.

> Young will not press Carter, publicly or privately, for the kinds of quid-pro-quos that invariably attend victorious political campaigns. What will Young do? Young: 'I will work for good government and to influence the quality of the Carter Administration.' 'The things I want are good for the American people. Carter couldn't betray me without betraying them.'[47]

Others, such as Julian Bond, disagreed with the "politics of trust" asking: "When Andy says Carter has made no promises to him, I believe it. But what about welfare, help for cities, the real policy questions important to Blacks?"[48] This was a fair question, since, as late in the primary season as early April, many Black leaders were unsure of Carter's stand on the Humphrey-Hawkins Bill, a jobs/economic development measure which had become the central issue in their public policy priorities. Carter had only issued a statement in support of it on the same day he apologized to Blacks for his reference to neighborhoods having the right to "ethnic purity," a view widely interpreted as racist.[49] Even then, some felt that his support for the bill was ambiguous.

No doubt, what made Carter feel confident in utilizing symbolic politics was the disorganization among Black leaders and the strong support of Carter by some, such as Rev. Martin Luther King, Sr. who publicly "forgave" Carter for the "ethnic purity" remark, a gesture which may have enhanced Carter's confidence. "I think the blacks just trust me to do what I say and run the government in a competent way."[50] Given the eventual strong support of Carter by Blacks, one would have to conclude that his strategy of the "politics of trust" was effective in the process of presidential selection.

1980

When the 1980 political season opened, Blacks were poised to be critical of the candidacy of Jimmy Carter because they had found many of his basic human needs policies as president alienating to their interests. Vernon Jordan, president of the National Urban League, as early as April of 1977 had the following view:

> There has been some disappointment and disillusionment
> with President Carter when you measure promises made and
> promises kept. There is intense feeling, certainly among the
> leadership in the Black Community that the president's
> economic message is inconsistent both with his commitment
> to them and to the Humphrey-Hawkins full-employment
> bill. He's saying, for example, that we have to delay imple-
> mentation of Humphrey-Hawkins for two years. That is
> bound to be a serious campaign issue.[51]

This disillusionment among Blacks with Carter's performance was the chief reason that in January, Data Black, a public opinion polling organization, found that most Blacks disapproved of Carter's efforts toward them (44%-disapproved; 38%-neutral; 23%-approved).[52]

The split between the Carter and Kennedy forces was also very much in evidence when the Black political leadership and 3,000 delegates met in February at the Black Democratic Caucus' National Conference on a Black Agenda in Richmond, Virginia. Mayor Coleman Young urged the delegates to support Carter, and it was clear at Richmond that the lack of consensus among the leadership on a presidential candidate posed a dilemma for securing a consensus commitment on the issue agenda proceeding from the meeting.[53]

In this considerable breach of opinion regarding which candidate to support, there was room for allegiance to a new candidate, as the poll also reported that Blacks preferred Senator Edward Kennedy by a margin of 48% to 32%.[54] The extent of the dissatisfaction was illustrated by an incident in June. When Carter's motorcade rolled through Miami, Florida's Black section of town, Liberty City, the scene of earlier civil disturbances, angry Blacks booed and threw bottles at his limousine.[55] At the same time, the Congressional Black Caucus had called for Black leaders to make no commitment to any presidential candidate until there was a commitment to Black issues. Congresswoman Cardiss Collins (D-IL), Congressional Black Caucus chair, had suggested throughout the campaign season that if there were "no contract" there should be "no vote" for such a candidate.[56]

The split in the Black community was reflected in the political leadership, as a group, headed by Walter Fauntroy, but including some civil rights leaders, key labor leaders and others, gravitated toward Kennedy. The impact of incumbency, however, was strong enough to convince the largest group of Black elected and appointed officials from the Carter administration to remain loyal to him. Andrew Young had pleaded for Blacks to remain with Carter at the annual Congressional Black Caucus Dinner in September 1979. Appearing to follow this suggestion of a former colleague, Congressman Rangel announced his support for Carter in December 1979 and was quickly followed by Tom Bradley, William Gray, Coleman Young and Jesse Jackson. While it often looks as though there is a "herd" mentality at work when Black leadership does make its choice of a candidate, the separate considerations which might cause each of them to choose one candidate over another are seldom available to public scrutiny, though obviously they are an important factor in their evaluation.[57]

Nevertheless, this movement of leaders appeared to have some influence upon the primary as Black voters began giving Carter a larger share of their vote than Kennedy, with the southern Black vote trending heavily for Carter while Kennedy took the northern Black vote.[58] At base, it appears that the process of presidential selection in the Black community in 1980 was securely related to the ability of the president to hold on to the most significant group of Black leaders who, in turn, were able to exercise their influence with the Black electorate.

THE CONVENTIONS

The Democratic convention in both 1976 and 1980 resulted in the nomination of the same candidate, but were significantly different in that the character of each administration and each of the different campaign opponents provided a different setting for comparison of the role of Blacks. In any case, I will describe each convention role briefly and then attempt to summarize these differences, using the contemporary record of the day, as well as surveys of convention delegates in 1976, 1980, and 1984 by the Institute for Urban Affairs and Research at Howard University.[59]

1976

The 1976 convention was simultaneously a test of the newly formed Black Democratic Caucus to effectively influence the further ratification of the party charter according to its own agenda, and to negotiate a satisfactory basis for ratifying the nomination of Jimmy Carter. Nevertheless, enthusiasm decreased somewhat when it became known that there were only 104 Black delegates and alternates at the convention, down to 10% from 183 delegates in 1972, amounting to 15% that year. This would lend additional anxiety to the task of the BDC in continuing its thrust to achieve party rules which allowed for the expansion of the Black role.

In general, the Howard University Delegate Survey (see Appendix) found that Black delegates supported the reform process with regard to delegate selection and a resolution supported by the BDC and passed by the convention was designed to expand Black delegate strength by having the DNC provide financial assistance for needy delegates to attend the convention. This resolution was necessary, from the perspective of the respondents, because of the differences in patterns of financial resources available to Black and white delegates and generally between rich and poor delegates.

Table 3.2 Sources of Democratic Party Convention Delegate Support (%) 1976: Blacks and Whites.

	Blacks	Whites
Candidate	21.2	29.7
State Party	41.6	28.4
Neighbors	57.6	52.3
Labor	22.1	19.4
Other	16.8	22.6

The pattern of support for delegates, shown in Table 3.2, is very similar, except for the wide disparity in support to Black delegates given by the state party organization, which has become the implementation unit for the state affirmative action plans. The fact that Blacks raise slightly more from neighbors than whites and that whites contribute slightly more from their own resources is consistent with the known abilities of both groups in this regard. For, even though Blacks were better educated and had higher occupational levels than whites, there was no significant difference in the income profile of our respondents.

The first issue Blacks faced was the fact that the response to the July 12 keynote speech delivered by Barbara Jordan, Black Congresswoman from Texas, had been so positive that it set in motion strong speculation among many delegates that she should be considered a vice presidential nominee. At the same time, Congressman John Conyers conveyed to the BDC that he was directing an effort to collect the required signatures to put the name of Congressman Ronald Dellums (D-CA) into nomination for vice president from the convention floor, essentially for the purpose of making an acceptance speech to set a progressive tone for convention issues.

The BDC interviewed Jordan with respect to her intentions and found that she was not intending to be a candidate. She released a statement to that effect the day following her speech. Within the BDC meeting, however, she said that she was realistic enough to know that neither the party nor the country was ready for a Black woman vice president, and that she did not want to be a "symbolic" candidate, but a real one. This done, the BDC gave its approval for the Dellums scenario. Consequently, Jordan's keynote speech, the first by a Black person, expressed both appreciation for the delegates' confidence in her and the belief that Carter had "in a significant way delineated his support for the issues that are of concern to (Blacks and women)."[60]

Here it should be noted that both Black and white delegates in our survey expressed a readiness to have a Black person for vice president, in response to our question regarding whether or not "the time was right."

According to the data in Table 3.3, Jordan may well have misread the attitude of a substantial segment of Democratic party activists on this issue in 1976. Whether or not Democratic voters, when faced with the actual choice, would have voted according to this attitude, or the extent to which this manifest attitude was shared

Table 3.3 Democratic Delegate Preference for Black Vice President in 1976 (%).

	Yes	No	No Response
Blacks	75.2	13.3	11.5
Whites	61.9	14.8	22.6

by a wider electorate are highly questionable. In any case, while some Black leaders suggested to Carter that Thomas Bradley, mayor of Los Angeles, should be considered for vice president, the Black respondents in our survey preferred Jordan for vice president over any other candidate (27.1%).

The prime consideration of the BDC sessions was the strategy concerning the Minority Reports coming from the Rules Committee, especially number 3 concerning "equal division" of the 1980 convention between men and women, and number 8 concerning the meaning of Black participation in "all party affairs." The Black delegates were instructed to support number 3, since the Women's Caucus had negotiated an exchange of support with the Black Democratic Caucus for its support on number 8. In fact, among Black delegates, the survey indicates that women were the most favored coalition group among a number of choices. At the same time, Black delegates indicated that among "the most important convention issues" the question of Equal Representation for Women ranked third (7%) behind the Party Platform (39%) and the Selection of the Party Candidate (19.8%).

The BDC, under the leadership of Richard Hatcher, had successfully established the principle of "goals and timetables" as the enabling feature of the affirmative action (Article 10) section of the charter, and this addition to the charter language was included in the Rules Committee Report to the convention.[61] The necessity for this addition is illustrated in a review of the language of the affirm-

Table 3.4 Coalition Preference of Black Democratic Delegates, 1976 (%).

Coalition Group	Preference Rating
Liberals	21.2
Candidates	12.3
Women	27.4
Minorities	17.7
Southerners	1.8
Labor	14.2

ative action plans to the 1976 convention from the state of New York, which begins with the goal that special efforts will be made to encourage full participation of minorities, Native Americans, women, youth and any other traditionally under-represented groups and to prevent discrimination on the basis of sex, age, race or social or economic status. This plan, which was similar to the Alabama Affirmative Action Plan, sought to "greatly increase" such participation with only the tools of publicity and public education and with no goals or timetable for achieving results, and with no penalty levied by the party for failure to achieve them.

Upon arrival at the Democratic National Convention in New York City, however, the complex political issues involved in bargaining with Jimmy Carter absorbed the attention of the Black leaders, who sought, unsuccessfully at first, to meet with Carter, even though one newspaper said that they had "shown an unflinching determination to play a meaningful role."[62] But, after submitting the Issue Agenda, resulting from the BDC conference in Charlotte, North Carolina, "for the record," they met with Black delegates to develop the actual agenda and a bargaining team (the Steering Committee).

BDC leaders wanted to meet with Carter to secure his commitment to a number of items, including: appointments in his administration and campaign, voter registration, the Humphrey-Hawkins Full Employment Bill, support for the Minority Reports, and others. However, the source of some anxiety lay in comments by Carter operatives immediately before the convention, that Carter would by-pass the Black leaders "and go directly to the people," and that "we want them (black leaders) but we don't need them."[63] Pehaps the basis of this feeling was that 78.8% of Black delegates had already decided to support Carter before the convention. It could also have been, as we have strongly suggested, the persistent thought that Blacks trusted Carter. Andrew Young seconded the Carter nomination and continued to exhibit his faith in Carter's promises to contribute to Black progress.[64]

There is some evidence in our study, that Black delegates actually trusted Carter because of their perception of his "honesty" (25.7%) and "personality" (15%). These character values, it will be remembered, were important to all Americans in the aftermath of the "Watergate Affair," and Blacks also placed great value on such personal qualities.

Black leaders met with Carter on July 12, and, according to one source, they "did not negotiate a compromise. They presented Carter with a list of their concerns and they said after their forty-five minute meeting that he committed himself to supporting most of their positions," leading the Steering Committee to say "that they would support him without reservation."[65] The Steering Committee reported back to the BDC that Carter promised:

1. "serious, hard-line commitment for the involvement of blacks and other minorities throughout the government."
2. "the biggest voter registration drive in the Black Community since 1960."
3. "continuing access to himself and to the policy makers in the upcoming campaign and in any subsequent administration."
4. the placement of individuals "who might serve on the fall campaign task force."[66]

The group also asked for the retention of Basil Patterson in his role as vice chair of the DNC and consideration of Tom Bradley on an equal basis for vice presidential nominee. However, it was unclear that these items were confirmed.

Two policy issues deserve mention from the perspective of the delegate survey. The first is the issue of employment. Jimmy Carter appeared to set the stage for his meeting with Black leaders by suggesting, the previous day on "Meet the Press", that President Ford's veto of the federal jobs bill was a "very serious indication of the President's insensitivity to people's needs," that it should be possible to develop jobs where people live. However, despite the various comments he made on the subject, there was still little indication of exactly *what version* of an employment program he would favor as president.[67] Yet, among platform issues, employment was favored by Black delegates to a degree (92%) that considerably out-distanced other issues of health (84%), taxes (62%), welfare (61%) and aid to education (57%).

Secondly, the issue of South Africa which would become very important to Blacks in the mid–1980s, lead Rev. Jesse Jackson, head of Operation PUSH, in 1976 to challenge both presidential candidates to respond to the recent violence occurring June 16, 1976 in Soweto, and to seek to have a resolution passed at both national party conventions condemning the South African Government.[68] A tough resolution on South Africa had also been proposed by the BDC for inclusion in the platform and party officials said they would review the platform as recommended by the convention Platform Committee to see if it might be included, since a procedure was in effect which outlawed amendments from the floor. Approximately 70% of those Black delegates responding to the Howard Survey indicated that they favored American corporations leaving South Africa, while 16.8% opposed such a step. The comparable figures for whites were: favor–46.4%; opposed–34.1%. The resolution, however, was never included in the platform of the Democratic party.

1980

Proof that the strategy of utilizing the rules to accomplish the integration of Blacks into the party was working surfaced with the expansion of delegates to the 1980 convention. Black delegates made up 14.4% or 778 of the 5,384 delegates and alternates, constituting a 58% increase in Black delegates over 1976. The South comprised a large proportion of this increase, since of the forty states with Black delegates, twenty-seven had increases, and nine of the eleven states with 20% or more Black convention delegates were located in the South. Such increases between 1976 and 1980 were especially true for states such as Louisiana (14.6% to 37.2%), South Carolina (22.6% to 43.2%), Alabama (17.1% to 37.7%), and the District of Columbia (47.1% to 63.1%). A Report of the Joint Center for Political Studies indicated that: "This very high level of black representation in 1980 results, in large measure, from adoption of a vigorous affirmative action program by the Democratic National Committee."[69]

This outcome may be attributed to the victory of the BDC in achieving its convention goals with respect to charter and delegate selection amendments, to the extent that the delegate selection rules for the 1980 convention included language calling for "specified goals and timetables," and defined "all party affairs" to apply to "party organizations at all levels . . . as indicated by their presence in the Democratic electorate."[70] In addition, the CRC had gained valuable experience which made for more effective monitoring of state delegate selection plans for minority participation.

Our survey findings support these outcomes. For example, under the delegate selection rules, the state party has a crucial role in balancing delegations for race and gender composition. Those responding to questions regarding the basis of their selection as delegates who said they were selected by the state party amounted to 7.1% in 1976 and doubled to 14.1% in 1980. However, this did not appear to increase state party financial support for Black delegate races, since party support decreased from 41.6% in 1976 to 33.2% in 1980. This could be accounted for by the larger number of Blacks running for delegate seats overall and the weak financial condition of the national party in 1980, racial discrimination, or other factors. There is direct evidence in the survey, however, that Black delegates felt that the rules were making a difference, and their overall approval of the changes registered 67.3%, the most important basis of which seemed to be minority affirmative action in general and more favorable opinions emphasizing attracting women delegates.

This last indicator highlights an important problem, since those delegates responding that affirmative action for women made the critical difference in expanding the delegate pool doubled between 1976 and 1980 (13.1% to 26.1%). Such an increase may have occurred because the 1980 delegate composition (and, thus, the survey) includes a larger proportion of persons who are both minorities *and* women. Women had achieved their important goal of "equal division" in the state delegations by 1980, and combining this with Black affirmative action requirements meant that an unavoidable emphasis is being placed upon attracting minority women as delegates. So, whereas the gender ratios in the previous conventions were heavily skewed toward Black men, the ratios in 1980 were beginning to favor Black women. Table 3.5 compares the actual gender composition at the 1974 Mid-Term Convention with that of our surveys in 1976 and 1980.

In addition, it should be noted that the increase in delegates may have increased the middle-class character of the Black delegate pool as the proportion of our respondents who had attended graduate and professional schools increased along with income levels.

The Black delegates arriving at the mid-August convention in New York City were split between President Jimmy Carter and

Table 3.5 Gender Composition of Black Democratic Convention Delegates, 1974, 1976, 1980 (%).

	1974	1976	1980
Male	58	56.8	44.7
Female	42	43.2	54.3

Source: 1974 data, Delegate Survey, Democratic National Committee, Washington, D. C., 1974.

Senator Edward Kennedy (D-MA) as reflected in our survey of pre-convention candidate commitment (Carter–55%; Kennedy–32%). In fact, in 1980 we found that 95% of Black delegates were committed to one or another of the candidates overall, reflecting an increase from 78% in 1976, a result probably stimulated by the intense competition for Black delegates by two strong candidates. Key Black political leaders were also split between the two, although Carter had the largest group of Black leaders due to the high number of presidential appointees in this group who were campaigning for him. For example, Kennedy had attracted key members of the Congressional Black Caucus such as Ronald Dellums, Cardiss Collins and State Senator Julian Bond, but Carter could call on an extensive list of leaders beginning with former U.N. Ambassador Andrew Young; Mayors Coleman Young, Richard Hatcher and Richard Arrington; Coretta Scott King; Rev. Joseph Lowery; EEOC head Eleanor Holmes Norton and many others.

This split challenged the effectiveness of the Black Democratic Caucus, as its initial sessions, beginning on August 10, were full of pleas and stirring speeches for Black unity. Nevertheless, the atmosphere quickly degenerated to one of mass confusion among Blacks when the two main presidential contenders began to impose discipline over their Black delegates, reflecting conflict over two key issues— Rule F3C and a significant employment program.

Rule F3C was a Minority Report from the Rules Committee which would have altered the practice of binding delegates to vote on the first ballot for those candidates to whom they were committed during the primaries. Instead, the Kennedy-sponsored measure proposed the concept of an "open convention," which would have released delegates to "vote their conscience" on all ballots. If this measure had passed, it would have given Kennedy another chance at the nomination; however, it failed.

After losing the vote on rule F3C, Kennedy resolved not to further contest the nomination, instead turning his energies to having language included in the platform that supported a strong job-creation program, together with budget increases in other human service programs. These initiatives were included in Minority Reports 1–5, and key Black political leaders were urged to support them.[71] In fact, Rev. Jesse Jackson had threatened to call for a walkout by Blacks if Carter did not address this important issue, and the tension was heightened by the fact that Carter had said that he would not meet with Black leaders until after his nomination was secure.

Jackson, however, had also been in discussions with Carter operatives and indicated at one point before the nomination in an interview on the convention floor that "the president had moved a long way toward a jobs-stimulation program."[72] Jackson later announced that the president had accepted seven proposals put to him by the group, some of which included:

1. a promise not to repudiate a minority report calling for a $12 billion jobs program;
2. a directive to the Department of Justice to move vigorously against the Ku Klux Klan;
3. a chair in the Department of Education to deal with increased appropriations to Black colleges;
4. a "generous grant" from the DNC to aid voter registration through Operation Big Vote.[73]

It was, therefore, even more disheartening to Black delegates for both Kennedy and Carter, when Carter announced in his speech accepting the nomination his repudiation of the $12 billion jobs program, the Kennedy proposal which was the center-piece of Black bargaining efforts. One delegate from North Carolina interviewed on the floor said that the jobs plank in the platform was "right but the President's response was fuzzy" and that "he represented poor Black people from North Carolina and doubted that the President's statement reflected their wishes."[74] In effect, it could be ascertained through discussions with other delegates that many Blacks felt they had been "double-crossed."

Perhaps, it should be suggested at this point that the political division among Blacks were more potent than the issue conflicts among them. For example, if we compare our respondents' views with respect to candidate preference, "open convention" resolution and the employment issue, Table 3.6 shows the result:

Table 3.6 Black Democratic Delegate Views on Candidate Preference, Open Convention and Employment, 1980 (%).

Candidate Preference	
Carter	54.9
Kennedy	32.4
Open Convention	
yes	41.7
no	51.8
Economy	
Carter version	36.7
Kennedy version	51.8

The table appears to confirm the view that *policy issue* positions among Blacks were not as seriously divisive as *political issue* positions, since their candidate commitment preference was controlling for the "open convention" response, but not for the employment issue where there was significantly more Black unity.

The essential problem, of course, was that political differences contributed greatly to the lack of Black unity, effectively destroying the Black bargaining position on policy issues in 1980. There is some support for the lack of unity proposition in our survey with respect to the attendance of Black delegates at BDC sessions. Table 3.7 shows the reported negative attendance pattern at BDC meetings during the week of the convention.

While we do not know if this pattern of attendance was generated by eccentric factors or whether it represents a normal distribution, it is suggestive that on Monday when the issue of Rule F3C was being decided attendance at the Caucus was low. Then, it is easily observed that Carter chose Friday morning to meet with Black delegates, a time when their lowest attendance at BDC sessions probably reflected their absence from the convention. Next, when asked what was the major issue in the Caucus sessions, they indicated first, "jobs" and second, "lack of unity" among Blacks. In addition, when asked why they did not vote in their state caucus according to decisions reached in the BDC, the dominant reply was that "blacks were disorganized." Then, since undoubtedly Carter and Kennedy exercised some influence upon their committed delegates, it is interesting to assess the source of that influence in Table 3.8 in response to the question: "When (State) delegations' and (Black) Caucus' positions were in conflict, did you usually vote as decided by the delegation, Caucus, other?"

The responses appear to indicate that the delegates rarely felt the direct impact of the candidate's discipline over their vote, rather it was channeled through structures closest to them, either their state

Table 3.7 Black Delegate Attendance at BDC Meetings of the Democratic National Convention August 11–15, 1980 (%).

	Yes	No
Monday	26.9	73.1
Tuesday	46.5	53.5
Wednesday	38.0	62.0
Thursday	32.4	67.6
Friday	16.9	83.1

Table 3.8 Black Voter Preference When State Delegation and Caucus Positions Conflicted at the Democratic National Convention, 1980 (%).

State Delegation	16.9
Black Caucus	25.4
Own Judge	22.5
Kennedy	2.8
Carter	1.4

delegation leaders or Black leaders. A further breakout of sub-categories, in an attempt to understand the nature of the Kennedy-Carter conflict upon Black delegates, indicated the existence of a strong cluster of variables which we have categorized as "hostility among blacks," caused by such representative factors as "suspicion of possible collusion between Carter and Kennedy" and the strong "tension between them," as elements in the Black perspective. A substantial majority of Black delegates responding to a direct question concerning the effectiveness of the Black Democratic Caucus felt that the BDC was not effective at this convention, implying that despite the conflict between Carter and Kennedy, the BDC might have been more effective with prior "planning."

CONCLUSION

The period from 1964 to 1980 was the culmination of an impressive struggle by Blacks to achieve the goal of political integration into the national Democratic party in order to attain equal status as members of its governing coalition. A prime assumption was that this posture would yield Blacks greater leverage in the political decisions which faced the party, thereby gaining political and policy instruments with which to improve conditions in the Black community. There was, indeed, in this period an expansion of Black participation in the national party organization in most activities. Similar in-roads were not made at the state level, and this goal is now further complicated, because the influence of the organization of state Democratic chairs has increased, creating an important counter to the influence of special party caucuses.

Our concern has been directed to the process of presidential selection and in that regard, it is striking that the participation Blacks have won within the institution appears not to have been translated into influence with the presidential nominees and their campaign organizations. Black party operatives appear not to have had sustained influence with the party chair, or automatic access to the party presidential candidates and nominees, and have only generated significant influence where the threat of disruption of party harmony was maintained as a credible option.

In the primaries, the process by which Black leaders selected Carter in 1976 was almost accidental in the sense that it was a result of an initial strategy to stop George Wallace in Florida, which developed into an almost personal decision by some Black Atlanta politicians to continue to support him. As a result, Black leaders were split over Carter, and primary voters exhibited the same confusion, which was not settled until just before the convention. By that time, however, important bargaining leverage had been lost and Carter was never specifically committed to what had been stated as the central propositions of the Black issue agenda in Charlotte, North Carolina. Most important, Carter was skillful in circumventing an unorganized Black political leadership, and developing his own organizational control of the Black vote.

Again in 1980 the bargaining results were vague and unsatisfactory, due partially to the lack of political leverage based on the incumbency of the president and, thus, his control over key Black leaders, together with the division of the Black delegation into two competing camps. Again, when the relatively weak concessions were made, they bore little relationship to those which had been described by the Richmond convention as the "Black Agenda."

The moderate success of the strategy of dependent-leverage through political integration into the party institution, together with the issue-bargaining confusion suggests that we concentrate next on the intended bargaining strategies by the initiators of the "Black agenda conferences" from 1972 to 1980. I will explore the questions whether or not the failure to effectively bargain these issues is inherent in the structure of the agendas or the political process of dependent-leverage. In any case, the issue conferences constituted an attempt at developing leverage and, thus, are ostensibly connected to the process of political bargaining. I will examine these aspects to see if they explain the unsatisfactory results from bargaining in the period under discussion.

Chapter 4

The Black Agenda-Building Process

INTRODUCTION

In the previous chapter, I described the tactic of Black political integration into the party as a logical extension of the grand strategy of dependent-leverage. However, Blacks have also historically felt the need for a "quasi-independent" leverage strategy of activities outside of the formal party structure. In the nineteenth century the National Negro Conventions and the various state Conventions of Colored Men were vehicles for addressing electoral strategy, and in the period of the "Nadir" Black exclusion from the major parties led to the creation of electoral conventions, such as those sponsored by the Black and Tans.[1] But the question we confront in the more recent period is why there is still perceived to be a need for tactics of political separation? Two answers come to mind: the first has to do with the function of the political parties and the second considers how to achieve Black electoral objectives such as agenda formation.

Almond and Powell find political parties to be a "specialized aggregation structure of modern societies," emerging "where the number and variety of interests being articulated becomes too great to receive satisfaction through informal interaction."[2] There is, nevertheless, always a tension in the way various interests are served in the formal "aggregation." If such interests are well served by the party, it may be a function of the effectiveness of the constituent group in having organized itself to compete with others within the party. Thus, in the Democratic party "coalition," organized labor,

Hispanics, Jews, Gays, and women, among others, are examples of constituent groups which have an extensive base of organization outside of the party. The party, then becomes an instrument of delicate mediation among these various internal interests in the act of furthering the ability of party leadership to successfully compete for power in the national political arena with which to implement its philosophy of government at various levels. The convention of the party is theoretically the place where the interests of the coalition members are formally aggregated, even though the constituent groups may have their own separate conventions as well.

Blacks have not maintained an organized electoral base outside the Democratic party historically, but have occasionally sponsored external forums such as conventions during an election year. The only organized political alternative was the Civil Rights Movement, which perhaps began the modern practice when it organized in 1960 a leadership conference as an adjunct to the Democratic convention. More than a decade later, as Black elected officials attempted to shape electoral strategy, these external conferences and conventions were sponsored by party activists who needed a legitimate forum from which to represent Black interests within party circles.

I will review the recent Black political (electoral) convention movement, encompassing the 1972 National Black Political Convention in Gary, Indiana, the 1976 Black Issues Conference in Charlotte, North Carolina, and the 1980 Conference on a Black Agenda in Richmond, Virginia, in order to understand how they furthered the agenda-building process of the Black community. This dictates an examination of whether or not the character of the set of issues themselves was viewed as legitimate by party leaders, or whether there existed sufficient linkages between the politics of the Black convention and that of the party presidential nomination process.

THE GARY CONVENTION

The National Black Political Convention held March 10–12 in Gary, Indiana was not only a "convention," but it was a singularly important event in an historical period because it symbolized the moment at which two types of political mobilization came together.[3] For instance, in some states, the process of organizing delegations according to the requirements contained in the Call that they should be broadly representative of the Black community, was controlled by youthful Black nationalist groups, while others were dominated by professional politicians. This led to some friction between these two dominant forces; the Michigan delegation was challenged as being unrepresentative since it was dominated by labor and other professionals. In response, the delegation was led out of the convention by Mayor Coleman Young and the challengers assumed their seats. Despite this display of friction between the two factions, the convention was attended by over eight thousand Blacks, about three thousand of whom were delegates and the rest observers. They would address at least three important issues.

The first issue was whether or not to place before the convention the question of supporting one of the announced white presidential candidates or any one of the unannounced Black contenders. The leadership of the convention, which included a small group comprised of Rev. Jesse Jackson, Congressman Charles Diggs, Jr., Black nationalist writer Imamu Baraka, and Mayor Richard Hatcher, were convinced that there would be a divisive and bloody fight if the issue were addressed by the convention. Not only were most of the Black would-be candidates in attendance (with the exception of Julian Bond), there was a strong Shirley Chisholm delegation lobbying, and there were some surrogates who served as lobbyists for Hubert Humphrey, George McGovern, and others. With these considerations, the convention voted, at the request of the leaders, to take no position on this issue.

The second major issue was the creation of a Black political party. Although strong sentiment had been voiced for such a step before the convention by persons such as Jesse Jackson, when the discussion came to the floor, Jackson and the leader of the Ohio delegation, Ron Daniels, strongly counseled delegates that a convention proclamation alone would not result in the formation of such a party. Rather, they suggested that if the grassroots work was accomplished which was considered to be a prerequisite to the formation of such a party, the party would naturally evolve. This evasive tactic prevailed, and the focus shifted to the details necessary to construct a continuing organizational mechanism for grassroots mobilization which would come to be known as the National Black Political Assembly.

The handling of these issues exhibited a very firm leadership style which drew a rebuke from many delegates as being too "heavy-handed," as the proposals were debated on the floor, and at one point the meeting almost broke up into confusion. This crisis led to the creation of a Steering Committee of state delegation chairs to improve communication with the floor and provide participation in major convention proposals. The committee structure was important inasmuch as these chairs were the embryo of the continuing national leadership of the assembly. It was also this body which decided such critical questions in the post-convention period as the final wording of the convention resolutions, the strategy of presenting the agenda to the major candidates and obtaining commitments on it, and the nature of the assembly.

All other issues being disposed of, the convention made the passage of the agenda its main focus of attention. In January of that year, there had been a preparatory session at Howard University at which policy experts discussed a range of issues such as political empowerment, economic development, human resources, environmental development, international relations, rural development, and communications.

It was originally planned that state delegations would submit resolutions to the Platform Committee, headed by Congressman Walter Fauntroy, prior to the convention. However, on March 11 at the convention the Platform Committee conducted a full day of hearings on issues which streamed-in from arriving delegations and, thus, no prior platform draft would have been useful. With this information, the drafting committee, headed by the remarkable Carl Holman, president of the National Urban Coalition, prepared the document, which was printed over night and ready for the delegates the next day.

As amendments began to emerge from the floor, it became obvious that the delegates' positions on the explosive issues of Israel and school busing were to become sources of severe conflict. Throughout the convention, a proposal opposed to busing was supported by the Congress of Racial Equality (CORE), but the convention eventually adopted an even more negative version offered by the South Carolina delegation which read:

> We condemn forced racial integration of schools as a bankrupt, suicidal method of desegregating schools, based on the false notion that Black children are unable to learn unless they are in the same setting as white children. As an alternative to busing of Black children to achieve total racial balance, we demand quality education in the Black community through the control of our school system, school districts and a guarantee of an equal share of that money.[4]

The proponents of this resolution, together with CORE, and the Black nationalist delegates coalesced to support this resolution, while opposing it were Black elected officials such as Henry Marsh, a Richmond, Virginia attorney and later mayor, who was in the process of suing the Richmond Board of Education in an effort to force busing to achieve racial balance in his city. However, the pro-busing Marsh resolution, as well as a sympathetic resolution offered by Jay Cooper, mayor of Pritchard, Alabama, lost on the floor.

This outcome was decried by Black elected officials, and led Roger Wilkins, then a black reporter for *The New York Times* to set the tone of criticism by charging that black separatists such as "Roy Innis (head of CORE) and his little band of bitter men" had, in effect, supported Richard Nixon's view that Black people also did not want busing. He reported the view of Walter Fauntroy who supported the Cooper position and cited a recent Gallup Poll which showed that 80% of black people supported busing.[5] Perhaps moved by the mounting criticism of both Blacks and whites, the Steering Committee of the Assembly met on March 24 to finalize the resolutions bearing on the agenda, and sought to "clarify" the convention position with the following language:

> Busing is not the real issue in American education today, and we condemn the dishonesty of the Nixon Administration and other forces in making busing an issue when, in fact, busing has officially been used to maintain segregation for many years in many sections of the country. The real education issue for the Black community is how do we get supreme quality education for all our youngsters. We condemn as false the notion that Black children are unable to learn unless they are in the same setting with white children; and further, we disassociate ourselves from the positions set forth by Nixon and Wallace.
> We cannot have Blacks disintegrated out of political power achieved by: (1) Nixon's plan to take us back to *Plessy vs. Ferguson*; or (2) the court's disintegration of our children into white-dominated school boards, budgets, curricula, etc.
> Our politics is that we must have control of our own education, with the options of transportation and any other tools which guarantee superior quality education and also protect all rights guaranteed under the Fourteenth Amendment.[6]

This statement attempted to answer the criticism leveled by such persons as Roger Wilkins (nephew of Roy Wilkins, the venerable head of the NAACP) who felt that the previous position had played into the hands of conservatives and racists, while the statement retained some of the assumptions previously adopted. Needless to say, this statement met with little more enthusiasm from the original critics than the previous one.

The second issue which remained unresolved by the end of the convention, and which caused much dissension, was the issue of Israel. On the final day, the heated floor debate on this subject was prompted by a resolution presented by a delegate from the District of Columbia, Rev. Douglas Moore, head of the local Black United Front, which stated:

> Whereas the establishment of the Jewish State of Israel in 1948 constituted a clear violation of the Palestinian traditional right to life in their own homeland,
> Whereas thousands of Palestinians have been killed, thousands have been left homeless by the illegal establishment of the State of Israel,
> Whereas Jews ruling Israel have demonstrated Fascist desires through the occupation of other Palestinian and Arab lands,
> Whereas Israeli agents are working hand-in-hand with other imperialistic interests in Africa,
> Be it, therefore, resolved:
> - that the United States Government end immediately its economic and military support of the Israeli regime,
> - that the United States Government should withdraw its military forces from the Middle East area,
> - that the historical land of Palestinian and Arab people be returned to them,
> - that negotiations be ended with the freedom of the representatives of the Palestinians to establish a second state based on the historical right of the Palestinian people for self-government in their land.[7]

This resolution called, in effect, for the dissolution of the State of Israel, or at the very least for the right of Palestinians to set up a sovereign state, a position which was patently unacceptable to both Black elected officials and, of course, to the Jewish community. In fact, some of the representatives of Jewish organizations were so upset that they made a frantic effort immediately after the convention to discover the specific source of the resolution by contacting members of the Platform Committee and convention staff. Again, at the March 24 Steering Committee meeting of state chairpersons, there was an attempt to arrive at what they believed was a "real compromise" in the language of the resolution, which finally read as follows:

> Whereas as an African people we fully support the struggle
> of oppressed peoples against their oppressors, and;
> Whereas we recognize that there is a crisis in the Middle
> East involving the oppressed people of North Africa, and;
> Whereas we support the O.A.U. as the representative body
> which speaks for our brothers on the Continent, and
> recognize that the position of the O.A.U. and the U.N.
> Commission on Human Rights are valid and fair;
> Therefore, be it resolved that the convention go on record as
> being in agreement with the O.A.U. position that calls for:
>   1. The Israeli Government to be condemned for her expansionist policy and forceful occupation of the sovereign territory of another state.
>   2. Measures to be taken to alleviate the suffering and improve the position of Palestinian people in Israel;
>   3. The National Black Political Convention resolves to support the struggle of Palestine for self-determination.
>   4. The National Black Political Convention concurs also with the U.N. position that Israel rescind and desist from all practices affecting the demographic structure or physical character of occupied Arab territories and the rights of their inhabitants.[8]

While this resolution was somewhat softer than that passed by the convention and reversed its stand on the dissolution of Israel, still, this revision was not reviewed without objection by Black elected officials and civil rights leaders. Because both of the above issues were contained in the National Black Political Agenda, two of the top three leaders of the convention, Richard Hatcher and Charles Diggs, issued public disclaimers of the Steering Committee position.

The Congressional Black Caucus went even further, and on June 1, 1972, issued its own version of an agenda—the National

Black Declaration of Independence and the Black Bill of Rights. These documents constituted a watered-down version of the Gary Agenda and were issued at a press conference where William Clay, Louis Stokes, Charles Diggs and Charles Rangel were the principle spokespersons. Questions arose in the press conference as they explained the document, concerning why it had been released and why it appeared that the "spirit of Gary and its strategy" had been violated. Clay replied that "any group could get together and adopt anything it wished, but that didn't commit either myself or the Caucus to that position. This is a statement of our position."[9]

Nearly two weeks, then, after the release of the Gary Agenda on May 19 (planned to coincide with Malcolm X's birthday), the Congressional Black Caucus had broken with the convention by withdrawing its support from the agenda. In any case, the strategy adopted by the Steering Committee, after eventual ratification of the agenda in a Greensboro, North Carolina meeting, was that it would be taken to *both* the Democratic and Republican National Conventions in an attempt to secure endorsements of its contents by leading presidential nominees. Then, based upon the strongest endorsement, they would support a particular candidate for president. This strategy, considerably weakened by the defection of the Caucus, was to utilize the agenda as the fulcrum of leverage with which to extract concessions from the political system by establishing a contract between it and the Black community through a potential president.

The first opportunity to test the strategy was at the Democratic National Convention in Miami, Florida July 10–14, and on the opening day, *Newsweek* Magazine carried an essay by Imamu Baraka, then secretary general of the National Black Political Assembly and a leading member of its Steering Committee, referring to some Black elected officials as, those "Negro leaders" who defended Israel as "Colored caucus-ians (sic)," who were "bought and paid for like them sleepy . . .ho's [whores] on Lexington Avenue near Grand Central."[10] But then, he talked directly to the point of why he and others had come to the convention from Gary.

> In the political year of 1972, during which time the symbolic power figure in American life will be elected (unless he is assassinated first), Black people, caught up in the media rush of exploiters and others aspiring to public office, must make certain that we come away from the political process having gained some essential goods, services and/or political advantage.[11]

Baraka continued to summarize the contents of the Gary Agenda for his audience, but it was clear that the tenor of the Black Democrats, many of whom had been at Gary, had changed. It was "every man for himself," rather than adherence to a grand strategy of bargaining and negotiations. One observer sarcastically characterized the mood as follows:

> (If you were one of those black leaders who had sold out) you acted as if the Black Agenda produced there [Gary] was never written. You revealed to a newsman that you had been asked to defend in Miami Beach, the Black Agenda's meticulous cataloging of Black negotiations with the Democratic and Republican parties. You explained that, on the contrary, your political assignment in Miami Beach was to handle yachts. And when you completed your assignment, you grinned triumphantly. You were going to get some more cheese and crackers.[12]

Unity under these circumstances was an impossibility, since it was clear that the politics of the Gary convention and the far more moderate strategy of the Black elected officials were at irredeemable odds.

Still, in the fifth session of the Black Democratic Caucus at the convention, as Shirley Chisholm made the proposal to operate a collective brokerage strategy for Blacks from the base of her presidential candidacy, Walter Fauntroy countered with the fact that McGovern had committed himself to both the National Black Political Agenda (excepting the resolutions on Busing and Israel), and the Black Bill of Rights, and had promised an additional six million dollars for campaigning in the Black community. The BDC voted to approve Baraka's proposal giving the Gary convention leadership the responsibility, along with the Black Democratic Caucus, for meeting with the presidential candidates to assess their commitment. However, since most of the McGovern surrogates had also been part of the Gary convention leadership and were for McGovern from the beginning, there was little leverage left for the hard bargaining.

In any case, since the Gary convention was a non-partisan affair, the National Black Political Agenda was taken to the Republican convention as well, which also met in Miami Beach in August. Black politicians there, however, effectively blocked attempts by the delegates to discuss new demands, being content to cite the previous record of the Nixon administration towards the Black community as a positive basis for renewed support of his presidential candidacy.[13]

CHARLOTTE 1976

On January 31, 1976 an ad hoc group of about fifty Black Democratic leaders, made up of various levels of office-holders such as congresspersons, mayors, and other officials, met in Washington, D.C. to consider how Black Democrats could influence the coming convention. The focus of the meeting eventually came to rest on delegate selection strategy and upon the critical policy issues. Congressman Charles Rangel presented a report relative to ten significant issues, but there was a clear consensus in the group that the Humphrey-Hawkins Bill was the number one priority.

In addition, the group adopted the recommendations contained in a report on delegation selection objectives by Mayor Richard Hatcher and a strategy report by Congresswoman Yvonne Burke. But an important decision, for the purposes of this discussion, was making Mayor Coleman Young of Detroit chairman of the Planning Committee for the Issues Conference at Charlotte, North Carolina, April 30–May 2. Needing a rationale for the Charlotte meeting, yet cognizant that the NBPA had planned a March convention in Cincinnati, Ohio, and respectful of the now-sensitive relations between themselves and the Black nationalist dominated body, they said:

> These efforts to organize in advance of the National convention [Democratic] in no way represents an attempt on our part to speak for all Black Americans or Black Democrats. Rather, we are motivated by the concern that the lack of such advance organization could leave Blacks with reduced influence at the convention.[14]

The statement went on to make a critical acknowledgment of its purpose in saying: "We do not plan to endorse any presidential candidate and strongly recommend that black delegate candidates run uncommitted or on the slate of any presidential candidate."[15] This statement had in the past been interpreted two ways: in one sense, it could have been a simple statement communicating that it was impossible to entertain a discussion about candidates, since the key actors were committed to different candidates; on the other hand, it could have been a bargaining strategy to force the available candidates to offer concessions to make delegates commit to their candidacies.

The Charlotte meeting was becoming the key mobilizational meeting for Black delegates to the Democratic convention, as there were twenty states targeted and an action/monitoring system set up by the BDC which fed into a "national reporting system" from which a roster of delegates was being compiled. The meeting, though not as well attended as some would have liked, was, nevertheless, well organized and attracted over 500 delegates. The meeting produced issue statements in the ten areas suggested earlier by Rangel: Full Employment, Welfare Reform, National Health Care, Africa, Education, Tax Reform, Economic Development, Equal Opportunity, Urban Policy and National Post Card Registration.

If we look briefly at the two issues which were the source of tension between the BEOs and nationalists, busing and Israel, we find that the education section of the Charlotte Agenda is extensive (having twenty-two subsections), but there is no mention of busing. Rather, busing is mentioned under the main section on Equal Opportunity, and contains the following language:

> Opposition to pupil transportation as a method of desegregating the public schools has steadily increased. Lawlessness and serious disruptions in the education process of school children has occurred in many communities. *Until such time that different approaches are found to effectively achieve school desegregation, we support existing law* (my emphasis). We also call upon elected and public officials at all levels to assist in finding additional methods consistent with the Constitution and the 1954 decision.[16]

The closest reference to busing, it should be noticed, is an admission of support for "existing law," meaning the *Brown v. the Topeka Board of Education* decision of 1954 and the means of achieving desegregated education—or busing—while calling upon BEOs to find other workable methods. This approach, of course, although moderated, was still in essential conflict with the NBPA position, which rejected both busing and the necessity for integrated education.

On the other hand, the Foreign Policy section of the issues document is much closer in tone to that of the NBPA, using as its theme the view that "U.S. foreign policy is an extension of domestic racist discrimination and economic inequities," and continuing:

> It is expressed by a set of priorities which allows the wasteful and redundant expansion of the budget for the military, moving us toward a garrison state, and causing us to act as the policeman of the world. These internal characteristics have been projected onto the international scene, and have

emerged as a reactionary policy toward the Third World, and the Black World, including the Continent of Africa.[17]

The other sections of the issue agenda are fairly consistent with the tone and substance of the Gary Agenda, though the one striking difference is that it is also less specific, omitting entirely any reference, for example, to Israel or Middle East policy.

The highlight of the public politics of the conference was supposed to have been the appearance of the major Democratic party presidential candidates such as Jimmy Carter, Birch Bayh, Jerry Brown and Morris Udall (this meeting differing from the Gary convention in that it was partisan in sponsorship). A committee of policy experts deliberated to construct "tough questions" for the candidates. However, the seasoned presidential campaigners took the prepared questions put to them by a panel and handled them in a predictably vague and non-committal manner. Their collective performance failed to distinguish clearly among them, and while Brown's performance was judged generally the better, on the whole, as one observer said, "We didn't lay a glove on them."[18]

Despite the fact that the public politics was an anti-climax, in private Jimmy Carter had asked for and received a list of potential Black administration appointees from a small delegation of leaders at the conference. Nonetheless, Black Democrats appeared to be in a good position for the ritual of the Democratic party platform deliberations when the 153-member committee met as Basil Patterson, chairman of the BDC Ad Hoc Committee, presented the Charlotte Agenda to the DNC Platform Committee on June 17. Although many of the issues in the Charlotte Agenda emerged as planks in the party platform, there was still the outstanding question of the commitment of the party's presidential nominee to them, when and if he assumed office.

RICHMOND 1980

In 1980, the Richmond Conference on a Black Agenda, held February 28 to March 2, was another attempt to forge a non-partisan "articulation of Black interests." Despite the obvious necessity of some sort of meeting to prepare a political response to the negatively perceived policies of the Carter administration toward Blacks for the previous three years, there was serious objection by some leaders to having such a meeting. Some Black politicians objected because they supported Jimmy Carter, feeling that there was no necessity to pressure or evaluate his policies, while others were committed to Kennedy and felt that such a meeting would be "too controversial" even for him, since it might prematurely push him too far to the left. Nevertheless, the persistence of Richard Hatcher and Carl Holman was decisive in providing the leadership for planning and executing the conference. Invitations went out to hundreds of heads of Black organizations, and elected officials and the meeting attracted over one thousand individuals.

At a February 28 press conference, a startling announcement confirmed the rumor that although all of the presidential candidates had been invited, all had declined to attend for one reason or another. Hatcher's statement confirmed the cancellation of the "Presidential Forum" featuring the candidates, pleading that "they be asked to explain to the American voter why they chose not to come to Richmond, why they reached that decision," and choosing not to further interpret their actions.[19] He suggested that the failure of the candidates to appear might be regarded by some as "an affront to the Black voter," but he continued to diplomatically avoid castigating the candidates, instead, emphasizing that "the message must be heard that the black voter is a force to be reckoned with this November."[20] The other way which the leadership sought to de-emphasize the declinations of the candidates was to re-focus the business of the delegates toward the more important task of developing an agenda of issues, and the unifying task this required.

This statement did not mollify many Blacks who had genuinely felt insulted by the absence of the candidates. Their dissatisfaction was registered through the press by a barrage of questions with undertones of disbelief, some asking whether or not the leadership had missed the opportunity to educate Black voters concerning the real reasons why the candidates had declined to appear. The Rev. Jesse Jackson accepted this challenge, replying:

> There is the attempt to make the absence of white people more important than the presence of Black people, and we are involved now in a struggle for the definition of our conference. If our adversaries can define us, they can confine us. Our agenda is our definition of *our* conference. One, we are successful, the purpose was to galvanize black leadership; two, to coordinate various information from our various appearances; and three, to put public focus on black concerns by mobilizing the media. . . .We will not be convinced of

our impotence by their absence because we know of the importance of our 10 million votes.[21]

Then, appearing to feel the necessity of talking directly to the point raised by the questioners, he said:

Let us put the onus where it really should be. Mr. Carter is not here, but he wasn't in Iowa or New Hampshire. It is his strategy now to stay in the White House; that throws the campaign somewhat out of kelter. Kennedy's basic strategy is that in New Hampshire he and Brown are competing for the same vote and for them to come here and have a blood letting, as he sees it, is a negative for him. A second reason is that he must confront the issue of (his lack of support for) Ed Brooke, he is a close friend of Strom Thurmond and as a result of those political considerations he is not here. As a result of Carter's political considerations he is not here. Considering their absence, putting the onus on us is putting it in the wrong direction in my judgment.[22]

These questions and answers were essentially repeated by many other reporters and representatives of the leadership, and one questioner asked whether or not a mass demonstration would be necessary to get the attention of the candidates. Rev. Jackson replied that some form of direct action would occur as a result of the frustration building over the lack of presidential leadership. Then, appearing to threaten the candidates, he suggested that, as a matter of strategy, "we can go Democrat, we can go Republican, or we can go home and either one will have a profound impact on the election."[23]

As obliquely as Rev. Jackson had opened up the question of strategy, Mayor Coleman Young did so aggressively in his presentation on the afternoon of February 28. In one segment of his remarks, Young said that the progress of his city could be directly traced to the policies of the Carter administration, and continued:

Now we came here to discuss an Agenda, so let's start off with the first . . . point, where do we go from here?
Who . . . are you going to support, brothers and sisters, and where are we going in 1980? Now if you don't address that, then I say that you're here finger-popping. So where do we go from here?[24]

Young made clear his feeling that there was a need for a tried and proven candidate who had a program for the cities and for minorities, saying, "No secret about where I'm coming from, who my candidate is, that's locked up. The only problem now is to write an agenda that that candidate can live up to." Proceeding further to pitch for Jimmy Carter, Young continued:

> If we are talking about anything in a national agenda, we are talking about which candidate in 1980 — because there is going to be a president — which one of the 18 will meet our needs — not the prettiest. We must address ourselves to the reality of what is before us. I'm telling you that based on his record, Jimmy Carter will be the next President of the United States (Loud booing!) For those who boo, I say you have a responsibility, when you get through booing. Who are you for? You can exorcise yourself if you want to. You can finger-pop here, but if we're talking about an agenda to take home for black people — black people are very practical — you're not going to drag them out on some limb because you're getting your jollies down here in Richmond. Where are you going? I'll tell you where I'm going, I'm going with Jimmy Carter. You make up your own . . . mind![25]

The reaction to Young's speech was almost uniformly negative in that those who were opposed to Jimmy Carter as a candidate were just as opposed to the mentioning of his name as those who considered that Young had broken conference protocol by mentioning the name of any of the candidates. This obvious breach was to provoke a great deal of heated denunciation by the delegates, but little by the leadership. No doubt, they were respectful of Young's role as vice chairman of the Democratic party, which made him the highest black party official there and potentially one with a great deal of influence over a possible president. This point is underscored by the fact that one month after the Richmond meeting, other Black leaders such as Richard Hatcher endorsed Jimmy Carter for president.

It was obvious that in the Richmond conference workshop on political parties, there was considerable visceral support for the idea that political parties were basically the same and that they had not facilitated the politics of Blacks at local levels. Because of this, several speakers reminded the audience that they were *Black first* and party members second, a sentiment also useful in creating a legitimate basis for the participation of Black Republicans in such gatherings, as indicated by the positive reception given the chair of the National Black Republican Council's remarks. Nevertheless, there was some slight dissent in the workshops to these ideas by some partisan party officials who felt that the essential route to political power was through the party organization. This idea is implied in a section of the final document devoted to political parties. One section of the final resolutions reads:

> Blacks should acquire a better understanding of the political party process in order to take maximum advantage of opportunities afforded by that process to achieve the goals and aspirations of Black people.[26]

There was some debate on the contradiction between affirmative action for minorities and the benefits of this program accruing to white women, and there was a lengthy discussion on the Strategic Arms Limitation Treaty as well as U.S. policy in the Persian Gulf, however, none of these issues were seriously contested. Considering the mild disagreements, including those about party politics and candidates, the process of achieving consensus on the issues was essentially free of rancorous conflict.

The result was that the agenda emerged framed under four broad headings: Economic Affairs, International Affairs, Political Affairs, and Special Workshops (ERA, Civil Rights, Black Youth, and the Media), and under each heading there were several resolutions. It is interesting that in the two areas in which there previously had been sharp differences of opinion, busing was not even mentioned in the fairly extensive section on Education and regarding Israel the International Affairs section began with the recommendation:

1. The United States must take concerted action to bring about a just and lasting comprehensive settlement of the Middle East conflict, including the resolution of the Palestinian homeland issue.[27]

The form of this document resembled a "wish list" rather than a platform with preamble, rationalized text and prioritized items. Even more important, there was no "grand strategy" for negotiating the document with any of the candidates, rather it was assumed that it would be presented to the Platform Committee of the Democratic party, as the 1976 document had been. However, when the Platform

Committee met in June, Coleman Young, its chair, frantically sent out a request for Black leaders to represent the issues in the Richmond Agenda at these sessions, but to no avail.

DISCUSSION

What is important about the articulation of interests is that it involves more than the act of merely expressing concern for certain issues. In the words of Almond and Powell, it involves "processing demands" made by certain groups through specific channels.[28] Therefore, such groups have to tailor the means for achieving interest articulation to the channels involved if real influence is to be the result, and for this reason we make a distinction between the mere presentation of demands (or issues) and the successful processing of demands through channels to the point that they become effective. In this sense, Almond and Powell are instructive:

> Mere achievement of articulation and of access is no
> guarantee of successful influence, but *to fail to gain articulation*
> even through sympathetic elite members is to forego any
> chance of shaping political decision.[29]

In this regard, Blacks have often utilized protest movements to make "effective demands" because such demands have resulted in the establishment of public policy. But the advent of the electoral politics movement has made it necessary for the new political leadership to adapt the skills of making effective demands in a new arena of action. As Almond and Powell suggest, the arena of Black political participation has changed from one of mass action, to the attempt to articulate interests to elites *through elite processes and institutions* such as political parties.

Cobb and Elder have referred to this as the "politics of agenda-building," and they have suggested that the extent to which demands are effectively articulated depends upon the prevailing balance of power in the political system and the resources which may be mobilized by subordinate groups to change the balance in their favor.[30] The authors define an agenda as "a general set of political controversies that will be viewed as falling within the range of legitimate concerns meriting the attention of the polity," and inform us that there is a distinction which may be made between the systemic agenda and the institutional agenda.[31] The systemic agenda is more abstract and issue-oriented while the institutional agenda is more process-oriented. The question of making effective demands often depends upon what happens in the "pre-political" informal polity rather than in the institutionalized system of politics; therefore, the systemic agenda often emerges from this environment rather than from the institutional arena. The problem, then, becomes how groups behave in the informal polity to legitimize their systemic agenda of issues, understanding that this is related to the legitimacy of the group.[32]

The core of this analysis applies rationally to our problem of understanding the determinants by which Black leaders have utilized the Black convention process to make effective demands through the instrument of various agendas. As this writer has suggested, the Black conventions have constituted an aspect of the informal polity through which Black political leaders have attempted to secure legitimacy for their agendas. Lenneal Henderson says of the caucuses:

> What is important to underscore about black political
> caucuses in presidential elections is the two-dimensional
> nature of their function. They simultaneously mobilize their
> membership and constituents to consolidate themselves inter-
> nally while seeking to affect productive exchange relations
> with other groups and institutions external to themselves.[33]

In order to "affect productive exchange relations" with other groups, however, Black leaders have had to substantiate the legitimacy which they have achieved as officials of various kinds by formulating their issue agendas through conventions of Black political activists, to gain racial support as a basis for legitimizing their own leadership within the party institution. Only then, would they have the necessary authority to affect exchange relations with the expectation that they would be productive.

The result, however, has been less than sanguine. In attempting to negotiate the elite politics of the Democratic party presidential nomination system, Black leaders have had great difficulty legitimizing (therefore making effective) demands to the point that they have been taken seriously as public policy issues either before the nominee took office or afterward. Why has this happened? There are two answers which may be given here, the first of which is the existence of objective problems with the Black conventions in relationship to the formal polity, and the second is the problem of political bargaining.

Objective Problems

Timing. Preparations for the campaign season by the candidates and the party actually never stop, but certainly by the start of the primary season in an election year, basic issue positions have already been identified, and the candidate field is settled. The three Black conventions under discussion were held in early March, late April, and late February, times when the presidential nominating process is in full swing, not in its preparatory stages. Doubtless, one of the thoughts of the organizers of these conventions was that an event held much earlier would miss primary election dynamics, such as changes in public sentiment, and possibly even the late entry of some candidates into the race. To hold conventions in the middle of the primary season gives the impression that the politics of impacting upon the general process of candidate selection by being prepared to influence primary election voting is secondary — or even sacrificed altogether — to influencing the party platform and rules deliberations after the primaries in June.

Sponsorship. It should be noted that the sponsorship of these meetings was transitory, being held in 1972 by the combined Black nationalists, Black elected officials and civil rights leadership; in 1976 it was sponsored by the newly formed Black Democratic Caucus, and in 1980 it was sponsored by a group mostly comprised of the Black Democratic leadership (although it was presented as a non-partisan meeting). In any case, it is most instructive that the group generally described itself, in terms of its temporary composition, as "ad hoc." The basic dilemma, which the ad hoc nature of the group attempted to address, was the lack of a comprehensive political structure in the Black community which could accommodate the combined pretentions to leadership by the new class of elected officials, from big city mayors to party activists and members of Congress.

Participants. The ad hoc nature of the leadership and the shifting basis of sponsorship led to confusion as to the immediate target audience of participants. Generally the invitations went to a wide variety of interested political activists (defined generally from elected officials to organizational representatives). The question most often asked of this group, however, was what its relationship was going to be to the political process already under way. The problem was that the sponsors needed to assemble a credible group of participants in order to legitimize the ensuing agenda product, but in so doing, an unfocused mass of people often assembled who were not directly involved in

implementing the agenda-commitment strategy. The difficulty here
was that the sponsors attempted to answer the charge of being too
exclusive, if the development of an agenda were the only issue of the
meeting, then it was unnecessary for the participants to be very
focused on implementation strategy. This, however, represents a
deficiency in implementation, since there was no strong linkage between the implementation strategy of the Black convention and the
party convention. In the Richmond meeting, for example, the convention adjourned without ever having adopted an implementation
strategy agreed upon by the delegates.

Agendas. The form of the agendas has been the subject of debate since
the 1972 convention, reflecting an essential difference of opinion between those who wanted the document to contain items addressed to
the Black community and those who wanted it to speak to the policy
system or government. Thus, it has tended to be comprised of both
strains, moving from the Gary Agenda which spoke equally to both
arenas, to the latter documents which were much more heavily
oriented to the public policy system. This outcome probably reflects
the increasing role of elected public officials in the leadership of
such meetings over time and their influence in shaping the agendas
to appeal to the institutions of which they are a part. Thus, tremendous differences exist among these documents according to the
strategic intentions of the meetings and their participants.

The critical problem, however, is the distinction between the
candidates and the party platforms which contain the substance of
the policy interests of Blacks. The difficulty we observe was in
evidence even when the Black leadership was united behind a priority item of policy, such as the Humphrey-Hawkins Bill in 1976, or
when it was not, as in 1980.

The issue of full employment had been a formal priority agenda
item of the Black community since World War II, but it surfaced
more strongly in the early 1970s due to the severe impact of the
economic recession occurring at that time. For instance, in 1975, an
annual Congressional Black Caucus Legislative Workshop covered
the issue of full employment, and the two main speakers were Congressman Augustus Hawkins, (D-CA) original author of H.R.50 and
Vernon Jordan, the then president of the National Urban League.
Likewise, in 1976, the CBC sessions focused on full employment in
the culmination of media events to spotlight the issue during that
year. This bill was designed to provide job expansion by requiring
the president to:

submit to Congress [annually] a full employment and balanced growth statement which will serve as the nation's economic blueprint. The report would contain target goals for employment, production and purchasing power and the President's proposed programs and methods for achieving those goals. The primary emphasis of the bill is to encourage employment in the private sector by stimulating business. Additionally, the [CBC designated] Hawkins-Humphrey bill would guarantee employment by establishing the federal government, through a job guarantee office, as the employer of last resort.[34]

The push for the bill continued throughout the election year of 1976, and, as we have suggested, became the central issue of the Charlotte convention, and eventually influenced the platform of the Democratic party. The Congressional Black Caucus noted: "The platform adopts the principles of Full Employment as the Democratic party's top priority without naming the Hawkins-Humphrey Bill."[35]

The fact that the platform did not specifically mention the bill was a result of the control of the platform drafting process by Carter operatives. Likewise, when the leaders of the Black Democratic Caucus announced after their meeting with Carter at the convention in New York that his support of "full employment" was one reason they supported him, there was no clear picture of which definition of this concept he supported. Just as important, there was little willingness on the part of Black leaders to pressure Carter into a definition, so that, by the time of his debates with Ford, he publicly admitted that he did not support a specific version of the bill since there was no clear consensus on the matter in the Congress.

Shortly after Carter's election, Congressman Parren Mitchell, (D-MD) chairman of the Congressional Black Caucus, wrote to him requesting a meeting with the Caucus on the subject of full employment. Carter replied that he would not be able to meet with the Caucus on this subject in the near future, but that it was high on his agenda.[36] After much evasion, the Congress passed and the president signed into law the *Humphrey-Hawkins* Bill, gutted of its essential provisions for specifying how to achieve its goals through comprehensive planning, while retaining the principles. The first budget passed under the act was in 1979, and while it specified the desirabil-

ity of achieving a 3% unemployment rate, the subsequent application of the legislation to the FY 1980 budget was carefully set aside
by Carter in 1979.

This chronicle of the political effect of electoral bargaining in
1976 is meant to suggest that one of the greatest obstacles, besides
the efficacy of Black tactics and strategy, has been the resistance of
the political leaders (Democratic party, presidential candidates and
presidents) to making a commitment. Therefore, the task of tactics
and strategy is how effectively to overcome such resistance through
the application of political resources. This study, however, has
revealed that it has been difficult for Black political leaders to overcome this resistance both because of their political vulnerability and
their ineffective use of bargaining strategy.

The first point is that there has been a persistent attempt by
some Black leaders to appeal to their colleagues not to give away the
bargaining leverage of the collective Black community by making individual commitments to the major party candidates in advance of
the candidate's public commitment to specific Black issues. In the
past this appeal has fallen upon deaf ears, largely because of the at-
tractiveness of private incentives and the vulnerability of elected officials to the power of a potential president. The process of becoming
a credible presidential candidate assumes that the candidate's
organization will attempt to exact the maximum amount of
discipline over the party apparatus, including political assets such as
convention delegates, leaders with constituencies, and the electorate. There will generally be an attempt to bind significant Black
leaders to a candidate's organization for the least possible inducements, so low-level individual and collective inducements are
utilized, such as those which routinely have become part of the
bargaining process.

Bargaining issues have generally fallen into three categories:
appointments (party, campaign, administration), voter registration
and get-out-the-vote funds for the presidential campaign, and a few
key policy issues. Of those items which have been the basis upon
which Black political leaders have bargained Black support for the
party presidential nominee, the policy issues have been far less emphasized than the immediate personal and political rewards. This
tension between what might be referred to as "private interest" and
"public interests" (actually the difference between individual and
mass interests) has led to severe limitations upon the independence of
Black leadership, creating deficiencies in the process of political

bargaining, by setting corresponding limitations upon the extent to which implementation tactics may be aggressively pursued.

Second, Black leaders have often dangled the bargaining resource of the Black vote before the party nominee. However, the party nominees have probably been aware that this vote is contestable in the sense that it is not organized by the Black leadership, and thus not directly available for them to use as a competitive bargaining resource. These leaders may make suggestions with respect to the power of the Black vote and, perhaps, how it will behave, but they cannot credibly bargain with this vote because they cannot control its behavior. Thus, *strategic* bargaining is not possible.

Carter proved in both 1976 and 1980 that it was possible to circumvent the established Black political leadership and achieve access to the Black community and, thus, to acquire its vote with minimal cost. *The Black vote, thus, is ironically postured as an important resource by Black leaders, but nearly useless to utilize in bargaining situations because of a lack of organizational control. In effect, these leaders yield control of the Black vote to the organization of the party nominee, by joining his organization, thus, exposing themselves to low-level private inducements and complicating the bargaining process on behalf of collective goals.*

The vulnerability of Black political leaders has also altered the nature of the Black convention as a place for sincere politics, in the sense that there may be no comprehensive discussion of the most effective means of implementing the agenda, because there can be no public discussion of the most political question — the preferred candidate. In this regard, Coleman Young forced upon the Richmond convention the consideration of an appropriate, and perhaps its most important subject — "Who . . . are you for?"

It is conceded that the drafting of an agenda in itself is legitimate if it has emerged from a base-line of consensus among Black political activists, regardless of whom they support. Nevertheless, the severe limitations of the forum as a thoroughly political arena also limit the possible achievement of the very issues which are presented as critical priorities for the Black community.

CONCLUSION

It is concluded, therefore, that these conventions are not, as initially suggested, part of an effort at "quasi-independent" leverage. Rather, since they have been directed essentially to the political system of the Democratic party, they may be regarded as an adjunct of the comprehensive party process of the articulation of interests. Almond and Powell suggest that one of the objective functions all parties perform is to organize the internal coalition interests into a set of comprehensible issues which are identifiable as the party's dominant ideology. In their view, the American party system is characterized by its "pragmatic-bargaining style."[37] The way in which these issues are presented to the party does not necessarily alter the role of the member group as a part of the coalition or, more important, affect its dependence upon the party to represent its interests in the various arenas of power politics.

Nevertheless, it does appear that the group in question must also exercise an effective *autonomous politics* in order to influence the party (including the party institution and presidential leadership) enough to ensure that its interests will be taken seriously. Perhaps one of the greatest tactical errors has been for the Black conventions to forsake the attempt to directly influence the presidential candidate's policy stance in favor of influencing the party platform, because of the effective distance which can be placed between these by a presidential campaign.

Then, the stunning absence of the presidential candidates from the 1980 Richmond conference, together with the lack of clear linkages among the Black convention agendas, party platforms, the candidates's views, or presidential public policy, lead to the conclusion that the conventions cannot even claim to be "political" in the sense that they impact upon such arenas of decision-making. As such, they are not instruments through which to make effective demands, but they could be considered the first stages of an interest-articulation process which includes serious second-stage bargaining activity within the party system. Alone, however, they are merely occasional policy conferences yielding moderate proposals without much political pretention, just as any other "convention" would be without its own presidential candidates or political party system.

Our inference about systemic connections is important, therefore, since the episodic nature of Black agenda-building activity might be improved by the strengthening of linkages between the politics of Black conventions and the presidential nomination process through the organizational advantages which come with the ability to maintain and enhance political memory, unique skills, and other electoral resources. One of the major contributions of the 1972 Gary convention was the establishment of the strategy which included flexible bargaining principles between both major parties, and an assumption that voting would proceed as a direct result of the bargaining outcome. The force of this contribution was lost, however, with the dissolution of the post-convention organizational effort. Lacking such organization, the process of agenda-building has been forced into a repetitive cycle of new beginnings, with the consequences we have suggested above.

Chapter 5

Independent-Leverage Strategies

INTRODUCTION

Now that we have examined the strategy which has guided the approach of Black leadership to participation in presidential politics, we must make a brief summary evaluation of its portends for the future. It is my conclusion that the "balance of power" strategy, as it has been implemented thus far, possesses serious limitations in the pursuit and achievement of political objectives, due, in part, to the use of dependent-leverage politics as the major implementing tactic. Since it would be more immediately profitable to think about restructuring past practice, I will focus here on correcting the deficiencies of dependent-leverage tactics by recourse to independent-leverage.

The idea of the Black vote being the "balance of power," we have found, has empirical validity in the sense that when in 1960 and 1976 it was added to the Democratic party coalition, it provided the "winning margin of victory," and in 1968 when it was withdrawn from the coalition, it provided the "losing margin of *defeat*" for the party candidate in the general election. Thus, the strategy has been strongly turnout oriented, and the mechanism for fulfilling public policy demands has been based on the sympathetic or "trustful" relationship of the Black leadership to the leaders of the Democratic party.

The strategy of political integration into the national Democratic party structure developed as an outgrowth of the increased institutionalization of Black elected officials, but it was not to provide much influence on the process of presidential selection because of the lack of comprehensive political organization among them. Even the establishment of the Black Democratic Caucus was not sufficient to provide the kind of internal leverage which would facilitate influence, because of the organizational limitations of the BDC and the dependence of key Black Democratic leaders upon major party candidates and their organizations. This was not as immediately reflected in Black strength within the party institution as it was within the Black caucus-sponsored issue conventions (or conferences) from 1972 to 1980. The various agendas failed to become the common currency of the party candidate's issues, and the post-election policy implementation in a Democratic administration was unsatisfactory as well.

Moreover, a serious deficiency in the dependent-leverage strategy as it has been practiced is that the political integration of Blacks into the party as a strategy for achieving influence and resources has not proven very decisive, since it has not facilitated other political objectives such as the slating of Blacks at the national level or their influence on the selection of the party presidential nominee. The impact of political integration was ironically minimal, especially when incumbent Democratic President Jimmy Carter was running for re-election, because many Black leaders who were either elected or appointed officials were in a position to be disciplined into developing a greater loyalty to the politics of the incumbent than to the interests of their own community. Blacks, for example, had achieved the highest number of presidential appointments in history, but were apparently unable to prevent the debilitating Carter budget cuts in social programs in 1979, a preview to later cuts by Ronald Reagan. Neither were they free in 1980 to support Edward Kennedy as a protest of the Carter policies. It might be that dependent Blacks develop greater interest in the establishment and maintenance of personal positions than in group policy and political resources.

A true "balance of power" system requires a neutral fulcrum in order for the leverage of each party to have an impact. When one party controls both its own leverage and the fulcrum, there is little opportunity for fair leverage to be exercised on both sides of the balance. Moreover, if the Black vote possesses little or no mobility there is little incentive for party leaders to attribute credibility to claims of the *exclusive* margin-of-victory role of the Black vote. The result is that post-election policy demands have been devalued by a winning Democratic president more often than they should have, given the impact of Black voting strength. Perhaps, as we have suggested, Black political leaders tolerate such a condition because they, too, believe they have no viable alternative to the "politics of trust," believing that tough bargaining inside the party coalition would prove unsuccessful in accomplishing policy demands.

Thus, the deficiencies in the system of dependent-leverage occur systematically: in the process of candidate selection during the primaries, in the process of issue-bargaining before (following the Black conventions) and during the party conventions, and in the reward posture following the general elections.

THE STRATEGY OF INDEPENDENT-LEVERAGE

If the primary weakness of the "balance of power" strategy as it operates within the Democratic party is in the necessity to make ex post facto policy claims, the satisfaction of which depends upon trust, then a strategy which extracts a previous commitment might be more effective in establishing a linkage to policy rewards. This would appear to depend upon the existence of an organizational manifestation beyond the mere chance of becoming the balance in the voter turnout. In fact, the concept of the "winning margin of victory" should, as we have seen, have the capacity to become either the winning margin or the losing margin, and thus, *the disciplined margin* which is the result of organization not coincidence. The challenge of disciplining the Black vote through organization is, therefore, the key to the exercise of independent-leverage, the meaning of which is that the Black vote will be controlled by the Black community rather than by the major Democratic party nominee. Shared control of the Black vote, or outright control of it by forces outside of the Black community, damages the credibility of policy bargaining. Autonomous control establishes a neutral fulcrum in the "balance of power" and provides the basis for making credible public policy claims based on the performance of the Black vote, because it is part of a "true leverage system." Control establishes leverage because it enhances the possibility of *direct*, rather than indirect or dependent, political influence. Thus, we perceive that two positive outcomes are possible through the autonomous control of the Black vote by Blacks: first, the satisfaction of policy demands and second, the side-benefit of political resources.

It should be clear at the outset that we do not mean by "control" of the Black vote a new form of "bossism," but the development of an instrument through which Blacks and their allies are able to democratically articulate demands, develop political resources and compete for power and influence in the political system. The form through which such control is accomplished should be constructed to achieve substantive objectives, such as those conceptualized by Lawrence Guyot and Michael Thelwell, two young organizers active in the Mississippi Freedom Democratic Party in 1966, who said that their task was:

> To establish and entrench in every Negro community the tradition of active participation in politics, in which the people will understand that their involvement and control of their own political organization is their strongest weapon.[1]

Their method of accomplishing this, at that time, was for the Mississippi Freedom Democratic Party to hold workshops about citizenship, to run local candidates for office, and to develop voter registration drives. A prime objective was to provide local community residents with a vehicle they could still utilize to negotiate with the "white power structure" from a unified base of support. They further said:

> Our job must be, then, to continue organizing these black voters into an independent political organ capable of unified action on the state level. So when this dialogue [negotiations with the white power structure] takes place it will not be to individual Negroes on terms of patronage and prestige, but to the true representatives of the community and in terms of governmental power. It is only in this manner that the vote will become an implement for social change in Mississippi.[2]

This sentiment was probably close to that expressed earlier by Martin Luther King, Jr. and Bayard Rustin, whose suggestion that Blacks should attempt to dislodge the entrenched corrupt party bosses who controlled the Black vote in local communities, strongly implied that such control should pass to Black leadership that was non-corrupt and democratic. But whereas these civil rights leaders saw the independence at the local level inter-locking with the Democratic party coalition at the national level, they were vague about the form of dependence there.

Observers such as Chuck Stone, this writer, and others have been more direct in the view that there should be a "Third Force" politics, which specifically meant the establishment of some form of Black political party, or otherwise an independent strategy. The basic motivation in such suggestions was reaction to the perception that the processes and strategies utilized by Black political leaders were dysfunctional, since the Black vote was so inflexible it had been less a strategic resource than it might have been. Therefore, how to make the Black vote a *strategic resource* in its ability to be flexible, to "oscillate" among candidates, and to re-align itself as the political situation demands, is regarded here as the essential route to achieving satisfactory ends in the electoral arena.

The dominant attempt at influencing the direction of the Black vote has been the Black political convention, a form of episodic organization which implied no necessary continuing structure (although some have often evolved). Although they may have been called to voice common concerns, such conventions also have had little direct connection to the most powerful elements of the electoral system.

The most conspicuous form of attempts at independent organization has been the Black presidential or vice presidential candidacy which has existed historically from the time of Frederick Douglass' position on the Peoples party (Equal Rights party) ticket as a vice presidential candidate in 1872. Blacks have, therefore, run against the prevailing political order, whether inside one of the major parties or outside. They have often had to mount independent non-partisan, or independent quasi-partisan (such as the Black and Tan or northern Black Democrat) candidacies.

These two political processes — conventions and parties — should logically function together but, except for a few brief attempts at national parties such as the Black and Tans and the Freedom Now party, they have often been separate activities rather than reflective of a genuine presidential candidacy. In subsequent chapters, we will explore specific case studies of the political party and the presidential candidacy as more overt forms of independence. Here, however, we will discuss them in general terms, seeking to clarify the distinction between a presidential candidacy *within* the Democratic party for the nomination, and a presidential candidacy *outside* of the Democratic party for the presidency in the strategy of minority group participation. In essence, this is an argument for the position that independent-leverage is achieved through the establishment of autonomous organization which acquires and utilizes political resources in the development of a disciplined Black vote which has the ability to become the "balance of power" through its flexible application to electoral coalitions as the strategic situation demands. Expectations that the winning party will satisfy the policy and political interests of Blacks are enhanced both by explicit bargaining and by the ability of their organization to levy sanctions as an accountability measure.

INTRA-PARTY PRESIDENTIAL POLITICS

In May of 1971, Rev. Jesse Jackson, head of the Southern Christian Leadership Conference's Operation Breadbasket, called a meeting of political leaders in Chicago saying: "We're going to talk about a black politician for President."[3] *The Nation* reported that Jackson felt that a Black candidacy would fill a moral void of leadership in the country to counter the Nixon administration, further commenting:

> We think that those who have a stake in getting rid of the moral crisis, which is an immoral circumstance, should have an obligation to look to new leadership, no matter what community it comes from. Young people and women have a real interest in a black candidate for President.[4]

This positive attitude appeared to be confirmed by *The Nation* which reported that a survey of *Jet* Magazine's readership released in the fall of 1971, showed that 98% felt that there should be a Black presidential candidate in 1972. The top choice was Julian Bond, who was only 31, and, thus, too young to legally be elected president. Congressman John Conyers, who had placed third in the *Jet* poll, believed that a Black candidacy "would stimulate registration and encourage many Black citizens to run for delegate seats to the national convention in larger numbers then ever. . . .and exert maximum leverage in the decision making . . . "[5]

By 1972, John Conyers continued to give legitimacy to the speculation over a Black candidacy by suggesting strongly that both Democrats and Republicans had failed Blacks, then posing a crucial question: "How do we maximize the power of twenty-four million Black Americans?" After searching through the alternatives of joining the Republicans, forming coalitions with other segments of the electorate, disassociating from electoral politics, or beginning another party, he discarded them all and settled upon his own choice: "I propose that we draft a candidate to run as the Democratic nominee for President. The candidate, running on a *People's Platform* would then enter selected statewide primaries between now and July 1972."[6] After further asking what might be the gains from such a strategy, whether or not the strategy would be limited to running in the Democratic primaries, and what other viable alternatives existed, he ruled out a Black political party, proposing instead that any strategy should capitalize upon the already heavy allegiance of Blacks to the Democratic party and, thus, intensify internal efforts.

With respect to the gains, he mentioned such measures as broadening voter appeal of Blacks by involving them in the campaigns of other candidates, having an impact upon the process of party reform, and expanding the Black role in the party convention process. These measures, however, do not constitute a sufficient picture of what could be achieved, other than to prove that Blacks can provide national leadership, nor how significant changes might occur beyond having a vague impact upon the party.

Shirley Chisholm, however, who had scored fourth in the *Jet* poll in 1971, took the occasion of a speech before the National Welfare Rights Organization that year to indicate her strong interest in running. As reported in January of the following year, her rationale was similar to that already outlined; she was attempting to use a presidential candidacy as a vehicle for party reform by building a coalition of the "discontented," including women, Blacks, and young people, to leverage political decisions about who would become the president and about the makeup of the governing cabinet.[7] By the end of the primary campaign schedule, Chisholm was still suggesting that she wanted to go to the Miami convention to "keep them honest" and "shake them up."[8]

The Chisholm candidacy for the Democratic nomination, however, never matured, since even among Black delegates to the Democratic convention the number committed to Chisholm was only 7%, fewer than those committed to either McGovern (21%) or Humphrey (before dropping out–15%).[9] Her pre-convention share amounted to twenty-six delegates and although she eventually acquired 101.5 in the floor voting, this was not enough support to achieve bargaining leverage.

Proof of this fact was that Chisholm sought and received support from the Black Delegate Caucus meeting to lead a bargaining strategy; however, she was outflanked in this endeavor by Congressman Walter Fauntroy who had already met and conducted negotiations with McGovern. McGovern would, no doubt, have reserved negotiating space for Chisholm if he had perceived that her delegate strength would be substantial enough to be interpreted as having political influence in the nomination struggle. Thus, the goals of bargaining were not realized because, although Chisholm's candidacy had been strongly supported by Blacks as an idea, they appeared unready to vote for Chisholm for whatever reason.

I would argue here that the results of the Chisholm candidacy were not idiosyncratic, but a natural result of the dynamics of dependent-leverage politics. Factors which played a role in the demise of her candidacy, such as the confusion in its base of support from the Black political leadership and the Black Democratic voters, spelled the failure of the campaign to attract the necessary legitimacy to be successful. Furthermore, the confusion among leaders was typical of their failure to mobilize sufficiently to take the initiative of choosing, either from within their own ranks or without, a possible nominee to support. In any case, we know enough of the model to make an attempt to characterize some of the systemic properties involved in both the dependent- and independent-leverage relationships to the party presidential nomination.

Presidential Nomination Politics

The Party System Level. Professor Charles Hamilton has wisely noted that:

> Gaining the right to vote does not, ipso facto, lead to the public goods and services needed or sought. More frequently than not, gaining the *right* to vote is only the beginning of an arduous task of transforming that tool into some meaningful substantive results.[10]

Referring to a heuristic device he called the "P" paradigm, he went on to posit a relationship among the factors Process, Product, and Participation, where process is defined as such activities as voting, marching and lobbying, and the product is the policy and material improvement.[11] It should be noted that Hamilton's interpretation of "substantive results" is strongly weighted toward improvements in political participation, and likewise, Henderson's model is also directed toward increases in voter turnout in the general election.[12] If one rearranges Hamilton's paradigm, there appears a model which emphasizes the dynamics that will make voter turnout "strategic."

Figure 5.1 Presidential Nomination Strategic Interaction Model

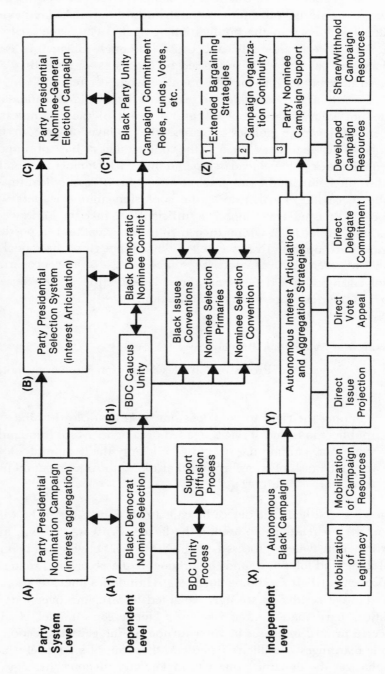

Beginning with the "party system level" of our model, a horizontal relationship can be said to exist among the variables of "participation" (voting, organizatonal mobilization, voter registration, etc.), "process" (the party political processes such as the primaries, the conventions, and the post-convention presidential campaign), and the "product" (policy, personnel, and resources). This is expressed in Figure 5-1 at (A) by the formation of presidential campaigns as a preparatory step to actual participation in the party presidential nomination process. The campaigns might be conceived of as an "interest aggregation" mechanism among the various party constituencies (ethnic, ideological, economic-class, etc.) At (B), the party "presidential nomination process" embodies the political system that results in deciding upon the nominee. This stage might be expressed as a "two-ballot scenario" where voters cast their ballots for their preferred candidate in the primary elections and delegates cast their ballots at the national convention. In addition, it is obvious that at each stage in what Kessel has called the "mist clearing process," much more than balloting is taking place, since in the competition among organizations there are winners and losers — causing the reformulation of some coalitions, further shifts in resources (financing, polling, and other technologies) and strategies, issue-bargaining, and corresponding adjustments in the media and the public environment.[13] Then, at (C) there is the post-convention period when the nominee has been chosen and the party is unified in the two-party competition for the presidency. This is the final balloting stage in what may cumulatively and symbolically be regarded as a "three-ballot strategic scenario" of political decision points in the process of deciding who will be President of the United States.

The Black Dependent Level. Most of this work to this point has been dedicated to an analysis of the dependent level and the way in which Black voters and political leaders have interacted with the main party political system of presidential selection. Therefore, at (A1) the assumption is automatic that the Black vote is to become an appendage of the coalition of one of the major white party candidates, and thus a process of "diffusion" of leadership and partisanship begins to occur in the process of candidate selection. We have seen that there are two tendencies at work, one of which is in the direction of unity under the direction of the Black Democratic Caucus, and the other which intensifies the diffusion of Black leaders and activists in the adoption of roles as "surrogate" to presidential candidates. Thus, at (B1) when it comes to Black participation in the party nomination system, the divergent tendencies of unity and diffusion contribute to such factors as the failure to devise and execute issue bargaining strategies to implement the agendas formulated at Black conventions, and the lack of an effective candidate selection method. At (C1) the Black leadership and voters become integrated into the campaign operation of the Democratic party nominee in an act of party unity, and that leadership, which then competes for the vote of the Black community, approaches it from the legitimacy of the nominee's organizational resource base.

The Black Independent Level. At (X), the mobilization of an autonomous Black campaign for the Democratic presidential nomination is also a process which requires the mobilization of the political resources in the Black community, and the mobilization of party and public campaign support. Given the results of the Chisholm campaign for the nomination, it is regarded as essential that the most critical element in the development of such an effort is the mobilization of *legitimacy*, without which other crucial resources will be withheld. This means that, at the very least, the candidate should have an undisputed leadership profile of a sufficiently high level within the community, and support from a substantial share of a wide variety of leaders necessary for mobilization activity. Then, the extra-community opinion-making publics such as party leaders and the media must credit the candidacy a potential influence role, even if it does not perceive that it might actually win the nomination.

Nevertheless, at (Y) a Black campaign is part of the competitive system of nomination politics in the "two-ballot scenario" of the primaries and the convention. In these arenas this campaign is able to directly project interests (issues/concerns) to the American people rather than to have them presented indirectly to the people through major white campaign leaders. There is also the opportunity to make a direct appeal for primary votes, and to seek commitments from convention delegates. Finally, at (Z) the autonomous Black campaign within the party has no further reason for existence, inasmuch as the nomination has been decided, so it dissolves and becomes integrated into the "party unity" movement in preparation for the inter-party campaign. Then, there are the mini-options at (Z1) of extended bargaining, a tactic to be used in the hypothetical situation which finds the Black campaign dissatisfied with the bargaining results in the post-convention period. The option at (Z2) presents the possibility that the Black campaign will not dissolve but continue its organization in some form. Nevertheless, in the competitive process of political organization and mobilization in conducting a campaign, important political resources are developed, such as state organizations with lists of voters, campaign contribution lists, skilled personnel, and leadership visibility. All of these resources may be utilized in an integrated fashion by the party nominee's organization in the final stages of the presidential campaign.

Two caveats should be added before closing this aspect of the discussion. First, although I have used the term and concept of a "Black campaign," it should be understood that this is a symbolic device, since, for example, from the very outset in the campaign of Shirley Chisholm she called for a coalition involving cross-racial constituencies. The campaign is, thus, "Black" in the sense that its leader and its base are located in the Black community. Second, the model is not static in the sense that these are the only possible variables. With respect to the level X,Y,Z or the "Black campaign," it should be recognized that it is possible to employ several other strategic options, in which case the model changes at this level. To the extent that relationships are also implied at levels A1, B1, C1, they may also change; however, there is unlikely to be much change in the basic system at A, B, C.

INTER-PARTY PRESIDENTIAL POLITICS

Blacks have run for president on third party tickets in recent times, however, these efforts have not been perceived as legitimate by either Blacks or whites, as seen from the results of selected elections shown in Table 5.1:

Table 5.1 Total Votes for Selected Black Presidential Third Party Tickets, 1960–1968.

Afro-American Party	1960 votes
Rev. Clennon King (Pres.)	1,485
Reginald Carter (V. Pres)	
Socialist Workers Party	1964 votes
Clifton DeBerry (Pres.)	32,720
Edward Shaw (V. Pres.)	
New Party	1968 votes
Dick Gregory (Pres.)	47,133
Mark Lane (V. Pres.)	
Peace and Freedom Party	1968 votes
Eldridge Cleaver (Pres.)	36,385
Peggy Terry (V. Pres.)	

Source: Historical Review of Presidential Candidates from 1788 to 1968, Congressional Quarterly, Washington, D. C., 5th Edition, January 1969.

It appears that regardless of whether the party was Black or white, in races where the total electorate was approximately 70 million, the figures shown in the table are utterly insignificant. Yet, sentiment for a Black political party as a mechanism of independent-leverage has existed for a considerable time, and while the more recent manifestations of this sentiment have been attendant to the rise of Black nationalism, older rationales were formed because of the stark fact of Black subordination by the major parties and the desperate search for strategies with which to exercise maximum influence in the electoral arena. Exemplary of the rationale for the Black political party as a leverage mechanism was the view of crusading Black journalist J. W. F. Foster, editor of the *Afro-American* newspaper, printed in the *Pittsburgh Leader* in November 1890.

> So long as the Negro is discriminated against in politics, religion and the industries, so long will there be a Negro problem to be solved. He has looked upon political parties to solve this problem, but they are no nearer bringing about its solution today than they were at any time previous. The only proper way to solve this problem is for the Negro to study his own relation to the country, and adopt a practical plan, and unite his entire strength for the accomplishment of that plan. He has reached that point in his history where he must or should unite himself politically, financially and socially to take care of his own interest, and until he does so but little will be done toward his own advancement. For twenty years he has been the ward of a political party, and yet if he stops to think a moment, he will realize that nothing has been done except what was necessary to forward party ends. He must endeavor to raise his interest above mere party lines, and form, if necessary a party of his own; enter into the various business enterprises among themselves and appreciate the institutions of his own creation. So the Negroes should now unite and elect their own men, nominate and vote for them whether they get defeated or not, and, as he holds the balance of power in their country, he could force the politicians to recognize his claim. But so long as he adopts no plan, continues to vote for one party and is merely looked upon as the ward of the party, so long will he fail to gain what is actually due him.[14]

Somewhat later, in 1916, Inez Milholland, a civil rights sympathizer, prominent feminist in the women's suffrage movement and founder of the National Women's party, made a speech in which she advocated the formation of a Black political party. W. E. B. DuBois supported this idea in the pages of *The Crisis* by setting forth the following principle:

> [The Negro's] only effective method in the future is to organize in every congressional district as a Negro Party to endorse those candidates, Republican, Democrat, Socialist, or what-not, whose promises and past performances give greatest hope for the remedying of the wrongs done the Negro race. If no candidate fills this bill they should nominate a candidate of their own and give that candidate their solid vote. This policy effectively and consistently carried out throughout the United States, North and South, by colored voters who refuse the bribe of petty office and money, would make the Negro vote one of the most powerful and effective of the group votes in the United States.[15]

Then, more recently, the view that there should be a Black political party, emerged from the Black Power Movement of the 1960s, as a recommendation put forth by journalist Chuck Stone in a 1969 article "Black Politics: Third Force, Third Party or Third-Class Influence?"[16] A more recent article by Stone still held that:

> Where pivotal politics demand it, Black voters should be prepared to boycott both major parties. This means supporting independent or Third Party candidates and laying the groundwork for a third Black Political Party.[17]

This view is consistent with those taken by this writer in a series of articles on this subject. However, other political scientists have attempted to evaluate the possibilities of this strategy, among them Professor Hanes Walton. Walton suggests from his extensive analysis that the former varieties of Black third parties were more localized in scope and of limited influence. But he also holds a positive view of the evolution of a truly national Black party, which suggests that:

> In many ways it [the coming of a national Black political party] will bolster the urge in black Americans to become an

independent force in American politics and use the American political system to remove some of the disabilities of black Americans.[18]

While accepting Walton's qualification that it would be simplistic to suggest that a Black party is the solution to the problems of Black people in America, there have been other views more decidedly negative. Professor Matthew Holden, for example, considers that the "idea of a *national* Black party is likely to be unproductive, or, at the least to jeopardize too many relationships which it might be better to cultivate."[19] Instead, he argues for the possibly more viable strategy of a third party movement which would not find Blacks isolated against the two major parties, but allied with others in a possible play against either one of the two or both.[20]

The ideas of Milton Morris appear almost identical to those of Holden, as he dismisses the possible utility of a Black political party both because of the difficulty of finding a consensus among Blacks and the possibility that a Black party could be isolated by a decision on the part of the two major parties not to compete for Black votes. Furthermore, he suggests that the function of such a party would be to raise race issues, and since they are already before the country, its function would, then, be marginal and efforts would better be aimed at a third-party, non-racial alliance of other minorities and the poor.[21]

Summarizing these views, it might be suggested that the issue of rigid Black exclusivity in the formation of a political party is passé in that, if its objectives are to express a sense of Black unity through an organization based on a common identity, it might profitably be exclusive. However, if its objective is to contest for public political power, then rigid exclusivity is contradictory, in that it limits the accrual of competitive resources.

Rather, the more productive scenario may be for Blacks to seek to become the leading edge of an alternative party movement which, if it succeeds in becoming significant, attracts other groups. So far, this view is close to that of Morris'. It differs, however, in suggesting that if Blacks are not able to attract stable cross-racial allies, then, because of the size of the Black vote, a Black party may still serve as a vehicle for operationalizing racial political strategies in an effort to directly project race and class-oriented issues into the political arena and become an effective balance of power based on the racial organization of the Black vote alone.

It should be obvious that the strategies for a Black political party have always included either running a Black candidate or utilizing the party base to support another candidate. Writing before the 1972 political conventions, Mark Levy and Michael Kramer took seriously the fact that there would be a Black presidential candidacy that year and analyzed some of the consequences in a section of their book entitled "A Serious Independent Black Presidential Candidacy Will Insure Democratic Defeat."[22] They constructed a scenario which found Blacks fighting for and winning seats to the Democratic National Convention, and once there, presenting demands upon the "unhappy" party which, faced with a possible walkout by Blacks, would probably concede.[23] That would be the case, they said, unless Blacks chose to nominate their own candidate in advance of the convention and attempted to construct a party as a brokering mechanism with the white major party candidates. In any case, they made the critical assumption that: "If an independent black presidential candidate can carry between 20% and 30% of the black vote, it will be virtually impossible for the Democratic nominee to carry nineteen states representing 285 electoral votes."[24]

The Kramer-Levy formula compared the percent of the Democratic vote in 1968 and the Nixon plurality over the Democrats to the Black vote as a percent of the electorate in nineteen states selected for their high Black VAP. The fact is that the Black vote as a percent of the electorate in these states could have influenced the percent of the Democratic vote and if withheld possibly could have provided the winning margin of victory for the 1972 Republican nominee. This analysis is very similar to our description in Chapter Two of the grouping of states which constitute the current claim to be the Black "balance of power" where Democratic party voting allegiance is concerned.

It should be clear that the effect of the Black vote as a balance of power factor operates whether Blacks are within the party or outside of it. The posture of independence is not only effective to the extent that the vote may be withdrawn or given to the candidate of any party, but that it may also facilitate multi-party bargaining.

Thus, the point here is that the Nixon vote in 1968 was a close vote and the calculation of the electoral effect of the Black vote is best illustrated as a balance when the vote is close—again, whether Blacks are inside of a major party or outside. Indeed, the balancing factor may become effective for possible Republican as well as Democratic party consent to Black objectives. In addition, the fact that there theoretically could be an agreement by both major parties to isolate the Black vote is only significant as a bluff. This turn-of-the-century "Gentlemen's Agreement" could not function now, due to the size of the Black vote, which gives it significant capability to intervene in the electoral system.

Finally, we have suggested that the independent party improves the bargaining atmosphere. One critical reason for the past failure of Black political party besides the efficiency with which it might affect the vulnerability of Black leaders to party leaders. The presence of Black leaders in a different organization, not subject to direct control by Democratic party leaders, would reduce the intra-party influence that is based on state party membership or national party candidate influence. In this circumstance, it is possible for Black party leaders to negotiate with the nominees of other major parties, given that it is the *candidate organization* which is more often than the party organization the decisive respository of political commitments.

There is another important reason for the development of a Black political party besides the efficiency with which it might affect electoral strategies. What might be called the "progressive coalition" constitutes a potentially important force in American politics — if organized to compete seriously for power. However, the effectiveness of this coalition depends upon a sense of permanence and the regular accrual of resources, just as it does for other organizations with dedicated political objectives. Progressive organizations representing poor and disadvantaged constituencies or advanced foreign affairs positions are dispersed into small research organizations, unions, publication collectives, and small political organizations. Thus, they often reflect the feudality of the political constituencies of the major party organizations, except on a smaller scale, a fact which is crucial to their political underdevelopment, since they also tend to attempt to form organic working relationships less frequently.

The institutionalization of this politics, then, depends upon the institutionalization of its national organization, which gives a systematic, rather than an episodic — every-four-year — quality to the competition. In addition, it is the only way that *political development* can take place which enhances political skills and resources necessary for effective competition with the other major parties. Most importantly, the existence of an institution carries with it the possibility that the American people will become socialized to the existence of an alternative political formation, challenging the mystique of the necessity and inevitability of the two-party system.

Given this foundation, the functions which the party must perform in competition with other parties during an election year, such as implementing a nomination system complete with a candidate selection process and a convention and the general election campaign, become routine. For example, such a routine process could obviate the necessity for the Black convention process, which has been a part of the party process of interest articulation, since the Black/progressive convention would presumably issue a platform of its own. Second, the bargaining arena would be removed from the Democratic convention and placed in a neutral arena accessible to both groups, where the political power of one side would not unduly influence the outcome. Third, in a strategy designed to utilize the leverage of the Black vote in the bargaining process, the timing of the Democratic party political calendar would be extended. For instance, if the Black/progressive coalition was dissatisfied with the results of the bargaining by the time the Democratic convention ended, the period from the end of the convention to the final vote in November would not only be available, but probably would constitute the most strategic period for productive bargaining because the nominees would be known and their issue-positions as well as their campaign resource needs clarified. Then, the nature of the bargaining issues would be clearer. If, for example, campaign funds and staff appointments were reduced in priority, the issues would be more closely related to the substantive character of the prospective administration.

The existence of an alternative political institution is important during national elections; however, it is also critical as a base for the coalition during non-electoral periods. The influence of the major party institutions has a rhythm which is highest when the opposing party is in power. With an opposing source of policy interests, the Black/progressive party institution would become both an accountability mechanism for issues agreed upon in the bargaining and a base from which to project additional issues as the policy environment changed. In this sense, the non-electoral functions of the party might be diverse and could possibly assume activities not characteristic of the existing major party institutions. Given the grassroots style of Black political behavior, the party might function very differently than either of the existing major parties does today.

OPTIONS

Heretofore, bargaining has been shaped by the narrow perception of major party leaders, the press, and Blacks themselves that they had few political options in presidential elections, especially if the bargaining was not favorable to their interests. Therefore, in a real sense, the expansion of bargaining leverage for Blacks depends upon the expansion of political options. Here I address the linkage between these two factors, previously discussed elsewhere, looking first at the question of political bargaining.[25] In addressing this question, I am really asking a larger one, "How does the party cohere?" One way, obviously, is through the formal mechanisms it has established in the nomination process which assume participation by coalition members in the act of achieving a consensus.

The other, much less analyzed, is the informal political process of bargaining by coalition members with the party leadership. Actually, the formal and informal processes at the party presidential nomination stage is one of the two critical stages of the distribution of benefits for coalition members, the second stage being the act of governing or being part of the governing process as, for example, in the distribution of policy benefits. In any case, because the party, as referred to by Kessel, is an "advocacy" organization, it attracts coalition members interested in the issue advocacy function. But because the institutional role of Blacks is not commonly decisive at the formal or informal stage of the presidential nomination, securing their advocacy interests in a way which fairly reflects their value to the party must often depend upon strategies more aggressive than trust.[26]

> [Loyalty] . . . is the principal reason that Negro political power has not been accorded its share of the political spoils. The fact that blacks have not been able to translate their vaunted balance of power at the polls into jobs after an election seriously calls into question the loyalty concept.[27]

Yet, bargaining is a part of the methodology by which similar interest groups secure their rewards. The mechanism which affected coherence among the various coalition members attracted to the Democratic party traditionally was the distribution of benefit by various Democratic administrations, and, as the party stayed in power, this was institutionalized by a system of patronage. Democratic party patronage systems, already operative in many states, have been much stronger at local levels where they have tended to be more ethnically homogenous.[28] Blacks, however, were only nominal members of this extensive system; but through the powerful forces of the Civil Rights Movement and the sympathetic public mood created by the death of President John Kennedy and Black loyalty to Lyndon Johnson, they were rewarded, as members of the winning coalition, with legislation.

Today political scientists have discovered stronger levels of consistency between the ideological predisposition of voters and those of the candidates, which is undoubtedly responsible for findings of stronger correlations between the mean policy preferences of the Democratic party coalition and its candidates.[29] This is, therefore, an age where the general relationship between voter issue preferences and candidate support is sharpening. As a consequence the competitive techniques of single-issue advocacy groups are having an enormous impact upon the political system, through the organization of Political Action Committees and their mobilization within presidential campaigns. In such an atmosphere, the methods of "political bargaining" by such groups to secure commitments from presidential candidates are extensive.

In a purely theoretical sense, an exchange of commitments is the mechanism through which coalitions are formed. Electoral coalitions are generally studied from the viewpoint of the socio-economic, ideological or demographic composition of the groups in a winning or losing election. Few studies, however, explain whether or not in the process of campaigning, the commitment of a given group was achieved through informal or formal processes of bargaining. This study takes the position that it is the "normal" substance of American politics for the commitment of groups viewed as strategic to the electoral victory of a campaign to be secured through a rather explicit exchange of commitments which may be either public or private. The strategic value of the group, like that in all game-theoretic situations, depends upon the distribution of power, and the quality of the power of the relevant groups affects the outcome of the bargaining.[30] The immediate group objectives lay in affecting a pattern of strategic interaction (political coalition) which is based on the reduction of the threat among members through establishing a shared interest in winning, so that each will realize its committed goals.[31] The mutual interest-benefit objectives, therefore, must be carefully understood, since some groups involved in strategic interaction "will often settle for the emotional rather than the payoff aspects of coalition decisions."[32]

We have argued that it is either dependent- or independent-leverage which has shaped the power quotient of a less powerful group such as Blacks, and that the organization of political resources into an independent posture is qualitatively more advantageous in securing rewards from this political system. A few examples of this process of exchange of commitments involve the recent campaigns of Jimmy Carter and Walter Mondale. Elsewhere, I have suggested that in 1976, the National Education Association exchanged its 1.7 million votes for a commitment from candidate Jimmy Carter to establish a new Department of Education, a commitment which was kept on both sides.[33] But, this organization, which had the largest block of delegates to the Democratic National Convention in 1980, also bargained with Walter Mondale in 1983, and in a closed door session on September 29, overwhelmingly endorsed his candidacy for President.[34] The point was made at the time that, with the endorsement of such labor organizations, the candidate received important political resources (or muscle) such as "direct mail computers, telephone banks, legions of volunteers, independent expenditures, etc." Although, the specific nature of the commitments exchanged at the time were not revealed, it is most certain that they existed.

Second, although Democrats are widely considered to have become the party of "special interests," Mondale complained after the election of 1984 that his approach was "a commitment to the public interest and not to the special interests, but I'm not sure that's the *way* to appeal to the American people."[35] Furthermore, he charged that President Reagan also made special interest commitments, citing the case of social security.

The day following the debate, I challenged Mr. Reagan to make the *commitment* that he would protect Social Security for those on and those who become eligible for Social Security, adjusted for inflation. His news secretary at the news conference said, 'I've just talked to Mr. Reagan and that's our *commitment*. We will not tamper with the program.' A few days later . . . he said, 'Anybody who tampers with Social Security will be gone in the morning.' There is no question that the President stated his *commitment* to protect Social Security adjusted for inflation, and having made that *commitment*—I dropped it as an issue. Now the election is over. The

senior citizens by a large margin voted for Mr. Reagan,
reassured by that *commitment*, and they've gone back on
it.[36]

The example of social security which Mondale used, and others
which might have been used as illustrations, certify that commitments are part of the normal discourse of presidential politics,
that they are publicly or privately made, and that they are difficult to
monitor in the absence of accountability structures in the post-
election period.

It is instructive that groups whose participation in the party
coalition is not decisive must engage in overt bargaining, while
decisive groups have the luxury of tacit bargaining that is often
systemic and, thus, hidden from public view. With respect to the latter, their influence is often publicly recognized at critical times, such
as in the acceptance speech of the Democratic party nominee. For
example, it has been widely reported that the Democratic party
Commission on Delegation Selection for the 1984 convention, headed by Governor James Hunt of North Carolina, was "stacked" by
representatives of Mondale, Kennedy, and the AFL/CIO. From this
vantage point, rules could be written which favored large, well-
organized candidacies with access to sufficient funding, and once
having participated in constructing such a system, labor support for
Mondale — the acknowledged "front-runner" in 1982 — was secured.
Without a full description of the relationship between the Mondale
organization and organized labor, the point here is that, given the
extent of labor backing of the Mondale campaign in 1984, bargaining most certainly occurred between them. It was not necessary to
execute the details in public because both were key "systemic" actors
in the party institution which governed the nomination process.
Below, I will address the basic elements of the bargaining process as
envisioned by the model at Figure 5.2.

The problem which requires bargaining has been the principal
concern of this work. It is the problem of how a minority such as
Blacks exercises influence in the achievement of its objectives
through political participation in the party presidential nomination
process. There is, then, an expectation that the reward from the process of participation directly impacts upon the group, and so its leaders
attempt to achieve these objectives in a scenario of conflict and cooperation with the party leaders, candidates, nominees, and presidents.

Figure 5.2   Political Bargaining

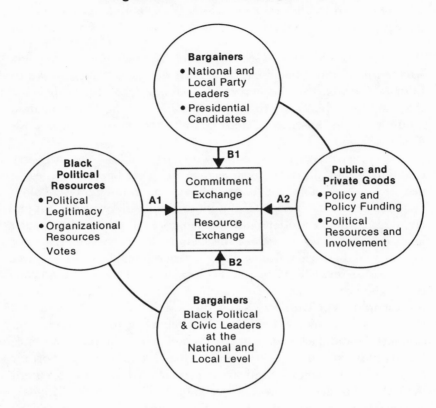

According to the model, the parties to the bargaining (B1,B2) are Black political leaders and the party representatives thus mentioned; however, we have shown that from 1972 to the present, at least, there has been some competition within the Black leadership for prominence in bargaining roles. The instability in this process is perceived to have relevance to the success of the bargaining strategy, for if, as we have suggested, Black bargainers emerge who are vulnerable to the party leaders, the bargaining will most certainly not be fruitful because of the party leader's ability to resist "hard bargaining" through holding out the hidden resource of private and personal incentives to vulnerable bargainers.

The basic element in bargaining is an exchange of commitments (A1,A2), the commitment of the party leaders to supply various kinds of resources in exchange for the political resources of Blacks. In what I have called the "three-ballot strategic scenario" the primary Black political resource is their vote (A1). However, the bargaining has often been unsuccessful because of the doubt that the Blacks leaders were fully organized in a way to effect sufficient registration and turnout of the national Black vote through their ad hoc structural relationship to it. As we have seen, in significant cases, the major party candidates and nominees have by-passed the Black leaders to establish their own relationship to the Black vote. Then, the resources to be provided by the major party leaders are such things as symbolic personnel assignments in their campaign organizations in the party institution or in the administration, campaign funds for voter registration and public policy. As indicated, policy considerations which are regarded as the most important outcome of participation, also have proven to be the most difficult issues about which to obtain meaningful commitments. Third, it would be interesting to know what incentives there are for major party leaders to bargain. It is the residual *threat* involved in the real and symbolic interaction between Black leaders and party leaders at the various stages of the presidential nomination process, as indicated below:

Table 5.2 "Three-Ballot Strategic Scenario" Voting Options.

Scenario	Resource	Vote Threat Option
candidacy	primary votes	yes/no
convention	delegates votes	yes/no
election	election votes	yes/no

This array, which also partially answers the question of *where* the bargaining takes place (scenario), suggests that the primary bargaining resource of Black leaders is their votes at each stage of the process. The threat to vote one way or another, however, can be refined. For example, the mere presence of a competitive Black candidacy in the race for the primary nomination is itself a threat because it competes for votes, and consumes precious legitimizing resources — media, money, political access, organization, etc. — which might otherwise have gone to one of the other candidates. Otherwise, it is the quality of the interaction at each scenario, such as the nature of Black turnout in the primaries and voter registration for the general election, that determines the possibility of Black leaders utilizing "backward leverage" or "forward leverage" in the bargaining.

Next, while delegate votes are a resource at the convention, another value of the delegates is their behavior toward the winning nominee, especially if their number was not enough to influence the nomination. Should they boycott the acceptance speech or give any other sign of disapproval, such behavior would be politically significant. Here, the resource might be characterized as the "backward leverage" of the Black delegates who have already won in the primary.

Finally, I have previously indicated that the period between the end of the convention and the final vote is obviously available, should the bargaining at other stages not have been successful. The nature of the threat at this point would be the "forward leverage" of the potential Black vote for the Democratic nominee in the general election. Whether or not Black leaders generally have the ability to "manage" the Black vote, which suggests that they might, for example, depress or increase turnout, is questionable, but for a nominee to ignore the possibility would be a risk to a presidential candidacy historically dependent upon such votes. The necessity to conceptualize all arenas as collective bargaining opportunities should further remove the major party convention from its role as the sole arena.

This brings us to the general election vote as the final opportunity to exercise political influence in the process of participation to secure political rewards. Since there has been traditionally so much emphasis on this vote, it is striking that there has been so little *strategic* consideration of how it might be used as a logical extension of the bargaining process. Perhaps, it has been felt that regardless of the results of the bargaining, Blacks would loyally adhere to the Democratic party coalition, especially when it was perceived that the Republican party provided little alternative to supporting whatever Democrat was running for president. But in fact, the disassociation of the results of the bargaining from the general election vote has bred an additional vulnerability in the bargaining process, in that the severe limits upon voter behavior have decreased the credibility of the bargaining threat. In other words, at this level, there has been an insufficient response to the old shiboleth that "Blacks have no place to go." Indeed, Figure 5.3 illustrates that, according to the results of the bargaining, there is a rich variety of "places to go," depending upon the strategic objective and methods one is willing to consider to get there. Such methods are considered here to be strategic voting.

Figure 5.3 Vote Decision Array

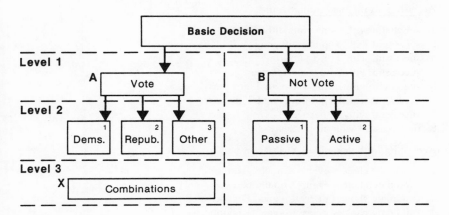

The Vote Decision Array is an objective illustration of the choices available in the decision to vote. At the first level, the choice begins with the decision of whether or not to vote at all, *as a matter of strategy* rather than for any other reasons, such as citizenship obligation, sentiment or symbolic rewards. Then, at level two, these basic vote options are divided, for example, into a party option if the decision is to vote, and to either a "passive" or "active" option if the decision is not to vote. If the decision is to vote, then one is faced with the question of how (or for whom) to vote in order to achieve one's larger objectives. Perhaps only the "active" option needs comment here, in that people who have decided not to vote — for whatever reason — are not accustomed to thinking of extra-voting methods to influence the interpretation of the action. If, for example, demonstrations or other such active mobilizations are conducted which are clearly related to the electoral process, then it constitutes "active" non-voting strategy under the intentions of this array. At the third level, a novel strategy would be to combine voting with the energies of those who want to participate by other collective actions. Nevertheless, it is most important to remember that between the vote and the results of the bargaining, at a given point lay the formulation of a strategy, the linkages of which might be illustrated, as in Table 5.3.

This is a fairly explicit schema with a number of hypothetical situations and choices involved which are intended to illustrate how such a relationship might be operationalized among variables such as the results of the bargaining, the strategy to vote, and the vote. Several brief points may be made about the variables listed here. To

Table 5.3 Implementation of the Vote Decision Array.

According to the bargaining results

1. successful with Democrats only
2. successful with Republicans only
3. successful with Third party only
4. successful with both major parties
5. successful with Democrats and Third party
6. successful with Republicans and Third party
7. successful with all parties
8. unsuccessful with all parties

According to the candidate evaluation

1. candidate choices even – equally good
2. candidate choices even – equally bad
3. candidate choices uneven – good Democrat
4. candidate choices uneven – good Republican
5. candidate choices uneven – good Third party
6. candidate choices uneven – good Democrat and Third party
7. candidate choices uneven – good Republican and Third party

Voting Strategy	Objective	Choice
1. vote Democrat	(discipline Republicans)	A1
2. vote Republican	(discipline Democrats)	A2
3. vote Third party	(own candidate)	A3, AC
	(discipline major parties)	A3
4. vote party	(likely to win)	A1, A2

begin with, it will be evident that the bias of this study, that voting proceeds according to the results of the bargaining, is no simple matter. In practice bargaining generally does not include all parties, perhaps because of the perception that the range of practical choice is not that expansive, especially when one considers elements such as the issue/ideology evaluation of the candidates and those likely to win. Also, the lesson at point number 6 under bargaining should be remembered, since success at any one point also implies the possibility of a lack of success. Thus, the *unsuccessful* bargaining result with Democrats, together with the evaluation that the Democratic candidate was the "best" (in terms of possessing a preferable issue/ideology profile) has resulted in precisely the strategic behavior I have described in this work. Nevertheless, given this norm and the ingredients of choice in the display, it is unlikely that the choices have had to be as consistently narrow as they have been historically. The most important point here is that the items at number 5 very closely resemble the current situation within which voting strategy now proceeds. Finally, the main "objective" is always to win (in terms of securing the policy interests), however, there are times when, as I suggested early in this work, the secondary (or tactical) objectives become simultaneously important. Often called "side-payments," voting is most strategic when it accomplishes the main objective and yields beneficial side-payments in the process.

CONCLUSION

The options listed in Table 5.3 are applicable to the act of "strategic voting," a term which is used to denote the maximum payoff expected from action which follows "strategic bargaining." By this logic, there will be many times when sincere voting — or voting directly for the voter's first choice — will not be possible, and second choice or third choice voting will be considered the logical thing to do in accord with the bargaining results. There is no certainty, however, that policy influence will be attained, even if logic prevails and strategic voting is accomplished, because Blacks are still a grossly outnumbered minority and the political environment, as we have seen, may be decisive for the majority as well as for the minority. It is a competitive game, demanding the highest degree of discipline from voters, which implies a high degree of understanding of tactical objectives. We have on numerous occasions witnessed the fact that Black leaders possessed the same objectives but have employed different ways of achieving them.

> Militant strategies have the virtue of effectively articulating demands in such a way that there is small danger that too little has been asked. They have the disadvantage that they may alienate the objects of their influence so that they get resistance where they could have had cooperation. Conservative strategies have the virtue of insuring maintenance of the channels of communication with the objects of influence, and maximizing the prospect of cooperation. It has the disadvantage that its realism may lead it to set its sights too low.[37]

I have argued that the policy results from the conservative practical strategies, used alone, have not been extraordinary and it may be a losing proposition to attempt more daring strategies, even considering the advantages in attempting to bring participation into accord with expectations. Nevertheless, we argue that more "militant" strategies, in the words of Keech, might yield greater policy results — depending, of course, upon the political situation as implied by the elements of strategic choice.

Chapter 6

Inter-Party Scenarios: The Black Independent Party

INTRODUCTION

Part of any "true" leverage strategy is the ability of the Black vote to exercise a "balance of power" position between the two major political parties. For this to occur, there needs to be some political organization capable of providing the option of running a candidate in the general election, or of throwing the organization's support to either one party or the other in accord with the outcome of the bargaining. Since the outcome of the bargaining might only be clarified as late as October of an election year the flexibility to change course or even to communicate a course of action upon short notice implies a high degree of organization, such as that afforded by a political party.

My case study of the recent Black political party movement must begin with the thought that many have conceived of it as a rational option of electoral strategy, as I have indicated. But its immediate antecedents have encompassed the fact that the Black political party was proposed to be both the electoral vehicle and a vehicle for community organization. The reason for the community organization approach is that, as a purely electoral strategy, the Black party concept has suffered from the tremendous alienation which grassroots Black community leaders have developed about dysfunctional "institutional" solutions to their problems and the politicians (Black and white) who are often identified with those institutions.

This discordant sentiment was perhaps best captured by Malcolm X, a former minister in the Nation of Islam, in his well-known 1964 speech, "The Ballot or the Bullet."[1] He presented the view then widely held among Blacks that in an election year (such as 1964), "white politicians will be back in the so-called Negro community jiving you and me for some votes," and that they would make "false promises, building up our hopes for a letdown with their trickery and their treachery."[2] Malcolm X also surveyed the congressional scene, decrying the control over legislation by powerful "Dixiecrats" who actually controlled Black economic opportunity through their influence on the federal purse strings and their opposition to civil rights. But despite this, he said, Blacks exercised their ". . . vote, your dumb vote, your ignorant vote, your wasted vote on an Administration in Washington . . . ," suggesting that there needed to be a new, aggressive strategy — "the ballot or the bullet." As the strategy concerned the use of the ballot, he says:

> The black man in the black community has to be re-educated into the science of politics so he will know what politics is supposed to bring him in return. Don't be throwing out [casting] any ballots. A ballot is like a bullet. You don't throw your ballot until you see a target, and if that target is not within your reach, keep your ballot in your pocket.[3]

We discover, then, in the powerful concepts of Malxolm X, the father of the modern Black Nationalist Movement, a rationale for both the attitude of opposition to white politicians (and Black alike) and for the more aggressive use of the ballot.

We should not be surprised, therefore, to find that in another speech, given a few days later, he based much of his confidence in the ability of Blacks to exercise unified and aggressive strategies in the electoral arena on the following view: "The Negro holds the balance of power, and if the Negro in this country were given what the Constitution says he is supposed to have, the added power of the Negro in this country would sweep all of the racists and the segregationists out of office."[4] In the early stages of the development of modern Black nationalism the acquisition of control over political office and office-holders was a goal shared by the younger lieutenants in this movement.

When the Black Power Movement burst upon the national scene in 1966, there was much speculation concerning whether or not it would be consistent with the former program of the Student Non-violent Coordinating Committee (SNCC), its progenitors. However, it was clear from the beginning that the philosophy of Black Power, as articulated by SNCC, entertained the acquisition of elected office as one objective. Stokeley Carmichael, then leader of the Student Non-violent Coordinating Committee, explained:

> . . . black power will mean that if a Negro is elected sheriff, he can end police brutality. If a black man is elected tax assessor, he can collect and channel funds for the building of better roads and schools serving black people — thus advancing the move from political power into the economic arena. In such areas as Lowndes [County, Alabama], where black men have a majority they will attempt to use it to exercise control. Where Negroes lack a majority, black power means proper representation and sharing of control. It means the creation of power bases from which black people can work to change statewide or nationwide patterns of oppression through pressure from strength — instead of weakness. Politically, black power means what it has always meant to SNCC: the coming-together of black people to elect representatives to speak to their needs.[5]

In this definition of Black Power, at the inception of the movement, we find an unmistakable emphasis upon electoral politics as an instrument of social change. The SNCC emphasis was logical since the organization had also participated in the formation of the Mississippi Freedom Democratic Party in 1964. The MFDP symbol was the black panther and it had conceived of the creation of a national electoral party even before Huey Newton and Bobby Seale founded the Black Panther party in Oakland, California.[6]

Because of the way in which the Black Panther party evolved and the decision by SNCC at a December meeting in 1966 to de-emphasize institutional politics, it could not be assumed that the dominant character of any national "political party" would be electoral. In fact, the report of that meeting suggested that the new national Black formation "would be all-inclusive political parties; namely, that these political parties would have within their structure a housing, a welfare, an education, a cultural, an economic and a youth division."[7]

The roots of this concept lay in the definition of "politics" by nationalists as a more comprehensive activity than that found in the electoral system. Then, as the movement became more international and Pan-Africanist in character, the model of the political parties leading liberation movements on the African continent and elsewhere unmistakably influenced the ideas of the leaders of the movement concerning the ends to which a political party should be dedicated.

In 1967, Congressman Adam Clayton Powell convened the Black Power Conference in Newark, N. J. Chuck Stone, his aide at the time, reported that the one thousand representatives and 228 organizations from 127 cities passed a resolution which emphasized that there should be:

> an immediate tripling of Negro representation in Congress; the election of Negro mayors in cities where Negroes are a majority in the population; a greater proportion of Negro state and city officeholders in top jobs; and more Negroes in high-level positions of responsibility in the Federal Government.[8]

The next Black Power Conference, held the following year in Philadelphia, adopted a similar resolution, but in 1970, at a Conference called "The Congress of African People" in Atlanta, a resolution was passed which stated bluntly, "Now is the time for a Black political party," and went on to indicate that although "a formal Black political party [may not be] feasible . . . we recommend that at least some sort of pseudo-party structure be planned through which the black political agenda can be expressed."[9] The activities such a party would undertake were construed to be comprehensive, as the resolution suggests:

> Since politics [implies] the gaining, maintaining and use of power, the Black political party must move to gain political power through four areas of political power: public office, alliances and coalitions, Community organization, or Disruption.[10]

In many of the discussions which led up to this resolution, Stone's ideas on achieving electoral influence played a seminal role.

The genesis of his "Third Force" concept was that the Black vote was not capable of performing the function of a true "balance of power" as long as Blacks voted overwhelmingly and "blindly" for either one of the major parties. As a consequence, he felt this behavior contributed to the powerlessness of the Black community and its "Third-class" influence. He defined the "Third Force" to be a "liberation party" which would be:

> . . . independent, unpredictable and totally black-oriented. It asks only one question: what do you intend to do for black people? A 'Third Force' is a cohesive vote which oscillates at will between the candidates of a Democrat, a Republican, or a Third party black man, depending upon which one the Black Third Party can more effectively control.[11]

The point we make here, then, is that by 1971, the idea of a Black political party had become an expression of Black independence in electoral politics.

Part of the urgency felt by those who proposed the strategy lay in the negative policy results of the first Nixon administration. It was an administration which had become characterized by Daniel Patrick Moynihan's phrase "benign neglect," as a description of its relationship to the Black community. It had attacked and attempted to thoroughly dismember the "War on Poverty" program, and had unleashed the federal police power to ruthlessly subdue radical organizations such as the Black Panther party.

When the National Black Political Convention met in 1972, there were two basic sources of tension which would affect the character of its consideration of a Black political party — the Black nationalist concept of a party and that of the Black elected officials. This tension would outlive the convention, color the politics of the Assembly and of the Black Independent Political Party, which Black nationalists eventually created in December 1980.

THE NATIONAL BLACK POLITICAL ASSEMBLY

The continuing mechanism of the National Black Political Convention of 1972 was its Assembly, constituted of 427 members representing 10% of the convention, and a governing "Political Council" of forty-three members or 10% of the Assembly. The formal leaders were Congressman Charles Diggs, Jr., president of the Assembly, Mayor Richard Hatcher, chairman of the Council, and Imamu

Baraka, secretary general (director of the Secretariat). The main agenda of the Assembly in 1973 was the development of state assemblies, the rationalization of the internal organization of the National Assembly, and the drafting of a charter which would govern the entire structure. The most significant decision that year, however, was made in a September Political Council meeting in Pittsburgh. In light of the fact that 1974 was an election year, a convention would be sponsored in Little Rock, Arkansas which would emphasize the "nuts and bolts" of political organizing in both electoral politics and community organization.

Despite the negative picture of the March 15 Little Rock convention by the press, the view of the participants was that the fifteen workshops were well-organized and highly substantive. The seven workshops on electoral politics, for example, emphasized such subjects as the process by which campaigns were managed, local accountability structures, tactics for elected officials, and funding of campaigns at various levels.[12] There were seven recommendations pertinent to electoral politics issued by the convention, and although they were not directed specifically to the presidential level, they provide a context within which to understand the thinking prevalent in the grassroots Black community among groups other than elected officials or party activists. The recommendations were:

1.   That local Assemblies should develop a criteria for evaluating candidates such as a rating system or other devices;
2.   That local Assemblies should insure that the process of community involvement is as open as possible;
3.   That candidates should be endorsed by the Assembly;
4.   That candidates should endorse the National Black Political Agenda before Assembly sanction;
5.   That candidates for office should be developed who might only serve the function of articulating major issues of concern to the Black community.
6.   That political education is a basic part of the responsibility of the local Assembly;
7.   That the local Assemblies should attempt to minimize multiple black candidacies for the same political offices.[13]

The negative picture, referred to above, was provided by press reports of division between militants and moderates and the lack of

Black elected officials and civil rights leaders at the meeting.[14] In fact, there were many Black elected officials present, although they were less well-known than the more highly visible leaders. Richard Hatcher's convention speech of March 16 reflected the tension to which we have referred, in remarks directed to this issue.

> The news that we bring to Little Rock is that everyone is needed, the politicians and the people, the activists and the pacifists, the moderates and the militants. We need our lions and our lambs. We need a united Black people and we need it now. We need Roy Wilkins now. It is time that Mr. Wilkins stop defending our grandfathers and started defending our children. We need Vernon Jordan now. We need Ed Brooke now. We need Floyd McKissick, Coleman Young, Tom Bradley. We need every Black man and woman who has risen from the ranks. We need them here in Little Rock now.[15]

Hatcher's plea for the return of many of the recognized Black leaders was warmly received; however, the fact could not be contradicted that their absence signaled the withdrawal of a segment of legitimacy that it needed from this effort. Specifically, the absence of Diggs, president of the Assembly, was a telling embarrassment, although he had released a statement saying that though he had not yet resigned, the pressures of his congressional duties had forced him to "phase out" his role as a leader of the Assembly.[16] Actually, as we have seen, the way in which the 1972 Black Political Convention had handled the issues of Israel and busing had negatively affected the attitude of the entire membership of the Congressional Black Caucus toward further participation. Therefore, the absence of moderate Black leaders heightened the presence of the Black nationalist element and their bitterness at the withdrawal of prominent Black elected officials. They desired unity, but not at a price that would diminish the "revolutionary" character of the Assembly. Owusu Sadauki, a leading Pan-Africanist, in his speech to the convention, said, if it "was not to be a 'fighting organization,' he would also resign."[17]

Finally, it was also clear that the press retained a certain expectation that a Black political party might be formed, and attempted to make this issue a test of the meeting's eventual effectiveness. Responding to questions at the first press conference, therefore, Hatcher said, "At this point, we're not talking about a political party as such. We want to bring an awareness to the people [of] what politics is all about."[18]

The issue did surface on the floor of the final plenary session, but it was treated in the fashion of the Gary convention, as being too premature since most of the state assemblies had not yet been activated. It was evident that there was a consensus when, at the closing press conference, Imamu Baraka made the observation that the refusal of the convention to approve a party indicated "remarkable maturity."[19] In addition, it had been said by many in attendance that the rationale for the absence of some prominent Black elected officials was that, indeed, a political party might be formed, and that, in the words of Professor Matthew Holden, too many of their existing loyalties would be challenged.

The period between 1974 and 1976 was filled with ideological conflict within the Assembly, then largely a Black nationalist organization. In 1975, the remaining Black elected officials departed and a conflict developed between the Baraka supporters (now Marxist) and the Black nationalists led by Ron Daniels, head of the Ohio Assembly, which resulted in the expulsion of Baraka from the leadership. The winnowing of these factions from the body, however, did not have the effect of strengthening the organization, but of reducing its visibility, seriously complicating its attempt to develop an effective program toward either community organization or the presidential elections of 1976. Nevertheless, in the breach of these considerable difficulties, plans were drawn up for a convention to be held in Cincinnati, Ohio on March 17. The other major decision was that of supporting a Black person for president on a Black party ticket, a step that was important inasmuch as it presupposed the formation of an electoral party not then in existence.[20]

The Black Presidential Strategy in 1976

On January 9, 1976, the executive council of the Assembly decided that, in fact, the convention would be held and that its choice for an independent candidate for president was Georgia State Senator Julian Bond. Bond had been considered, both because he had taken a position critical of Jimmy Carter for the Democratic nomination, and because he was a young politician who had been involved in SNCC and who was thought to possess both the visibility and the understanding of the Assembly's politics to make the commitment.[21] The other central issue was the Constitution of the

Assembly which had become complex because many members believed that one source of the Assembly's difficulty lay in its maintenance of a troika structure. The other fact which gave the constitutional issue some prominence was the struggle to define the Assembly in such a way that it would facilitate running a candidate for president. The by-laws of the organization stated:

1. The NBA (National Black Assembly) will be considered a *pre-party* structure (my emphasis).
2. The NBA will, therefore, dissolve itself at the point where it is determined that a national Black Political Party can and will replace the NBA.
3. At the time of the dissolution of the NBA, the NBPC will be continued as the governing structure of the party, having the same function and relationship to the party as it has/had with the NBA.[22]

The plan which gave the executive council confidence that it might in fact proceed to a resolution of dissolution in 1976 was worked out in a series of meetings in 1975. A Strategy '76 Committee had been formed by the Assembly under the leadership of prominent nationalist Mtangulizi Sanyika (Hayward Henry). Its recommendation to the council was that instead of dissolution, the presidential campaign would be run by a "National Committee for Peoples Politics," a multi-racial and progressive organization which would have branches in the various states. The Assembly's contribution to this coalition would be a Black political party known as the Independent Freedom Party.

Although a meeting with white activist groups was held in Washington, D. C. in February 1976 to organize the coalition, in fact, it was never really functional. Thus, by the time of the convention in Cincinnati, the Assembly had made itself responsible for the overall conduct of a presidential campaign and negotiations had commenced with Bond, as well as with other possible candidates, such as Congressman Ronald Dellums, John Conyers, and Richard Hatcher. The council resolution, released on January 21, 1976, read:

> Georgia State Senator Julian Bond shall be the NBPA nominee for president of the United States as an independent in 1976. The nomination shall take the form of a draft movement which will bring together black, Third World and

White organizations and persons into a National Committee for People's Politics (N.C.P.P.) which shall seek ballot status for the candidate in 30 states.[23]

Bond, however, responded that he was "flattered by the interest shown" in the possibility of his becoming a candidate for the presidency in 1976, but that "until the 1976 legislative session is over in March (1976)" he had no plans for being involved in any candidacy except for his state senate seat.[24]

Perhaps it was the vagueness of Bond's response, or the persistence of the NBPA leaders in a "draft" strategy that continued the illusion of his candidacy. In any case, the illusion was destroyed when the NBPA failed to gain ballot status for Bond in any state, or to deliver a campaign-ready organization. Thus, by the time of the convention, Bond had finally withdrawn his name from consideration, stating that he would run for a seat to the Democratic National Convention pledged to Morris Udall. Bond, nevertheless, did come and address the Cincinnati convention, and departed after a brief note of thanks and polite encouragement.[25]

The spotlight was, then, focused on the second choice, Ronald Dellums. As the convention sessions began, negotiations were still being conducted, and Dellums, not having withdrawn his name from consideration, came and addressed the convention. The mood of the convention delegates was heightened by the prospect that Dellums was coming and that he might actually agree to become the Assembly's candidate. However, in an emotional speech to the convention, he also declined, saying, "It is not my moment, it's not my time."[26]

Dellums' message gave the delegates a dose of political reality. In effect, he was being asked to give up a seat in Congress and his constituents in California for an organization which was unable to get on the ballot in any state, or to fund a campaign adequately. Dellums' declination led to the death of any serious attempt to organize a presidential strategy by the Assembly, although it eventually selected Rev. Frederick Douglass Kirkpatrick, a relatively unknown activist from New York City, as a "candidate," largely to represent the Assembly's point of view at a number of political forums around the country.

THE NATIONAL BLACK INDEPENDENT POLITICAL PARTY

Enthusiasm for the Black Political Assembly subsided between 1976 and 1979, its credibility greatly diminished by the failure of the

1976 presidential strategy. However, with the coming of the electoral cycle, interest was rejuvenated in 1979, as a successful meeting of Assembly activists was held in Pittsburgh. Plans were made at this meeting for an August 1980 convention in New Orleans and, to the surprise of its planners, over 1,000 delegates attended.

Two things quickly became clear at the New Orleans convention (attended by few Black elected officials): in the wake of their alienation from both the Democratic and Republican parties, the delegates wanted a strong political response, which meant a radical reform of Assembly politics. Secondly, they wanted a Black political party to replace it.[27] Thus, on August 23 a motion made by well-known activist Rev. Benjamin Chavis for the establishment of a party passed the body overwhelmingly, and set a three month deadline for the convention leaders to hold a founding convention.[28]

The deadline was deliberately set *after* the November elections in an effort to signal that the formation of the party was not intended directly as a response to the Carter administration. Nevertheless, urged to take a position on the election, at a press conference on September 4, Assembly chair Ron Daniels indicated that Carter's actions in cutting the social budget constituted a "betrayal" to which Blacks should respond by "a massive Black voter turnout on November 4," but "Black voters should not vote for the office of president at all or vote for any third party, or independent candidate."[29] His statement was intended to avoid alienating Blacks who wanted to vote, but urged them to express their disapproval of both major candidates by a boycott of the top of both tickets.

Again, the central questions to be addressed were the character of the new party organization and its relationship to electoral politics. The Charter Commission, charged with bringing the basic draft constitution to the founding convention, reached a compromise on these questions. The compromise was that an "Electoral Politics Study Commission" would study the problem and make recommendations on the way in which an electoral organization might associate itself with the party, but that the main body, The National Black Independent Political Party (NBIPP), would not be an electoral vehicle but a broad-based organization devoted to community organization and civil rights. Thus, they were returning to the earlier solution. The case for an "organic-styled" political party (with strong ideology governing more than electoral activities) had been argued as early as April 1980 by black activist Professor Manning Marable, and this view controlled the first party congress in August 1981.[30]

By 1981, the NBIPP had attracted forty-six chapters in twenty-seven states and established a national office in Washington, D. C. However, the same pattern of ideological in-fighting overcame the organization's forward momentum, and by 1984, it was, ironically, too weak to respond when the Jackson campaign attracted the attention of the national Black community as an independent Black presidential candidacy, albeit within the Democratic party.

DISCUSSION

In the previous chapter, I introduced the theory upon which a Black political party is based and presented a short history of the idea. With this case study, however, we should obtain a better understanding of the problems inherent in the more recent attempts to construct such a party and, thus, the conditions under which it might actually materialize as a legitimate strategy for the Black community. Logic suggests that it is likely to materialize in one of two ways: either there exists a popular basis for the creation of such a party within the Black community or it will exist as the only course of action, thereby, forcing such a choice upon Black political leaders.

With respect to the first course, the criticism is accurate that the idea of a Black political party as not "practical" has rested, in part, on its lack of credibility among Black voters. This has led to the belief that there has not been a workable constituency for the idea. Proponents of the idea have often been more enthusiastic than regular Black Democrats, as indicated, for example, by the fact that the turnout of delegates at both the New Orleans Black Political Convention and the founding meeting of the party in Philadelphia topped 1,000 and 3,000 respectively. These equalled or exceeded any other Black political meeting held that year, including the 1,000 largely Democratic delegates to the Richmond Convention on a Black Agenda. But while the Assembly's convention drew participants who were more highly representative of the grassroots Black community, the BDC convention was more reflective of electoral leadership constituencies with connections to approximately three hundred organizations. Thus, they represented the breadth of the Black community while the Assembly represented its smaller progressive/activist segment.

Still, the informal evidence in 1980 found many Black Democrats interested in an alternative to the Democratic party, as indicated by the contacts made to representatives of NBIPP in an effort to establish linkages and gather information about its local and national plans. The scientific evidence, however, confirms the overall impressions reached regarding the attraction of the idea. For example, national polls of the Black community have asked, with increasing frequency, whether or not the respondents would support a Black political party. The poll by *Black Enterprise* listed in Table 6.1 is biased in that the respondents pool was its readership.[31] Nevertheless, the results favorably compare with the National Black Election Survey (NBES) of the University of Michigan, which was performed as a scientific study with over 1,150 Black respondents nationwide.[32] Moreover, the individuals who appeared to have the strongest orientation to the idea of a Black party appeared to also believe that:

- the black vote makes a difference in presidential elections;
- Black elected officials have no power;
- the Black vote makes a difference in local elections.

The high "factor loadings" which produced the above listing of variables indicating that the Black vote makes a difference in local and national elections, but that Black elected officials have no power, seems to suggest that those supporting the formation of a Black party would be attempting to resolve the contradiction of potential power and the dysfunctional performance of Black political leaders through such a vehicle, a formulation which has been favored more by the progressive intellectuals than by more practical Black politicians. Then, the Joint Center Survey results are inexplicably the lowest of all.[33]

Here, then, is an essential conflict, the basic foundation of which is the disorientation of the highly ideological progressives

Table 6.1 Preference for a Black Political Party

	Yes	No
Black Enterprise Magazine Poll (1985)	22.7%	74.8%
National Black Election Study (1984)	29.1%	70.9%(1)
	24.9%	75.1%(2)
JCPS/Gallup Poll (1984)	18.0%	– – –

Note: The first (1) result from the National Black Election Study is from the preelection survey performed before the 1984 general elections, while the second (2) was obtained soon after the elections.

toward the existing system of institutionalized politics and the strong
orientation of Black elected and appointed officials and party activists toward this arena. Although I will not offer any serious discussion of the dichotomy between militant and moderate orientations,
they are easily available in other works.[34] I might make two points
here, the first of which is that the split has historical roots, as we have
seen in the dichotomy of strategies between the progressive activists
of DuBois' day who supported independent strategies and those of
the party operatives who supported dependent ones. The orientation, then, appears to conform to Professor Holden's observation
that a main difficulty of the independent party strategy is that it
would be disruptive of too many kinds of relationships, many of
which do not exist for community activists. So, the question of
whether or not leaders may espouse and pursue political dependence
or independence, in this light, cannot be viewed apart from the
tangible network of political relationships within which each group
exists.

The idelogical problems have bred subsets of other problems.
Within the National Black Assembly, the strong representatives of
nationalists, politicians and Marxists fought it out until the
moderate Black elected officials and Marxists were eliminated, even
though the Assembly began with an "all-inclusive" philosophy.
Although there was some truth to the charge that part of the ineffi-
ciency of the party's adminstration was caused by a "three-headed
monster" of leadership, the effort to restructure the constitution in
this regard was also a way to deal with the problem of ideological
conflict. The result of this conflict was that the Assembly was
destroyed and, thus, its credibility to mount a 1976 presidential
strategy so undermined that from the start the project was a grand
illusion.

The second level of conflict was external in that the National
Committee for Peoples' Politics implied the formation of a multi-
racial coalition, but the level of racial alienation bred such distrust
on both sides that no meaningful coalition was possible. The conse-
quent lack of external political resources threw the problem back
upon the Assembly, which eventually assumed responsiblity for the
1976 strategy directly.

The third problem was the lack of competence in mounting a
presidential campaign. In 1976, the departure of elected officials
meant that the technical problems of campaigning were being
overlooked, and problems such as ballot-access within states, which

were imposed by the requirements of the political process, were addressed as problems amenable to the internal manipulation of the Assembly's constitution. Thus, the highly important element of the legal competence necessary to comprehend the growing requirements of the Federal Election Commission with respect to the definition of minor parties and their conduct under the law was largely absent.

In any case, it is unlikely that the Assembly would have gained ballot access in the required ten states, and thus, there would have been no matching funds, since it would have been difficult to attract the necessary 5% of the national vote. In 1976, minor party candidates had no advance matching funds. Under the law (PL 93–443), they would have had to receive 5% of the total (nearly 3.5 million votes) and complete the campaign with debts in order to submit requests for federal reimbursement. Thus, the campaign would had to have been financed on the strength of Assembly resources, and it does not appear that the base existed for such funding, with the regular Democratic Black leadership strongly committed to Carter.

The final element, however, in determining the relationship of the Assembly to Black presidential politics was its stunning refusal to become involved in the elections of 1980, and the exclusion of electoral participation from the party charter in August 1981. This was the clearest signal that the new formation, ironically, was not going to participate in the activity which constitutes the major political behavior of the Black community.

CONCLUSION

I conclude this discussion with the disclaimer that it is not intended to constitute a comprehensive critique of the NBIPP or Black nationalism (which was the driving force behind the Assembly's politics). Rather, the NBIPP has been evaluated from the narrow basis of its attempt to create a Black political party which might have had some impact upon national presidential politics. From this perspective, it can only be concluded that the effort failed basically because Black nationalism contains a strong strain of anti-institutional politics, which is incompatible with the requirements of this system-oriented process — perhaps the strongest system-oriented process in the entire American political system.

This conflict has unearthed, however, a fundamental disagreement within the Black community over the utilization of a Black political party, as indicated by the struggle over its definition and role. The conflict is epitomized by the attempt on the part of progressive activists to create, in the words of Professor Harold Cruse, a "new organization," such that "it has to be the consensus that the Black political party is organized for the purpose of dealing with the myriad problems of the Afro-American minority group, first and foremost."[35] It is of no little note that this characterization of the intended function of the "new organization" is also resonant with the definition by Black progressives of "new politics" itself. In the official document which guided the work of the Assembly, politics is defined as follows:

> Black politics is the process by which we establish goals, identify issues, problems and Black interests, set priorities, and develop strategies, tactics, projects and programs to achieve and defend our interests as a National Black Community. Black Politics involves electoral politics, various forms of community struggles, and whatever other mechanisms and methods are necessary to justly fulfill our goals and interests as a National Black Community.[36]

This is moderate enough, but when the goals of Black politics transverse the scale from the total liberation of Black people to the necessity for the development of a "new" society that will make a priority of humane values at home and support Third World human rights abroad, much more than electoral participation strategies is implied and intended. This definition implied a vast undertaking, as recognized in the section of the party constitution on "Black Political Strategies." When it comes to the question of electoral independence, the documents says:

> our position must be one of maximum flexibility as it relates to the two major political parties, and any other parties which might emerge. Our politics must be dictated by interest, and in that regard we may elect to utilize existing parties, but we must never come to depend on them as the primary or only vehicle to promote our political interests.[37]

Thus, philosophically the new party aligned itself squarely with the historical sentiment of the older progressives and the newer "Third

Force" concept, at least in the posture of an organization seeking to achieve a "true balance of power" model for the exercise of the Black vote in elections. However, because the Assembly was not prepared in any respect to engage in elections, this conceptualization was largely symbolic.

One should not, however, diminish this symbolism since it provides an important indicator for evaluating the NBIPP's response to the direction of society. In a rationale for the origin of the party, Ron Daniels, for example, cited the elements of an emerging conservative political trend: the 1968 campaign of George Wallace for president, the election of Richard Nixon, the attack on affirmative action, the Carter proposals for increases in the defense budget, and the apparent immobility of the Congressional Black Caucus to provide leadership in the face of it all.[38] The precedent set by other third parties gives us a guide to the character of its activity if the Black political party engaged in the presidential nomination process. Frank Smallwood, delineating the historical functions of third parties, writes:

> Because the major parties have often tended to ignore or minimize controversial social issues in their efforts to occupy the safe middle ground of American politics, pressures have built up within disaffected groups to organize their own parties in an effort to promote their goals. These protest parties have provided minorities with access to the political arena, thus enabling them to work legitimately within the confines of the American political system.[39]

This type of Black political party, however, would not necessarily conceive of itself as acting within the context of the American political system. It would be taking advantage of the opportunities afforded by the general liberal access to the right of participation to expose what it conceives to be the anti-humanitarian cast of the political system. In this sense, it comes close to Smallwood's typology of a protest political party. Even here, there is ample room to distinguish the purely protest party, which does not envision governing or participating further in the American political system, from the kind of Black party which fully conceives of the possibilities of sharing in the process of governing and, at its maximum, considers its activities directed toward fully utilizing the instrument of the political system to achieve whatever ameliorative gains are possible for the Black community.

On the other hand, to the extent that Black elected officials have considered the function of the party, it has been conceived to be a more specialized organization for competition in the electoral arena. For them and for many other Blacks, party membership and participation define their national electoral politics. Thus, since Black political allegiance has remained strongly Democratic, any new party formation which duplicates this function poses an inherent conflict of loyalties. Democratic party allegiance can be strong because of its narrow function, but it is also nominal in that it does not represent the interests of Blacks in many other arenas of life. This may provide an opening for the Black party. Nevertheless, there would have to be an overridingly powerful reason for a transition in party loyalty. Otherwise, flexibility might occur in the pursuit of different strategies without changes in fundamental party allegiance.

Given the experience of other organic parties, it is not an open question as to whether or not a multi-purpose organization can also compete successfully in the electoral arena at the presidential level. It is, however, less questionable that the ideological character of the organization will pose severe limitations upon the adoption of such a strategy. Cruse, who has had much experience with European-style organic political parties, has also indicated that the effective functioning of such a party was best left to persons with "maturity."[40] Although Cruse literally meant adults, the political meaning of this concept is applicable in the sense that a mature Black nationalism might have permitted the implementation of a strategy of independent politics in national elections, but the immature strain emerging from the 1960s may have made such implementation "premature."

At least elements of political maturity may be conceivable as they apply to the future, and then only narrowly as they relate to the attempt to build an independent Black political party which has some relationship to presidential politics. First, there is the necessity for all groups to conceptualize the electoral arena, not as that arena where the maximum payoffs will be attained relative to other arenas, but as a legitimate arena of political struggle. There are many things which make the electoral arena less than democratic, such as the funding of some campaigns by the government, business, organized labor and professional political action committees, all of which may have access to larger resources than the average citizens group. There are also rules which prohibit easy ballot access to presidential candidates of minor parties and which limit the ability to register for minorities, the handicapped, and the day-time employed. Nevertheless, it is also an arena where ideas may be tested and where the skills of grassroots political organization are as relevant as in any other place.

Secondly, the great irony of the electoral market place is that Blacks perform in this arena with greater frequency than in any other institutionalized part of the political system. As such, groups which have outlined community organization programs must recognize the relationship between the acquisition of external resources through the political system and the goal of internal resource mobilization to achieve their ends. This means that while moderate political leaders and more progressive activists may not ultimately be able to share the same organization, they may, since they have similar objectives, find a profitable relationship in coalitions between and among them, especially since both have practiced the politics of multi-racial coalitions. Here, it is tempting to speculate on the electoral effect of such a coalition. In our concept of "forward leveraging," for example, we found that in 1984, Jesse Jackson might have attracted as many as six million votes in a general election contest. This result, which may have been peculiar to one election and one candidate, nonetheless, represents a significant share of the Black vote and poses the possibility that even if a Black political party draws between 25%–50% of the Black vote in support of an independent candidate, it could achieve some tactical and strategic objectives. For example, it could split the solid Black vote, and although we have argued that splitting the vote would ordinarily be dysfunctional as a two-party strategy, it might threaten to depress the Democratic vote (possibly inducing bargaining) and simultaneously provide votes to a third party candidate as a sincere choice. Such a move might also initiate a process of dealignment from the Democratic party into a more independent position.

Lastly, it is generally possible to enter into this arena and compete without loss of principle, since it is not necessary to participate through party organizations. In fact, the case could be made that such groups, by organizing to assess the record of presidential candidates on terms constant with their own program and policy objectives, may provide an important political accountability service for the community at large.

Realism about the demise of the attempt to build a Black political party in the 1970s and early 1980s, however, suggests the likelihood that at this period in history none of this was possible, since it took place at the apex of the ascendancy of two types of politics within the Black community. Perhaps with the perspective of time, the elements needed to develop maximum support for such an effort among various segments of the politically active might benefit from the experience of the period under discussion.

Chapter 7

Intra-Party Scenarios: the Jackson Campaign for the Democratic Party Presidential Nomination

INTRODUCTION

In 1984, the campaign of the Rev. Jesse Jackson for the Democratic nomination for president of the United States constituted a major variation in the way in which Blacks have participated in the process of candidate selection. Of all the tantalizing questions it presents, it is *the strategic value of the campaign as a leverage strategy in the process of political bargaining* that is important for this study. Normally, there are very few mysteries about the function of a presidential campaign. Either it is a dedicated campaign for the presidency, or it is essentially a bargaining vehicle; in any case, even if it were basically a bargaining vehicle, it would have to be managed as though it were a dedicated campaign for the presidency in order to make it credible.

The "abnormality" in this case is the highly problematic question of whether, in the foreseeable future, a Black person Would win either of the major party nominations or be elected president in America, even though the data indicates broad-based acceptance of the idea among the white population and an even more significant share of Blacks. For example, Table 7.1 shows the results when the

Howard University Convention Delegate Surveys of 1976 and 1980 asked respondents whether they thought it was "time for a Black candidate for president?" Democrats are fairly consistent, with little significant difference between their 1976 and 1980 views. The low response rate in 1976 for white Republicans and the high rates for Black Republicans may be accounted for by the fact that they were faced with the possible choice of a Black vice presidential candidate in Senator Edward Brooke. Thus, behavior may change substantially from the norm when voters are actually presented with the opportunity to vote for a Black candidate for president.

It has been established that the major function of the independent-leverage tactic is to operationalize the balance of power strategy, and although the Jackson campaign was still within the Democratic party, it was independent because it was an autonomous campaign. Thus, I will consider, in this case, the utility of independent-leverage within the Democratic party, in an effort to determine to what extent it was directed to the function of becoming the balance of power within the party nomination process in order to establish a bargaining environment for the exchange of commitments. In evaluating the campaign, I have utilized the concepts applied to this study and, even more specifically, the model developed in Chapter Five.

Mobilization of the Campaign

The first aspect of mounting an autonomous campaign was for Jackson to "mobilize the legitimacy of the idea" of a Black man running seriously for the Democratic nomination as a rational and popular strategy, since it had been called into question by the previous campaign of Congresswoman Shirley Chisholm. In the spring of 1983, the Black leadership was fearful that the Democratic party leadership was going to take the Black vote for granted as in-

Table 7.1 Democratic and Republican Delegate Preferences for a Black Presidential Candidate.

	1976		1980	
	Yes	No	Yes	No
Black Democrats	47.8	38.9	49.2	27.1
White Democrats	42.6	33.5	40.6	35.0
Black Republicans	57.1	14.3	35.5	32.3
White Republicans	25.0	50.0	44.4	30.6

dicated by Senator Edward Kennedy's endorsement of Mayor Jayne Byrne of Chicago for re-election and Vice President Walter Mondale's endorsement of Richard Daley, Jr. That neither of the presumed presidential candidates endorsed Congressman Harold Washington, the ultimate winner, sent a powerful signal to Blacks.[1] Furthermore, Harold Washington in Chicago and Wilson Goode, the new Black mayor of Philadelphia, had both been obvious vehicles for the kind of enthusiastic mobilization which gave Black leaders the feeling that the trend toward a political movement was a national manifestation.[2]

Thus, a series of meetings was held beginning in March of 1983 and ending in June at which the idea of a Black presidential candidate was thoughtfully entertained by a group of twenty-five Black leaders, headed by Rev. Joseph Lowery of the Southern Christian Leadership Conference, and representing a cross-section of institutions. The discussions reviewed various rationales, such as the possibility that a Black candidacy would get the attention of party leaders because it would increase voter turnout and that it would be a bargaining tool. A report prepared by the Joint Center for Political Studies on the background issues for the presidential elections held that such a candidate would run well in the South and that a Democratic victory in 1984 would be inconceivable without a strong showing by the party in the South. It also held that Blacks were pivotal voters in fifteen of nineteen swing states, and they could play a role in the nomination process by having as many as 200–400 Black delegate seats at the national convention.[3] As such, the convention delegate emphasis as the function of the Black candidacy was a bargaining tactic. During the debate which developed over the strategy, the writer suggested that

> a black candidate might run in 15–20 primaries in 1984 to attract a multi-racial pool of delegates to the convention committed to a bargaining strategy.[4]

Others, however, suggested that the candidacy might take votes away from more "serious" candidates, that Blacks should be in all camps, and that in any case, Jesse Jackson, in particular, could not win.[5] Therefore, the tactic of the Black leaders was to separate the discussion of the idea of the Black presidential candidacy from the person who might operationalize it, and on June 20, 1983 at a meeting in Chicago the idea was approved, while the group took no action to name a candidate. By leaving it open they hoped to provide a fair opportunity for anyone who wanted to do so to run. Rev. Jackson, reacting to a statement by Rev. Joseph Lowery that the positive decision gave a "green light" to any Black who chose to enter the field, formed an exploratory committee headed by Mayor Richard Hatcher, declaring that the decision "made it highly likely" that he or some other Black Democrat would run.[6] This statement, then, meant that an important milestone of legitimacy had been passed, at least among a critical group of Black leaders and that the remaining aspect of the legitimacy of the candidacy was that of the candidate himself.

In practical terms, the idea of the candidacy could not be separated from Jackson, thus his own strategic ideas were important. For example, he had often suggested that the relationship between Blacks and the Democratic party had to be "re-negotiated" toward parity, which is to say that a reciprocal relationship (or a bargain) should exist which recognized the value of the Black vote in exchange for fair rewards. There were those, however, who held to the traditional politics of seeking access to a potential winner with the best civil rights record, in an effort to perform brokerage roles as special surrogates to the Black community. Therefore, tactics of dependent- and independent-leverage were in conflict, a fact which was often masked by interpretations which held that the conflict was essentially over personalities. For example, Andrew Young, Martin Luther King, Sr. and Coretta Scott King had all endorsed Walter Mondale out of a genuine belief in the tradition that the way to exercise leverage was from inside the organization of the potential winner. Thus, in addition to whatever other reservations they may have had, it is more important that they also did not believe in independent-leverage tactics.

Again, at the August 1983 Convention of the National Urban League, in a workshop on "Presidential Politics" as a panelist, the writer again presented the basic rationale for the Black candidacy, by associating the Black vote with policy rewards, suggesting that "A black candidate would induce a 'bargaining situation,' the basis upon which you transfer the agenda of the black community into the agenda of the person who will be the party standard bearer."[7] These ideas were countered by another panelist, a well-known Chicago journalist, who said:

> Don't ever develop a strategy that assumes that you have to use gimmicks to get people out to vote. For us to play games

about a black candidate that we admit can't win, we're in-
sulting black people. We're out here to win tangible victories.[8]

Vernon Jarrett went on to say that it was important not to follow
symbolic politics because the issues, such as appointments to the
Supreme Court, were too critical. In practice, it was difficult to
divorce the issue of the Black candidacy from the feelings of those
opposed to it on its merits, because some were opposed to Rev.
Jackson. Nevertheless, it appeared that some who were dependent-
leverage traditionalists were just as sincere as those who were willing
to attempt an independent strategy.

By October 1983, the results of a poll by *Ebony*, the magazine
with the largest Black circulation in America, indicated that 67.1%
of its readers approved of the idea of a Black candidacy, and 61.6%
believed that Rev. Jesse Jackson should run, a remarkably strong
and therefore important confirmation of the "fit" between the idea
and the person.[9] The results of a David Garth poll showed that nearly half of the 61% of whites who were aware of the potential Jackson
candidacy viewed him favorably.[10] Other polls were showing Rev.
Jackson third in national popularity behind Walter Mondale and
John Glenn, suggesting that by the summer of 1983 the Black campaign idea was, indeed, legitimate, and that it had even more
credibility with Jackson as its organizer.

Jackson himself understood the stage that his "exploration" into
the possibility of a candidacy had reached, as he said that there was
"substantial evidence" that if "the masses began to move from the
bottom up" it would have an effect upon the leaders, and the enthusiasm he sensed for the idea meant that the impact of the campaign
could cause an increase of three million voters, electing many more
Blacks to office. Thus, he suggested:

> My running will stimulate thousands to run for [elected
> office]: it will make millions register. If you can get
> your share of legislators, mayors, sheriffs, school-board
> members, tax assessors and dog-catchers, you can live with
> whoever is in the White House.[11]

Professor Martin Kilson's comments would seem to confirm the level
of legitimacy the candidacy had achieved in the mind of the public,
as he indicated that the bargaining strategy was at the heart of this
Black candidacy, and implied that perhaps no one but Jackson

possessed the "charisma" and "popular appeal" necessary "to smash black voter apathy and thereby affect the outcome of a bid by President Reagan for a second term."[12] Kilson further suggested that, "Victory for a Jackson candidacy should not be measured traditionally. Mr. Jackson seeks to nurture new notions of what is politically possible among Afro-Americans while gaining new respect from the established political parties."[13]

The mobilization of resources is the second critical step toward organizing a Black candidacy, and, as important as endorsements were, campaigns generally need funds for staff, travel, communications, and other tangible resources. In June, Congressman Parren Mitchell said that a Jackson campaign would need "a million dollars in seed money, a tightly structured national organization, and a major voter registration drive," and of the two, only the voter drive was beginning to emerge.[14] The fact that by late October, a close adviser would say that Jackson could qualify for federal matching funds and raise "five million" for the contest, showed the growing optimism of those around him that indeed the financial resources could be found.[15]

Such optimism was not without foundation, since one week after his announcement Jackson's appearance before the National Conference of Black Mayors drew pledges of an estimated five thousand dollars.[16] In early December, the endorsement of the National Organization for Women (narrowly won by Walter Mondale) was actually a two-man race between Mondale and Jackson, the significance of which helped to legitimize his candidacy among white female voters.

By far the most important resource was that provided by Rev. Jackson's natural base — the Black church. For example, Rev. T. J. Jemison, president of the National Baptist Convention U.S.A. Inc., endorsed Rev. Jackson, a fellow Baptist minister, a step which was interpreted as placing the forty thousand-church, 6.8 million-member congregation at the disposal of the Jackson candidacy. Jackson himself said that the endorsement meant that these Baptist churches would provide the core organization for his campaign in each state, beginning with their role in helping the campaign to acquire federal matching funds by immediately raising at least five thousand dollars in each of twenty states.[17] Apparently as a result of Rev. Jackson's successful venture in returning Navy pilot Lt. Robert Goodman to the United States, Rev. J. O. Patterson, Primate of the Church of God in Christ, Inc., a three and three-quarter million member Black congregation, offered Jackson his gratitude and support. The report of this offer also indicated that its Division of Urban Affairs would appeal to the church's assembly for a commitment to the campaign in April.[18] In fact, data from the Federal Election Commission indicated that in the October-December 1983 period, the campaign spent $183,085.13, and by March spending had increased steadily: January - $425,847.23; Februray - $714,667.34; March $907,148.58.[19]

This pattern of support from religious leaders and institutions continued and increased. For example, as the Jackson campaign moved into New Hampshire, twenty-four religious leaders from across the state met at St. Anselm's College in Goffstown to endorse Rev. Jackson.[20] The denominational importance of the group was that it spread considerably beyond the Baptist, being largely comprised of white United Methodist and Congregational churches, but including an expanse which ranged from the Mother Earth Indian Church to the Unitarian Universalists. Many of the volunteer staff of the campaign in New Hampshire were observed to have been sent by one or another of these churches. By March 11, as Jackson faced the critical "Super Tuesday" primaries in Alabama, Georgia, and Florida, the Black churches were poised to participate. A survey of Black congregation leaders in these states appeared to confirm Rev. Jemison's estimate that by this time 90–95% of the pastors in his organization supported Jackson, and the survey continued:

> In black churches in Alabama, Georgia, and Florida—the
> three southern states holding presidential primaries
> Tuesday—the talk was as much about voting as about
> religion. The churches that were the base for the civil rights
> movement in the 1960s are now the base of the voter
> registration movement of the '80s. And Sunday the word
> went out.[21]

Although the word was that parishoners should "vote your conscience," there was little confusion about what conscience dictated, as Rev. T. L. Lewis of Birmingham said: "I tell them that a homegrown tomato is always best."[22] The Jackson campaign, indeed, met the qualification for matching funds to begin the race, and, by its performance in the March 11 primaries, qualified to continue further. This base of religious support was fundamentally important in providing the resources.

It was the national campaign organization, however, that was responsible for utilizing the resources in a way which would make a successful campaign possible, and, to that end, by September 1983 a small core staff was assembled from the exploratory committee. However, the full organization was not in place until January 1984. The schematic outline for the organization is shown in Figure 7.1.

The National Committee of fifty persons was established by the campaign to represent a broad cross-section of constituencies within the Black community and outside of it, in an attempt to create a "Rainbow Coalition." Care was taken to assure that the coalition was comprised of three categories of representatives: male and female, ethnic/racial, and issue representation. The concept was unique in that of the twenty-seven special categories of Rainbow representatives, more than half were represented by desks within the campaign structure, reporting to a director, who operated at the deputy campaign manager level. The work of the five official campaign managers was supplemented by a comptroller, management team, volunteer coordinator, press office, and scheduling unit.

As of January 1984, there were thirteen states which had established campaign offices, twelve of which had applied for official status and had been approved, and by the end of the month chairs had been selected in thirty-four states. By the end of the primary campaign, units had been established in forty-four states. There was a recognized "interface" between the national campaign office in Washington, D. C., the state units, and the "road campaign," and

Figure 7.1   Jackson Campaign Organization

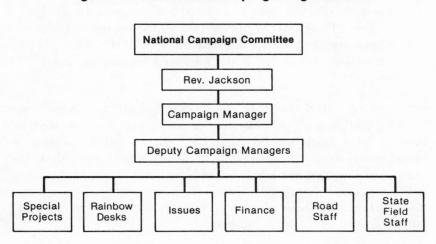

although the coordination was not as smooth as necessary, the chaos became more understandable as reports indicated that it was a generalized phenomenon and that some campaigns were even less organized. The importance of the candidate's road schedule demanded the kind of competence gained only through trial and error experience, which did not make possible a credible campaign operation until the early April primaries.

Nevertheless, the challenge raised by journalist Howell Raines in June 1983 that Jackson "Must Prove Candidacy's Credibility," had been met by the end of March 1984, in the widely respected journalist David Broder's eyes: "He has won the battle for credibility, he has won the struggle for survival and he has won a position of influence greater than any black politician of the past."[22] This statement by Broder was based, not only on the fact that the candidate had developed the rudimentary infrastructure necessary to mount a credible campaign, but that its reception by a substantial segment of the American people made it credible as well.

THE TWO-BALLOT STRATEGIC SCENARIO

The mobilization of an autonomous campaign makes it possible for the Black candidate to compete, like other candidates, in the primaries and caucuses in an offensive effort to obtain visibility for issues and the acquisition of votes, and convention delegates. These are the primary instruments through which the campaign seeks to articulate the interests of its constituency. In doing so, however, the defensive strategy is operationalized which totally denies political resources to any one of the other candidates, and competes for them at each point in the scenario, therefore, posing a "threat" at each of the main points of interaction — the primaries and the convention — according to the model in Chapter Five.

The overall threat is that of projecting strongly organized Black constituency interests in the political competition with other interests. Before the campaign began, Rev. Jackson sought to articulate the interests associated with it as gaining influence in the party presidential nomination process, in order to achieve political and policy rewards. In making this interpretation, the writer is aware that the visionary statements of any candidate are most often addressed to the nation through a specific focus on the ultimate prize of presidential office. Thus, while some of these remarks are related to the instrumental value of the campaign, others paint a much broader picture on a much larger canvas, yielding the ultimate vision of what they would like for America. It is, then, necessary to somewhat disaggregate and reconstruct those statements by Jackson in which he entertains a conception of the value of his campaign.

> A Black candidacy would dramatically increase voter
> registration and participation. There are 18 million eligible
> Black voters, but only 10 million are currently registered.
> A combination of Reagan's negative incentive and a Black
> candidate's positive incentive could take us from 10 to 15
> million registered voters.
> Blacks must run to get their program and agenda on the
> front burner.[23]
> This campaign is not about getting a seat in San Francisco,
> it is about a battle your constituents are having getting a seat
> at home.
> It is not about having access to some man, it is about having
> access to a plan.[24]

Jackson maintained that if voter registration expanded, then Blacks would be in a position to be the balance of power by being able to provide the winning margin of victory for the Democrats in several states. For example, similar to the Kramer-Levy formula he pointed out that in 1980, Reagan won in Alabama by 17,500 votes, but there are 272,000 unregistered Black voters; by 5,000 votes in Arkansas where there are 85,000 unregistered voters; and by 165,000 votes in New York where there are 900,000 unregistered Blacks.[25]

Finally, in his announcement statement of November 3, he repeated that one of the political dividends of his candidacy was that it would stimulate many others to run for a variety of offices. He felt that the ultimate destiny of the campaign was to empower a "rainbow coalition of the rejected," such that a broad emphasis on domestic and international policy changes would be sought. Consequently, he said:

> My concern is to chart a *new* course, to lift the boats stuck
> on the bottom; to fight to provide education based on one's
> ability rather than the ability to pay; to fight to provide
> health care for all Americans on the basis of need and not
> wealth; to provide a fishing pole, not just more fish, in a
> campaign to rebuild our cities and end the slums; to provide
> a strong and adequate national defense, but end the massive

waste, fraud, abuse and other unnecessary costs of the military; to campaign on behalf of a rational and fair immigration policy; to move beyond our current common-ground; and to change the present course of our foreign policy, so we can again be respected in the world community, not just feared.[26]

If we reconstruct these statements it is possible to determine that they fall into a systematic pattern, as expressed below:

Figure 7.2 Campaign Rewards System

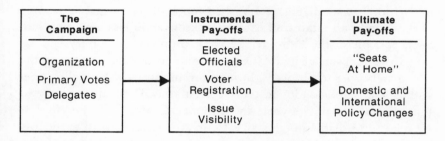

The Campaign	Instrumental Pay-offs	Ultimate Pay-offs
Organization Primary Votes Delegates	Elected Officials Voter Registration Issue Visibility	"Seats At Home" Domestic and International Policy Changes

We suggest, then, that the broad goal of the campaign, through the mobilization of its resources, was to articulate the interests of its constituency and to achieve immediate pay-offs which would enable this constituency to achieve its ultimate pay-offs — a better quality of life. This process, described in Chapter 5, may approximate what might be regarded as the act of "empowerment" through the process of presidential selection, as especially indicated by the "Participation, Process, Product" model of Professor Charles Hamilton, cited earlier in this work.

Primaries

One of the most important activities during the primaries is the opportunity for the candidates to express their views on various issues and to have these views carried by the press. Although Jackson was a novelty and considered a good interview by reporters, the campaign did not possess the kind of budget with which to process endless timely press statements or to purchase expensive advertisements. One substitute for such funding was the fortunate characteristic Rev. Jackson possessed for obtaining free press coverage by "making news." For example, on January 4, Rev. Jackson returned triumphantly to the United States, after a five-day trip to Syria to bring home Navy flier Lt. Robert Goodman, Jr., who had been captured and imprisoned. This act won him national acclaim, an invitation to the White House from President Reagan, and improved his standing in the polls in New Hampshire.

On February 13, however, *The Washington Post* first published a story indicating that Rev. Jackson had used a derogatory term—"hymie"—in reference to Jews, and "Hymietown" referring to New York City, in a private conversation with a Black *Washington Post* reporter. This incident and the way in which it was highlighted by *The Washington Post* in another story on February 22, and picked up by other news media, diminished much of the positive coverage of the Goodman affair and caused Jackson to do less well than had been possible in the February 28 New Hampshire primary.

Rev. Jackson visited Mexico at the end of May, stood on the Mexican border to propose a humanitarian immigration policy, met with Soviet Ambassador to the U.S. Anatoly Dobrynin to request that the USSR not boycott the summer Olympic Games in Los Angeles, and made an extensive Latin American tour in early July covering Panama, Nicaragua, El Salvador, and Cuba. Again, much of this favorable press coverage was muted by press attention to controversial statements by Muslim Minister Louis Farrakhan, head of the Nation of Islam, for whose statements the press attempted to make Rev. Jackson responsible.

The more formal arena for the presentation of the campaign views of Rev. Jackson, however, was the seven nationally televised debates involving all the Democratic candidates. By the fourth debate on March 11, in Atlanta, Georgia the field had been cut in half. Thus, the additional focus on the views of Rev. Jackson made it possible for him to acquire more media attention for issues associated with his campaign, such as proposals for a 25% cut in the military budget and support for a nuclear freeze, a stronger American position on divesting from South Africa, opposition to the Simpson-Mazzoli Immigration Bill, support for the Contadora initiative in Latin America, normalization of relations with Cuba, a more balanced policy in the Middle East involving the legitimate views of the Palestinians and their representatives, and an industrial policy which emphasized full-employment, penalized run-away shops, and provided funds for youth education and job training.[27] The campaign, then, afforded Rev. Jackson and his constituency the opportunity to appeal directly to the public in competition with others regarding the solutions to the problems of the country, rather than hoping that they would be addressed indirectly through another candidate.

The very favorable showing of Rev. Jackson on the campaign issues he presented to the public, doubtless, had an impact upon his ability to attract votes during the primaries and caucuses. However, studies by researchers at the University of Michigan have found that the position on issues was less salient as a predictor of voter choice of Jackson than other factors such as perceptions of Democratic party treatment of Jackson, party identification, perceptions of ideology, and a common fate with other Blacks.[28] Such factors may well have accounted for the startling increases in Black voter turnout in the primaries.

After winning only 5.3% of the vote in New Hampshire, 5.0% in Massachusetts, and 7.6% in Vermont, the election turned South, and there Jackson did very well, as indicated in Table 7.2.

With over one-third of the primaries and caucuses accounted for by March 21, the Jackson campaign had won ten congressional districts, seventeen counties, and had scored the striking support of 90% of eligible Black Chicago voters and 360,000 votes in the state of Illinois, reaching nearly one million total votes. In addition, the campaign had come in second in both South Carolina and Arkansas, and second to Mondale in Mississippi ("Uncommitted" came in first) in the overall popular vote. This showing was evidence of a dramatic rise in voter registration and support from first-time voters, many of whom were college students and youths.

The impact of Jackson's attraction was registered in the fact that he was competing with Mondale for the Black vote and winning it in both the South and the North, as Black voters in New York and Philadelphia increased their turnout over 1980 by 124% and 32% respectively, boosting the state results for Jackson to 25.6% and

Table 7.2 March 13 Primary Results: Jackson Black Vote in the Selected Southern Primary Elections (1984).

State	Vote %	Delegates	'80–84 Vote Change
Alabama	19.6	9	+ 87
Florida	12.4	1	+ 38
Georgia	21.0	17	+ 14

Source: Compiled from Congressional Quarterly, June 16, 1984, p. 1143; Lorn Foster and Thomas Cavanagh, "Jesse Jackson's campaign: the Primaries and Caucuses," Joint Center for Political Studies, Washington, DC, 1984, Table 2, p. 17.

16.0%. As a result, Jackson clearly established his predominance over the Black vote nationally and this underscored the national character of his campaign.

By the end of the campaign, Jackson had scored clear victories in the Virginia caucuses, the District of Columbia and Louisiana primaries (uncommitted came in first), and achieved respectable showings in other important Democratic primary states such as Tennessee (25.3%), Maryland (25.5%), North Carolina (25.4%), New Jersey (23.6%), and California (19.6%), the latter exhibiting concrete evidence of the existence of a multi-racial vote of Blacks, Hispanics, and Asians which comprised his "rainbow coalition." Moreover, the total number of votes was nearly 3.3 million, with victories in sixty-one congressional districts, yielding 384 convention delegates.[29]

The Convention

This better-than-expected showing by Jackson was far from the nomination, but it did have the strategic effect of denying the front-runner, Walter Mondale, the legitimacy of having won the Black vote as he claimed the nomination. Similarly, Black votes were denied to runner-up Gary Hart, preventing him from achieving what would possibly have been a disastrous defeat for Mondale.[30] More importantly, it set up two critical bargaining situations for the convention.

The primaries ended with the following delegate totals: Mondale - 1,635; Hart - 1,160; Jackson - 352; but by the end of June the unpledged "super delegates" made the totals: Mondale - 2,061; Hart -1,247; Jackson - 384. Considering Mondale's slender lead and the fact that delegates were not formally bound, both Hart and Jackson refused to concede him the nomination and instead prepared con-

Table 7.3 Black Voter Preference, March–April, 1984.

State	Jackson	Mondale	Hart
Alabama	50%	47%	1%
Georgia	61	30	5
Illinois	79	17	4
New York	87	8	3
Pennsylvania	77	18	3

Source: CBS/New York Times exit polls in Foster and Cavanaugh, "Jesse Jackson's Campaign: The Primaries and Caucuses," Joint Center for Political Studies, Washington, D. C., 1984, p. 24.

vention strategies focused on denying Mondale a first-ballot victory. Jackson's strategy was directed at establishing a degree of harmony and understanding of the bargaining with the Mondale Black delegates, as well as attempting to attract the Hispanic delegates.

Perhaps here, however, I should briefly introduce the conflict over the party rules concerning delegate presidential preference. The Jackson campaign was greatly disadvantaged by the relationship between his total primary vote and the party formula requiring each candidate to achieve a 20% threshold of votes in each congressional district in order to obtain delegates.

The Jackson campaign argued that a fair (proportional) system would have yielded the same number of delegate votes as the total vote — challenging the rules on this basis as early as December 3, 1983, one month after joining the race.[31] Thereafter, many subsequent meetings were held to further elaborate on the problem and seek remedies, beginning in January 1984 and continuing throughout the campaign.[32] The case was made that the threshold requirement unfairly penalized voters with the socio-demographic profile of Blacks and other urban minorities who are concentrated in congressional districts. It was further argued that the threshold unfairly discriminated against both the delegates and the presidential candidates. The unfairness of this method, it was suggested, was further exacerbated by the addition to the convention delegations of a racial and gender unbalanced group of "super-delegates" of elected and party officials. Moreover, other schemes such as "bonus delegates" enhanced the distortion of the "one-person-one-vote" principle.

In response to these arguments, promises were made by chairman Manatt to ask both congressional Democrats and state Democratic delegations to commit some of their "at-large" delegate slots to Jackson in order to correct this situation; however, no meaningful number of delegates were transferred.[33] As a result, while Jackson won 18% of the total primary vote he was awarded only 8% of the convention delegates.

Nevertheless, meetings were held between the Mondale and Jackson Black delegates at the convention in an effort to strike a unified posture which would make possible the use of "backward leverage" bargaining. It should be noted, however, that the most direct leverage upon Mondale was his own Black delegates — who ironically refused to bargain with him. The only additional flexibility was in the possible shift of Hispanics to the Jackson column on the first ballot, a scenario which potentially made both the Mondale Black delegates and the Hispanic delegates the *most strategic* of all.

There were 208 Mondale Black delegates, and another 140 (mostly Mondale) Hispanic delegates, while Hart had 26 Black and 77 Hispanic delegates, for a total of 234 Blacks and 217 Hispanic delegates, or 451 combined. When Mondale finished the primaries, his "margin of victory" (or distance from the number required to be elected) was 341, and even on the first ballot at the convention he only exceeded the number required by 215 votes (his winning margin largely made up by the "super-delegates"). Some combination of the Black and Hispanic vote was strategic, then, in the development of a scenario which might have prevented Mondale from winning the nomination, thus inducing serious bargaining in the process. The convention was, indeed, theoretically brokered, but the brokering situation was never realized or consumated, because the Mondale Black and Hispanic leadership were still wedded to the "politics of trust," the dependent-leverage tactic which eschewed hard internal bargaining.

Although the Hispanic delegates attempted to boycott the first ballot to register their dissatisfaction with Mondale, in part because he had not attended the National Hispanic Leadership Conference in April, the strategy of withholding their votes could not make an impact because of their small numbers.[34] Jackson's appearance at this conference, however, and his record on Central American and domestic Hispanic concerns made it possible for him to appeal for Hispanic votes on the first ballot, but he did not receive their support.[35]

Second, Jackson attempted to utilize the "forward leverage" of the number of votes his primary constituency might represent in the general election to remind Mondale and the party leadership of its importance and, thus, of the need for bargaining.[36] The question of "forward leveraging" the Jackson vote in the general election was more credible than it appeared at the time, since a poll as late as May of that year had indicated that 25% of those surveyed would have voted for Jackson in a contest with Reagan, a figure which translates into an estimated 17 million votes, and the same poll revealed that 27% would be "more likely" to vote for a presidential candidate endorsed by Jackson.[37] The view inside the Jackson campaign was that he could probably have influenced six million votes, in a conservative estimate of the value of the 3.3 million primary votes.[38] In addition, the National Black Election Study at the University of Michigan, found that 59% of the 1,150 Blacks surveyed would have followed Jackson into the general election as an independent. Six of every ten Black votes also amounts to six million votes.[39]

Bargaining

The fact that Jackson did not bargain with any of the other Democratic contenders during the primaries, but competed on an equal basis, meant that he was running a "dedicated" campaign to win the presidential nomination and only began to consider bargaining when it was clear that his convention strategy would not yield sufficient delegate strength to be successful. Thus, amid calls for "party unity," he indicated that his campaign had bargaining leverage "at the apex of the triangle," (figuratively in the triad of Mondale, Hart and Jackson) and that, therefore, he would continue to seek "party justice before party unity." At the annual convention of Operation PUSH on May 8, he indicated that "party unity now may cost party victory in November because it will be a unity without substance," and set forth ten goals he believed to be continuing and problematic issues between his campaign constituency and the party. They were support for:

1. Ending the system of delegate thresholds;
2. Voting rights enforcement;
3. White voter support for black candidates;
4. Integrated slate-making;
5. A peace plank in the platform;
6. A jobs plank in the platform;
7. Passage of the Equal Rights Amendment;
8. Human Rights as the basis of foreign policy;
9. Corporate responsibility;
10. A new emphasis on helping the poor.[40]

The character of this listing, however, was misread by the press as "demands" Jackson was making upon the convention, when in fact it contained concerns, some of which were already a part of the proposed convention platform. The listing had been general enough, for example, to include his four Minority Reports to the platform: the affirmative action language of the 1980 platform, elimination of the "run-off primary," adoption of a pledge of "no first use" of nuclear weapons, and "substantial real reductions" in military spending over five years. Having lost on all of these issues (except modifying the affirmative action language), he was left with the political issues outstanding on his bargaining agenda after the convention.

Before the convention, he had begun to seek negotiations with rivals Hart and Mondale, and had prepared by getting the support of such groups as the Congressional Black Caucus. A June meeting in Kansas City with Mondale having resulted in an inconsequential "feeling-out" session, he held a press conference at the convention in San Francisco to indicate his view that the delegates had not put Mondale over the top, and that both Mondale and Hart should meet with him in an effort to resolve existing problems in a way which would recognize the contribution of the Rainbow Coalition to the party and preserve the candidate's self-respect.[41]

At the same time, for those Blacks who were fearful that his attempt to have the party adopt ultra-liberal positions would play into the hands of Reagan and cost the Democrats the election, Jackson said:

> We cannot become so afraid of Ronald Reagan that we
> leave our backs wide open to Democrats. That would push
> us back into the bag of allowing the Democrats to take us for
> granted on the assumption that we have no where to go and
> we'll be driven by Reagan mania. That's not right. We'll be
> driven by a quest for justice, which is a positive motivation,
> and not by Reagan mania, a negative stimulus.[42]

Despite the strength and logic of his rationale, Jackson was not successful in achieving a bargaining relationship with either Hart or Mondale at the convention, since Mondale preferred, instead, to deal with such issues after he had secured the nomination. Rather than use his role in the convention, as some had predicted, to lead a walkout if he were dissatisfied with the bargaining results, Jackson attempted to use his speech to "unify" the party and to make an appeal, in his words, "to heal the party."[43]

Neither Jackson nor his constituency was rewarded by the contents of Walter Mondale's nomination acceptance speech, which contained signals to various constituencies such as women, labor, and others. Although Mondale mentioned the Rainbow Coalition as being vital to the Democratic party, his speech contained no substantive line of policy proposals directed to Blacks. Indeed, this was a significant test of dependent-leverage, since one of the traditional roles of Black party insiders since the time of Booker T. Washington has been to suggest motivational language directed at the Black vote for inclusion in the party nominee's acceptance speech. In a meeting of both Mondale and Jackson Black supporters at the convention, it was admitted that the Mondale Blacks had abdicated even the traditional bargaining roles.[44]

The model in Chapter Five (Figure 5.1 at Z1) indicates that if the bargaining strategies of the convention are not successful, then the process can continue into the post-convention period. Jackson did, indeed, conduct a form of public bargaining with Mondale in the absence of a face-to-face meeting, which Mondale's advisers believed might alienate Jewish and other constituencies. Jackson signaled his displeasure with the lack of Black involvement in the Mondale campaign by saying, on July 25, that "the Rainbow Coalition was still waiting for the party to make a commitment to its involvement in the campaign"; that Mondale's appointment of Congressman Charles Rangel to be a co-chair of the campaign was a "step on a thousand-mile journey"; that he "reserved the right" to continue to criticize Mondale; that his "enthusiasm level would be nil if Mondale had not appointed more Blacks and women to the campaign by Labor Day"; and by August 16 that he "was not really aboard" the Mondale campaign.[45] Mondale withstood the pressure of these comments with growing irritation, and although in mid-August he hired close Jackson associate Ernest Green, he also rejected a proposal for a federal jobs program for the hard-core unemployed.

Finally yielding to the pressure to deal with Jackson's demands, Mondale held a bargaining session at North Oaks, Minnesota with Jackson and a core of their respective key Black supporters on August 28, 1984. This six-hour meeting, held a critical six weeks after the convention, was less than successful, possibly because of the lack of unity within the Black delegation. Mondale's Black supporters, again, argued against pressing him to make commitments, while Jackson supporters sought them against Mondale's resistance. In the end, Mondale agreed to some additional political appointments to his campaign and an autonomous role for Jackson as head of the Rainbow Coalition, to which Jackson agreed.

Whether or not the bargaining was sufficient must be balanced against the requirements of the model presented in this study, since in this respect, the most important result of the bargaining was the glaring omission of policy and program commitments. This result, in strategic bargaining terms, is evidence of the fact that Rev. Jackson was not prepared to fully utilize the "forward leverage" of his theoretical votes in the general election, together with tactics which would have made credible the threat to deny these election resources to Mondale. This could have meant an "exit" by Jackson from the party into some form of general-election-targeted action, but this was a step which Jackson had precluded at the announcement of his candidacy.

On the other hand, while the Mondale campaign had to balance the cost-benefit risks of drawing too close to the Jackson campaign and alienating some supporters, there was still a pointedly significant loss to Mondale in not bargaining earlier with Jackson and reaching some form of agreement. By concluding the bargaining so late and on such unsatisfactory terms, he was unable to utilize in the general election the Jackson campaign's resources which were accumulated during the primaries. The result was that, compared to previous campaigns, little campaign activity was conducted in the Black community by the Mondale forces.

According to the Federal Election Commission regulations, the Jackson campaign had to demobilize itself after the convention; however, the organization still possessed skilled staff workers, and an organizational apparatus in forty-four states. This resource was not fully mobilized for Mondale, because Rev. Jackson had indicated to his state chairs that they were to "wait for the signal" which concluded successful bargaining—a signal which came very late in the election and was very weak. Thus, the residual support of the Rainbow Coalition as a cohesive force was diffuse. Some high-level officials and staff members of the coalition became staff members of the Mondale campaign, and thus achieved a partial integration into its activities. However, as turnout figures illustrate, during the general election Black voter participation, though greater than the 1980 levels, was not comparable to that achieved during the primary campaign in the same year, a considerable anomaly in American politics.[46]

CONCLUSION

Admittedly skimming the surface of the Jackson campaign, this work has, I hope, provided enough of a description to evaluate it in light of the theory of independent-leverage. To what extent a campaign may be said to be "independent" while still within the party process is simple and yet complex, in that it bears the same relationship to the process as all other campaigns, but as a vehicle for the mobilization of a distinct constituency, there is an unavoidable "separateness" involved in the motivation, style and results of the activity. It should be clear, however, that Jesse Jackson himself considered the campaign to be independent in a larger sense.

> The message to white Democrats is that black voters can no longer be taken for granted because they have 'no where else to go'. We had to break the dependency syndrome. We moved from a relationship born of paternalism to one born of power.[47]

Yet, despite its independent features, at every point in the major scenarios of the election process there is an interactive relationship implicit in the functioning of our model between the Jackson campaign and the political process. For example, the primary process is governed by party rules and thus is an obvious extension of the party system, as the myriad meetings between the Jackson campaign and the Democratic party leaders suggest. In a sense, the rules issue was important in creating a sympathy factor for Jackson among Black voters, as the University of Michigan Survey indicates, and in giving him a way to establish greater independence by appearing to "run against" the party institution as a true insurgent. This posture of running against the party may have been an attractive feature to many who were first time voters with weak party identification, who had otherwise been alienated from party politics.

In the convention process, the dependency factor was evident in the extent to which the process of participating in the development of the Democratic party platform resulted in Jackson's four Minority Reports. But the status of the campaign was nowhere more evident than in the post-convention period when its demobilization was required out of deference to both Federal Election Laws and the Mondale campaign, which at that point represented the Democratic party.

Besides this structural dependence, there was the dependency of the extent to which the interaction of Jackson with the other candidates, especially Hart and Mondale, bred both competitive and cooperative lines of action. They were obviously competitive in the televised debates, but they were also cooperative in establishing the rules governing them. They were competitive in the convention balloting, but they attempted to compete in a manner which promoted "party unity."

Another set of interactions, however, were those of the Black delegates in the various campaigns, who were unaccustomed to the dichotomy of dependent- and independent-leverage. While the Jackson campaign staff, for example, attempted to maintain contact with Blacks in the other campaigns, these staffers were often at lower levels than the Jackson staff in the hierarchy of authority and in the control over comparable campaign resources. For the first time there were substantial differences in political access to presidential election resources by Blacks involved in the various campaigns.

The power valence also worked in the opposite direction, as there were Mondale and Hart Blacks who were able to push for Jackson delegates to the convention in the "at-large" contingent of their state delegations. In addition, the Jackson campaign was assisted by some Black mayors who were themselves otherwise committed to Walter Mondale, as their institutional roles as mayors demanded a different pattern of political allegiances — they could not always act as "Black" politicians, but had to be institutional politicians first. Thus, because of its popularity with their city voters, there were many instances where Black mayors did not fight the Jackson campaign, although they were on opposite sides.

As Jackson also discovered, while the presentation of issues to the public is perhaps the freest arena of the political process, it may also become extremely confining if the candidate makes a mistake. Although the presentation of issues is as unregulated by the party as the candidate's daily schedule and style of activities, all of these activities occur in the "goldfish bowl" of scrutiny by powerful news organizations which can exact a demanding standard of public accountability.

These are some of the many reasons why, although the campaign was regarded as "independent" by its candidate and others, the degreee of its independence was limited by the general parameters of the political system as long as it operated as a part of the formal presidential nomination process.

As we have seen, what occurs in the post-convention period may test the limits of independence, according to the results of the bargaining. Mondale's refusal to bargain with Jackson formally in the post-convention period provoked a counter-refusal of Jackson to cooperate with Mondale's campaign. At any time, Jackson possessed the opportunity to exercise one of the strategic voting options discussed in Chapter Five as a sanction, especially when faced with Mondale's rejection of important items such as a jobs program. That this did not happen suggests the self-imposed dependence which Jackson exercised in this period in the name of party unity. This should cause us to reinforce a useful distinction: there are two concepts of independence at issue here, independent-leverage within the party, and outside of the party in the general election competition for president, especially if convention bargaining is unsuccessful.

Results

Public evaluations of the Jackson campaign and other such contests could well rest on such factors as Black pride in the candidate having done well and an outstanding convention speech, among others, if it were not for more careful analysis. For example, one public opinion poll was split (hurt-42% to helped-43%) on the question of whether Jackson's candidacy helped or hurt Democratic party chances in the November election.[48] However, Black respondents in the University of Michigan Survey on the question whether it was good or bad that Jackson ran, answered overwhelmingly in the positive, and it appeared that those most supportive of Jackson were also most identifiable by their strong association with the variables "power/discontent."[49] Without a complete analysis of this variable, the response may signify that an important segment of the Jackson constituency evaluated the campaign on the basis of (power-achievement) result-oriented criteria—and may do so in the future. This study has suggested the strategy of independent-leverage as determined by the results of political bargaining in 1984 and previous presidential campaigns.

What, then, were some substantive results of the campaign? The first was the achievement of political organization out of the mobilization which occurred. The campaign represented the first time the Black community was substantially organized to compete through an autonomous campaign. The "organization" was manifested in the campaign staff and officials, the state campaign units, the voters and delegates, and in the many sympathizers who may have contributed resources of time, money, and other forms of support, but who may not have even participated in the process in any other role. Second, while the creation of an organization was in itself important, its ability to conduct a serious campaign with so many staff members inexperienced in presidential-level politics was an accomplishment which ultimately created a collection of individuals in the Black, minority, and white progressive communities with presidential campaign level political skills.

Then, out of the successful conduct of a campaign, substantial political resources materialized, such as funding which amounted to $3.5 million, nearly 3.5 million votes, almost four hundred delegates, and a campaign schedule of events maintained in at least forty-four states and six foreign countries. Also, there is credible evidence that "the Jackson candidacy did, indeed, mobilize large numbers of new Black voters and, according to election-day exit polls, about 12% of Black voters were voting for the first time."[50] There is little doubt that this turnout in the primaries and in the general election helped to fulfill one of the campaign goals of "having the widest coattails," by helping to elect more Black officials, as the increase of about thirty-one Black mayors in 1984 was the largest in history, and the annual percent increase in the total number of Black elected officials went from 1.7% in 1983 to 6.2% in 1984, the largest overall increase since 1976.[51] Finally, there is direct evidence that "rainbow" candidates won office in many official party posts at the state and local levels in states as different as Vermont and Mississippi.[52]

Most important, with such organizational resources, high-level bargaining scenarios were established in the campaign. For example, although a candidate may present issues directly to the public in the hope that they will attract voters, these issues may become the subject of bargaining among the candidates. But they may also be adopted on the "open market" of ideas by any decision-maker; thus, an important "side-payment" may be the equality of access to the media afforded by the status of a credible candidacy. Here, the high-level strategies available derive from the options of candidates from this leverage to speak directly to other candidates, to the current President of the United States and the Congress, to the American people or to foreign audiences. This is no revolutionary finding; nonetheless, within the context of Black or minority politics, to be able to operationalize this level of political involvement is a quantum leap in political strategies, which at least holds out the prospect of better returns in the future.

Candidate bargaining, however, did occur, as the North Oaks meeting suggests. Jackson, clearly on the horns of a dilemma which, on the one hand, ran the risk of disrupting Democratic party unity and, on the other, in not achieving his bargaining objectives, opted for party loyalty in the final analysis. It may be concluded then, that given the strategies available for taking advantage of the high-level bargaining scenarios thus established, Jackson's option of party loyalty resulted in the failure of the policy commitment aspect of the campaign. This confirms my original thesis that assent to dependent-leverage results in low-level bargaining results.

The Jackson Factor

One fundamental dilemma in speculating on the future success of independent-leverage within the Democratic party is the calculation of how it would work without a candidate such as Jesse Jackson to energize it, and absent the equally negative factor of a president strongly unpopular among Blacks. These two factors were responsible for what I have elsewhere called the "emergent mobilization" stage of the Black community which formed the basic environment from which the Jackson campaign was created.[54] In fact, the view of University of Michigan researchers that there are few direct variables which account for the differences noted between Jackson voters and others may be related to the complexity of social movement analysis.

I would argue that the Jackson campaign was a political movement which surfaced within the unlikely environment of the electoral arena, even though the Civil Rights Movement has always focused upon such issues as voting rights, elections, and community empowerment through the production of elected officials. As such, it is uncertain, to the extent that we have attributed success or failure to any aspect of this enterprise, what part of it may be accounted for by the movement style of its mobilization. Thus, it is equally uncertain whether the independent-leverage tactic within the party has a certain future, based upon adherence to the strategy or allegiance to the leader of the movement alone. This would appear to depend upon whether or not the campaign-movement is capable of institutionalization by the leadership of the Rainbow Coalition, and the dynamics which will occur as a result of the attempt to do so.

Chapter 8

Leverage Strategies and the Future of Black Politics

INTRODUCTION

I consider that the "balance of power" concept has served more as philosophy than strategy, but that this philosophy has been correct, not only because it has conformed to the logic of the Black political relationship with both major parties, but also because of the perception that it has occasionally provided the leverage which has given substance to Black public policy demands. The long struggle of progressive Black leaders has been to improve upon the occasional performance of the concept by turning it into a strategy which demands more rigorous tactical formulations. These recommended formulations have included a shift in voter support to the Republican party, support for a third party or a Black political party, and the sponsorship of Black political conventions and Black presidential candidacies. A few of these formulations have been considered "impractical" by some politicians in the Black community, who have largely stuck to a moderate course of supporting one major party, attempting to utilize dependent-leverage political strategies.

Today, however, in view of the decline in the Black voters' recent policy influence, there appears to be a readiness to adopt more aggressive strategies of electoral participation which have the promise of yielding greater substantive mass benefits, rather than merely individual or group symbolic rewards. Thus, there has arisen a debate over political dependence and independence, and over what constitutes substantive and symbolic gains from the process. Although this debate hasn't fully matured there is, nevertheless, an increasing consensus about the need to obtain more from presidential politics.

The Republican Option

Inasmuch as this study has been concerned with events after 1960, it has naturally emphasized Black political behavior within the Democratic party. The basis of that behavior, however, lay in the extent to which Blacks have not conceived of the Republican voting option as a realistic strategy in achieving a "balance of power" position. Professor Pearl Robinson's analysis of this problem invokes the ideas of conservative Black economist Dr. Thomas Sowell, who says that only split-ticket voting or a "vote that could go either way" provides Blacks with the necessary "bargaining leverage to force Democrats to take them seriously."[1] Calling this a "political exchange" relationship, Robinson suggested that while some Black leaders have seen the two-party option as a strategic situation, ironically, the Republican party has entered into a conservative realignment which has devalued this option for Blacks.[2]

Actually, a theoretical Republican option has existed at least since 1978, when Blacks became increasingly disenchanted with the politics of President Jimmy Carter.[3] Robinson suggested that in order for them to have taken advantage of this possibility, Republicans needed to adopt a profile which would appeal to Blacks on such issues as full employment, health insurance, income maintenance, and others. But because such a profile was soundly rejected by the 1980 Republican party platform, she concluded that: "On the whole the Republicans' approach to economic problem solving restricted the party's potential black supporters to a very narrow constituency."[4] Thus, in the off-year elections of 1982, Blacks resoundingly voted against Republican candidates, as they had done in 1980, causing Housing Secretary Samuel Pierce, Jr. to sponsor a post-election meeting of Black Republican party loyalists, to enhance the White House rationale that Blacks had not understood Reagan's policy objectives.[5]

Indeed, by the end of his first term the net effect of President Reagan's policies had proved extremely damaging to Blacks. For example, a 1986 report of the National Urban League indicated that in almost every category the Black community had lost ground since

1980.[6] Thus, while the 1984 level of Black family income as a percent of white family income had fallen to levels which prevailed at
the beginning of the Civil Rights Movement in the early 1960s,
decreases in the funding of education have contributed to a reduction
in Black college enrollments, and the proportion of Black families
existing in poverty has grown. Authoritative reports have found that
a cumulative effect of the impact of Reagan's first-term policies is
that the average Black family (including two-parent households) lost
$2,000 of income.[7]

Adam Herbert summarizes the impact of these policies in
several major points.

1. Blacks believe the economic policies of the Reagan
    Administration have been harmful to them;
2. The administration has not made a conscious effort to
    maintain a dialogue with the leadership of the Black
    community;
3. The administration has made a number of policy
    judgments in civil rights which have given the impression
    of its hostility to existing law;
4. The Republican party has not developed a clear ap-
    proach to attract the Black vote;
5. Well-off Blacks are more likely than comparable whites
    to have their assessment of voter support influenced by
    the status of their group members.[8]

Then, in a revealing essay, Black Republican J. Clay Smith,
Dean of Howard University School of Law and former member of
the United States Equal Employment Opportunity Commission,
pointed to aspects of the administration's policy which were "antithetical to the core of Black aspirations," emphasizing its across-the-
board attack on civil rights policy, as well as its rejection of moderate
Black Republicans.[9] This is a critical factor in the attraction of the
Republican option to Blacks in general, because the first point of
success in attracting mainstream Blacks should logically be in gaining the support of most Black Republicans. The Howard University
Survey shows that the views of Black Democrats and Republicans
are closely associated. From Table 8.1, it is possible to determine
how far apart the responses of this set of party activists happen to be.
The mean difference was calculated between responses of Black
Democrats and those of white Democrats, Black Republicans and
white Republicans, according to the categories of issues in the table.

Table 8.1 Issue Preferences by Race and Party, 1980.

Issue	Black Democrat	Black Republican	White Democrat	White Republican
Full Employment	92	87	69	50
Tax Cuts	41	77	27	80
Low Prices	51	61	39	39
Health Insurance	75	32	56	3
Welfare Reform	42	61	52	69
School Funding	62	61	36	14
Handgun Registration	38	32	49	19
ERA	71	68	60	33
MX Missile	13	19	14	25
Military Capability	18	71	28	83

(Responses represent "yes" preferences to the query "most important issue.")

The results are shown in Table 8.2. As is readily evident, while there are some significant differences in the responses of Black Democrats to white Democrats and Black Republicans, the greatest difference in positive responses is between Black Democrats and white Republicans. Upon closer inspection, however, there appears to be little significant difference in the responses of Black Democrats from those of Black Republicans and white Democrats on economic and social issues, while the differences with white Republicans remain considerable.

This finding confirms the long held assumption that the views of Black Democrats and moderate Black Republicans on the basic social and economic issues facing the Black community are very similar. The essential difference today is the emergence of a relatively small group of highly visible conservative Black Republicans whose views are consistent with those of very conservative white Republicans. Thus, it is also evident that the views of these conserv-

Table 8.2 Average Difference in Responses to Issue Categories by Race and Party (%).

Category	BD–WD	BD–BR	BD–WR
Overall	13.7	18.2	37.6
Economic	16.0	17.0	31.6
Social	15.4	14.4	40.8
Defense	5.5	29.5	39.5

(BD – Black Democrat; WD — white Democrat; BR – Black Republican; WR – white Republican)

ative Black Republicans may lie far outside of the consensus of mainstream Black opinion as a whole.

Nevertheless, Black Republican spokespersons could still be heard to suggest that, in spite of the administration's strategy of transferring the access traditional Black leadership has had to American presidents to more conservative Black leaders, it might be possible to have a "summit" of Black Democrats and Republicans to rectify the "predictability" of the Black vote in presidential elections.[10] But, upon what basis might such a "summit" proceed? Speculation abounded in February 1985, when it was discovered that in some public opinion polls the Black approval rating for Reagan had approached nearly 40%, that a reappraisal of Reagan might constitute the basis of a Black Republican party realignment in presidential politics comparable to that of whites. However, the approval ratings have since decreased to the low 20% level by late 1986 and, in any case, it is not clear that for Blacks overall job-approval ratings are a more salient predictor of voting behavior than Reagan's civil rights ratings which have remained consistently low.[11]

There has been little opportunity to use the "balance of power" strategy which might have affected Republican policies in the last two elections, because they both were won by landslides. Still, it is worth noting that the tendency toward strong Democratic party allegiance by the Black vote would have prevented Republican initiatives in any event, while a flexible and independent Black vote would present more of a threat to both major parties. In this light, Professor Sowell's advice to execute occasional split-ticket voting is consistent with our view, while other Black Republican admonitions to permanently split the Black vote more evenly between the two major parties is not. The nearly structural prohibitions to widespread Black Republican voting, however, severely limits the degree of this practice.[12]

There has also been the intermittent suggestion that if Blacks were to realign party preferences with the Republicans, middle and upper income Blacks would take the lead. However, as we have seen from Adam Herbert's comments, middle-class Blacks have been the most critical of the Reagan administration record, such that there appears no foreseeable Republican option for Blacks as long as the party's presidential candidates maintain the current profile of policy positions.

The Democratic Party Realigns?

The Democratic party has responded to being out of power for twelve of the past sixteen years by vascillating between the politics and policies of the New Deal and those of the new Republican era. Jimmy Carter came to office as a Democrat but also a fiscal conservative whose economic policies were moderate, a fact which must be appreciated since he has been far out-spent by the Reagan administration. Nevertheless, the Democratic nominee in 1984, Walter Mondale, inexplicably chose to make the problem of *inflation* his primary economic issue at the same time that opinion polls were showing that *unemployment*— a traditional Democratic issue — was the priority national concern. During the presidential election process, neither Carter nor Mondale committed himself to specific policies which had the potential to reverse the economic and social decline in the fortunes of the majority of the Black community.

Perhaps presidential candidates have a natural aversion to making binding commitments in order that they may have the greatest flexibility in dealing with issues which might arise should they become president. It may be that this rationale, together with the conservative tenor of the present political environment which appears to reject "special interest" politics and public policy, has reduced presidential candidates to making symbolic appeals to groups which either might or must accept them.

In 1980, for example, Jimmy Carter did make some public commitments to Blacks during his campaign, among which he explicitly promised, on one occasion, to put "the unemployed back to work" and to put the Ku Klux Klan "back in its grave."[13] These vague and emotional appeals may also be heard with regularity when presidential candidates appear, for example, before national conventions of major civil rights organizations — often to considerable applause. Without an analysis of the correlation between this apparent support and actual political support for such candidates based on these emotional appeals, perhaps Blacks often react positively to such symbolism based on the historic rationale that it is offered by a candidate who represents the "lesser of two evils."

Many Democrats in Congress have also aligned themselves with Republican party positions on vital issues. For example, not only was there a strong Democratic vote in both the House and the

Senate for the FY 1982 Appropriations Bill which began the Reagan budgetary revolution, in 1986, Democratic Senator Ernest Hollings (SC) was co-author with Republican Senators Phil Gramm (TX) and Warren Rudman (NH) of budget-balancing legislation. It should also be noted that twenty-one other Democrats provided the margin (61–31) for passage of this bill that intended to effect additional deep cuts in programs beneficial to Blacks, other minorities, and the poor. Thus, it is questionable, now that the Democrats have regained control over the Senate, that congressional policy will change substantially in this present political atmosphere. The dilemma for Blacks posed by the strong conservative ideological influence over both parties is whether allegiance to the Democratic party or, indeed, to any party should rest on a policy of *trust* by Black political leaders.

Although independent-leverage strategies are favored in this work, the comprehensive answers to the question of party allegiance are far more complex than we have sought to address here, since they related not only to the preconditions for initiating Black strategies, but to the larger environment of social and economic issues. For example, some political scientists consider this to be an "anti-party age" in which the parties are losing their effectiveness as vehicles for political mobilization and influence because of the encroachment of such phenomena as strong candidate organizations, financing by Political Action Committees, and powerful media technologies and events.[14] We have not sought to address the relative effect of these forces upon the political arena, though most certainly their influence is assumed in our emphasis upon improving the competitive strategies and resources of Blacks through autonomous organization.

That the concept of autonomous Black political organization may be threatening to some interests reveals not only the continuing influence of the habit of dependence, but a defective understanding of what makes party coalitions optimally functional. There are at least two levels of political coalitions, the first of which is the theoretical coalition such as that described by Seymour Martin Lipset in the 1980 presidential election where the "winning" and "losing" sides are described by their socio-ethnic composition.[15] The other level of coalition is that described by Wilson Carey McWilliams referring to the organic intra-party issue-political behavior of the Democratic coalition in the 1984 presidential election.[16] I have suggested that the ultimate collective vote of the coalition is the manifest expression of its power to mobilize voters, but the substantive power resides in the relative ability of each coalition member to utilize organizational resources (mobilize) *outside* of the party base. Therefore, success in the intra-party competition, as well as in the external political mobilization of each coalition member depends upon the strength of both their intra-party integration *and* their autonomous organization.

Black political leaders have only made half-hearted attempts at autonomous political organization outside of the party system; rather, they have concentrated most of their energies on intra-party integration. This has left them in the position of attempting to substitute the currency of an uncontrollable vote for the organized political resources which other groups possess. To be sure, Black influence cannot be based only upon the financial contributions of its meager business structure, but working Blacks do contribute considerable sums to the Democratic party in the form of union dues — which they do not control — and, thus, their political influence is not registered as the influence of the Black community, but that of "organized labor." These strategies of the total integration of Black political resources into the party structure and into organized labor have obscured the existence of formidable political resources that constitute potential Black systemic influence.

Political integration strategies by themselves are yielding fewer returns. For instance, in 1985, the Democratic National Committee disregarded the recommendation of the party's Black Caucus and elected its own Black candidate to be vice chair.[17] Then, in 1986, despite the overwhelming desire of most Blacks to either eliminate or reduce the convention delegates selection threshold in congressional districts to 10%, they were defeated on a vote of the Democratic National Committee which lowered it to 15%.[18] These steps, together with the general objective of deemphasizing "special interest" caucuses, points the Democratic party in a decidedly different direction from that envisioned by most Black party activists.

The 1984 Election

Various dimensions of the need for an effective strategy may also be summarized with respect to the results of the 1984 election. Reagan's victory in the 1980 election was regarded as a landslide because he had an 8.5 million vote margin and 91% of the electoral vote, but fifteen of the twenty-nine states won by Reagan had relatively thin pluralities of from 50% to 55% of the vote. In 1980, then, it was significant that Blacks were voting 85% for Democrats while whites were voting nearly 60% for Reagan. In 1984, Blacks were voting 87% Democrat, but whites were voting 66% for Reagan, doubling his popular vote margin to 17 million, increasing the electoral vote to 98%, and making the Black vote inconsequential.[19]

Citing the outcome of these elections does not suggest that Blacks should have voted Republican in those contests, but rather provides evidence of an increasing racial polarization in society which is only *reflected* in the electoral process rather than a product of it. The degree of this polarization indicates that both major parties may be inhospitable to organic coalition interaction with Blacks, and that only first level — or theoretical — coalitions may be possible. Theoretical coalitions may be entered or rejected more easily from an autonomous base depending, as had been shown, upon the nature of the political situation.

On the other hand, such recent electoral polarization may be the culmination of a trend which has been a structural fact of elections since 1948, the year of the South's defection from the Democratic party because it extended an olive branch to Blacks.

Figure 8.1 shows that with the exception of 1964 (and almost in 1976), more whites voted for the Republican party than for the Democratic party, in part because of the large number of southerners who joined the Republican presidential voting coalition. It is also instructive that in both elections mentioned, the Democratic presidents who won had southern accents, leading some strategists to suggest that in order for the white South to rejoin the Democratic party's electoral coalition, there needs to be a southerner on the presidential ticket.

This sentiment has provoked a debate between the northern and southern wings of the Democratic party over a 1985 proposal by its southern legislators and party officials for a regional primary in the 1988 presidential elections, with the prospect that as many as fourteen states would hold their primaries in the second week of March. Southerners have argued that a regional primary would force Democratic party candidates to tailor their messages and their political resources to attract the votes of the region and influence the choice of a conservative to moderate nominee.[20] Those opposed to this plan have suggested that liberal candidates would not be prevented from winning southern primaries, especially after a good showing in New Hampshire. Others have referred specifically to the fact that this scheme heightens the political influence of Black voters,

Figure 8.1 White Margin of Votes for Democratic and Republican Presidential Candidates, 1948—1984

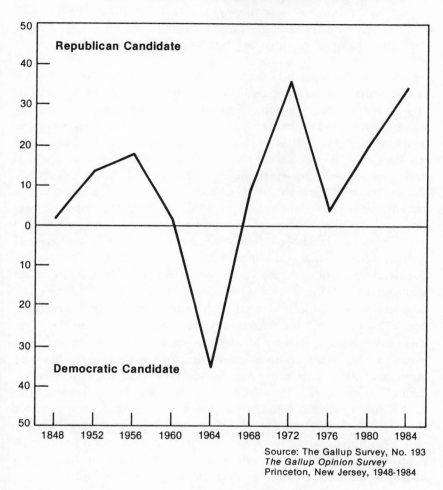

Source: The Gallup Survey, No. 193
The Gallup Opinion Survey
Princeton, New Jersey, 1948-1984

as it did in 1984, and would aid the candidacy of a Jesse Jackson.[21] It remains to be seen which of these points of view will prevail, but it is certain that the regional primary would enhance the competition for the Black vote, raising the question whether it would be controlled by the party leaders or *would control itself*, as was largely the case in 1984.

Future Options

In a very important discussion of the possibilities of a Black realignment, Professor Diane Pinderhughes has suggested that a strategic conflict for Blacks is created by the fact that:

> Both parties offer an unpalatable range of policy options, or
> one offers none and the other, accepting the black vote as a
> given, proposes fewer [policy] positions within the party and
> offers less attractive substantive benefits knowing its [black]
> allies have no credible or obvious reasons for exit.[27]

Against this background, she says, "Blacks must calculate the costs
and benefits of remaining loyal, or of exiting from the party," but in
any case, as one option, "attempting independent strategies,
whether within a regular party structure or outside of it, has certain
benefits and risks and is more likely to be successful under certain
conditions."[23] In describing the pertinent conditions under which
such independent strategies might be considered, however, she of-
fers the parameters of electoral balance (or the idea of considering all
candidates as potential choices), the policy appeal of competing parties, and the likelihood of policy implementation, as criteria.[24]

This study has been attentive largely to the benefits and risks of
independent-leverage strategies, which necessitate the expansion of
the parameters of strategic voter decisions to scenarios both inside
and outside of the party. Consideration of both environments,
however, places a premium on such factors as "timing," "organization," "bargaining," the "three-ballot scenario," and the like. The
three criteria suggested by Pinderhughes, while useful, continue to
imply a defensive posture characteristic of dependent-leverage
strategy, rather than an offensive one. For example, the obvious
benefits of organizing the Black vote so that Blacks are in command
of their own political resources suggests that *deliberate preparation* for
competition should be a given. This makes *timing* important, since it
will be impossible to decide whether or not to operationalize a
primary election campaign within the election year, so this criteria
alone forces critical choices of strategy before the final electoral
balance may be known. Then, at the point of decision, only the
policy appeal of the available candidates may be known, and, in fact,
the likelihood of implementation completely unknown.

Indeed, one of the great weaknesses of any leverage strategy is
the *lack of certainty* regarding whether or not commitments made
within the political arena will be eventually honored, and the effect of
whether or not they are honored on subsequent political decision-
making. So, strategy should proceed as though implementaion will
be resisted (or on the basis of a "worst-case" assessment) and attempts made to build in accountability safeguards geared to the

four-year period a party controls the White House, or to the subsequent presidential election, or preferably both. The result of the party nominee bargaining is, thus, a vital parameter for ultimate strategic decisions on the voting options in the general election, and on political activity after the election.

Since a Black presidential candidacy within the Democratic party in 1984 was a powerful vehicle for constructing bargaining options—even though they were not followed to a logical conclusion—we must reaffirm this version of independent-leverage as a viable strategy, largely to accomplish the organization and direction of Black political resources. At the same time, it is necessary to reaffirm that the logic of the bargaining results should dictate the approach to strategy in the general election. In this light, the discussion of "exiting" proposed by Pinderhughes takes on truly dramatic proportions. For example, if the hypothetical assumption is entertained that by the end of a given presidential nominating convention the bargaining results are unsatisfactory, the question is "What next?" In order to attract leading Black Democrats to his campaign, Rev. Jackson made a pledge at the time his candidacy was announced in 1983 that he would not "exit" the party and run as an independent. Rather, he continued to attempt to bargain with Mondale in the post-convention period, finally opting to achieve "party unity" by supporting the Democratic party ticket. However, if "exiting" the party and either changing the basis of support to the Republicans or moving into an independent campaign for the presidency positioned between the two major parties is to be a credible move in setting up a final bargaining scenario, then it must be done immediately after the convention. The ability to react quickly to the hypothetical outcome above presupposes the existence of an independent organization which might, for example, be able to convene a leadership meeting on short notice and make strategic decisions in accord with the situation.

The drama is futher enhanced by the prospect of the wrenching effect such a change of strategy would have on the relationship between the independent actors and the party loyalists. Whereas the leadership differences within the Black community in 1984 over the Jackson campaign were within the Democratic party, "exiting" the party altogether by one group would, undoubtedly, provoke considerable tensions among those who were unfamiliar with or who would not support such a strategy.

This experience, however, partially hypothetical and partially real, suggests that the initiation of non-traditional strategies will re-

quire considerable re-education of Black voters and political
leaders, in an effort to understand the difference between the forms
of leverage, their implementation, and intended results.

For example, large segments of the leadership of Black tax-
exempt organizations are voter-registration oriented, and are legally
prevented from partisan advocacy, a fact which complicates their
ability to openly support party candidates. Yet, as we have seen, the
civil rights leadership was instrumental in constructing the Black
role in the Democratic party coalition, so it is certain that most of
those whom they register will vote for the Democratic presidential
nominee. However, their legal posture does not prevent them from
espousing independent strategies; inasmuch as they have been
prevented from fully entering into the political process in the past,
independent non-partisan organization would appear to strengthen
their role in community political leadership. Yet there is a lack of a
consensus on the value of independent strategies. Rev. Joseph
Lowery, President of the Southern Christian Leadership Conference, was head of the group which approved the Black presidential candidacy in 1984, while Rev. Benjamin Hooks, President of the
NAACP, opposed it.

It will be recalled that some Black leaders thought that the
Black voter was too sophisticated to need the "gimmick" of a Black
presidential candidacy to stimulate voter turnout.[25] Blacks not only
turned out overwhelmingly in the primary elections, but the Jackson
campaign proved that large numbers of people may also be cost-effi-
ciently registered to vote within the context of a candidate-driven
program. This suggests that Black voters will both register and vote
in larger numbers where there is the possibility of enhancing their
sense of political efficacy through the opportunity to cast a "sincere"
vote, rather than an indirect vote for a candidate or an issue.

In addition, a serious impediment to strategic thinking is
detected in Hooks' view that an independent campaign would be
merely symbolic. Although Hooks later moderated his view of the
Jackson campaign, still his initial attitude illustrates the existence of
a gap between the low-level "turnout-only" conception of the impact
of the Black vote, and the secondary and tertiary benefits associated
with bargaining, which connects turnout to concrete rewards.[26]

Thus, I do not view the autonomous institutionalization of
Black political resources as symbolic, but as a necessary process
through which to make credible the envisaged connection between
the Black vote and tangible rewards. With such credibility it would

be possible to even mount *non-voting* strategies directed at the electoral system, as was suggested in Chapter Six. However, civil rights leaders who have struggled so valiantly to secure the right to vote and to eliminate the remaining barriers, may conceivably feel at odds with a strategy which might call for withholding the vote in a given circumstance. The strategic use of the vote presupposes that the electoral arena is like any other in attempting to expand the range of effective political options. Therefore, as we have suggested, both the predictability of Black allegiance and the predictability of voting itself must be evaluated if the full strategic value of voting is to be achieved.

In any case, problems notwithstanding, the necessity to achieve political re-education is being forced upon Black leaders by the natural transition in the interests of many party activists from primary concern with integrative issues such as affirmative action in state convention delegations to the mechanics of acquiring delegates committed to the Black agenda. This, in my view, represents a maturation of Black politics as it moves from the posture of attempting to benefit from the use of power by some other party to one of wielding autonomous power itself.

The Democratic Primaries

The logic is inescapable that with even modest changes in political behavior, Black political influence would be enhanced. For example, following our thesis that Blacks cannot use the political system in the same manner as the majority, I would challenge the practice of Blacks following white voting patterns in the Democratic primary presidential elections. The natural division of the white vote by the Democratic and Republican party presidential primary elections creates a strategic opportunity for Blacks to exercise a balancing role. White voter turnout in the 1984 Democratic primary as opposed to the general election stood at a ratio of approximately 3:1, while the Black ratio is estimated to have been the same. In the general election, however, the Black vote constitutes 10% of the total electorate and a stable 25% of the Democratic electorate; but with the white turnout depressed in the Democratic primaries, the total Black Democratic vote of over 10 million could have amounted to as much as 50% of the total Democratic vote in the 1984 primary election. Realistically the Black turnout in the Democratic primary would be far less than 10 million voters, but even if it was considerably less—at a level of 6-7 million—it could often be decisive, provided the white vote remained the same. Walter Mondale's primary vote in 1984 was 6.9 million votes and Gary Hart's was 6.4 million; with a Black Democratic vote of 6-7 million a candidate supported by Blacks could win. At the very least, in multi-candidate situations, such a total Black vote would perhaps exercise a decisive influence over the choice of the party nominee. Then, if the white Democratic vote increased in response to higher Black voter turnout the additional factor of other coalition votes in the "rainbow" might offset such increases.

It is, therefore, crucial for Black leaders to understand the potential power of their electorate and the opportunities to exercise the "balance of power" role. In many cases this might mean changing aspects of past political behavior and, thus, shedding tradition. We have seen how difficult it has been historically for the practical politicians to seize such opportunities and even where they may have ultimately made sound political decisions, such decisions have worked in a terribly incremental fashion to enhance the social progress of Blacks.

BEYOND LEVERAGE STRATEGIES

There is a strange sense of historical deja vu in the way in which this era of American politics is beginning to effect the Black community. As I indicated in the earlier chapters of this work, it has not been adequately appreciated how the rejection of the Black community by both parties in the late 19th century forced Blacks into a period of independent politics. This historical fact may once again sorely test the limits of the concept that a semi-permanent party coalition role for the Black community is the only viable form of presidential politics. In fact, future circumstances may warrant the experimentation by Blacks with an independent third party, since, as has been stated, the sheer size of the Black vote prevents it from being neutralized. At the same time, any significant portion of the 10 million votes cast by Blacks in 1984 that is taken away from a presidential contest may be decisive considering the fact that since 1960 there have only been four landslides out of seven contests, and each of the remaining elections were decided by less than 10 million votes.

As a modern phenomenon, the Black political party would undoubtedly include whites and others in a coalition form—similar to the "Rainbow Coalition" which emerged from the Jackson   campaign. This multi-racial feature was present not only within the Jackson campaign, but, it will be recalled that the National Black Political Assembly attempted to establish a "National Committee of Peoples Politics" to accomplish a similar form of organization. The potential maturation of the "rainbow coalition" concept pressages the possibility of replacing the old Democratic party coalition with a more modern version to suit the politics and changing issues of this age.

Despite the acceptance of the necessity to form multi-racial coalitions, however, substantial risks are entailed in the management of its internal politics. Samuel Eldersveld's point is well taken that a party is basically a social group with "reciprocal deference" relationships which must be observed.[27] Whether or not a Black-led multi-racial coalition will be any more successful than the Democrats in mediating this internal deference system is an open question given the existence of racial antagonisms even among progressives. Dr. Barry Commoner, Citizens party presidential candidate in 1980, was one of the few prominent whites to argue forcefully (and publicly) for the necessity of whites to follow Black leadership during the Jackson campaign.[28]

It follows, then, that there may be inherent difficulties in sorting out problems based on whether the roots of disagreements are basically ethnic/racial or ideological. Also, the complexity of the "rainbow" concept complicates the management process, since it cuts across racial, ethnic and issue axes, enhancing the difficulty of finding a stable set of consensus principles around which to build an institutional manifestation of the coalition.

Yet it is obvious that the potential for a significant new political coalition exists. For example, one of the largest and increasingly salient "rainbow" groups is Hispanics, who often manifest a similar socio-economic profile to Blacks and urban poor groups, and like Blacks they are often concentrated in a specific geographical areas of the country. A picture of the distribution of Hispanics is presented in Table 8.3. In many of the states listed in Table 8.3, the Hispanic population is concentrated in urban centers such as those listed in Table 8.4.

Blacks vote three times as often as Hispanics in presidential elections, having voted 10.2 million in 1984 to three million for Hispanics. Nevertheless, Hispanic turnout has been increasing on all levels. The congressional vote improved slightly from 22.9% in 1974 to 25.3% in 1982. The presidential election turnout declined from

Table 8.3 Distribution of the Hispanic and Black Voting Age Population by Selected States, 1984 (%).

State	Hispanic VAP*	Black VAP
California	16.1	7.1
Delaware	1.3	14.2
Colorado	9.8	3.2
Florida	8.5	11.3
Illinois	4.6	12.9
Nevada	5.8	5.3
New Jersey	5.7	11.0
New York	8.3	12.4
Ohio	0.9	9.2
Texas	17.7	11.1

Source: Current Population Reports, Bureau of the Census U. S. Department of Commerce, 1982. *(VAP – Voting Age Population: combined total of at least 10% of the state VAP)

37.5% in 1972 to 29.9% in 1980, then rose to 32.7% in 1984.[29] In addition, the growing base of Hispanic political power has been reflected in the election of local officials such as new mayors in Miami and El Paso and members of the City Council of Los Angeles. There are six Hispanic mayors in cities over 100,000 population and altogether about half as many Hispanic elected officials as Black (6,424 to 3,147), the combined totals of which still amount to less than 2% of all elected officials. Unlike the Black population, however, there has been an Hispanic governor, Toney Anaya of New Mexico.[30]

Table 8.4 Distribution of the Hispanic Population in Cities above 100,000.

City	Population
Albuquerque, New Mexico	112,084
Chicago, Illinois	422,061
Dallas, Texas	111,082
El Paso, Texas	265,819
Houston, Texas	281,264
Los Angeles, California	815,989
Miami, Florida	194,087
New York, New York	1,405,957
San Antonio, Texas	421,774
San Diego, California	130,610
San Jose, California	140,574

Source: Current Population Reports, Bureau of the Census, U.S. Dept. of Commerce, 1982

The Black and Puerto Rican Caucus in the city of New York and in that state has attempted coalition politics for some time. Although results have been spotty, there are still occasional attempts to influence the election of city and state officials. The Hispanic vote also played a major role in the election of Harold Washington as mayor of Chicago in 1983, and it is poised to play such a role in the regional politics of the Southwest in future presidential elections.

There are still important social, economic, and cultural differences between Blacks and Hispanics that are manifest in their political behavior, and substantial differences among Hispanics themselves with respect to ethnicity, ideology, and socio-economic status. Thus, while Blacks were voting for the Democratic presidential candidate in 1984 by 85%, Hispanics were also voting Democratic, but at a rate of 20% less.[31] In any case, a political coalition between Blacks, Hispanics, and other elements of the "rainbow" grouping could seriously influence traditional politics at all levels of the political system, at least in the geographical areas cited in Table 8.3.

The Stakes of a Black Presidential Candidacy

In view of the possibilities of forming a viable "rainbow coalition," I have attempted to examine the value of a Black-led political party as a practical proposition in the arsenal of leverage strategies. Yet I have steadfastly resisted the temptation to treat as an immediately realistic possibility the achievement of the presidency of the United States by a Black person, the question of its desirability aside. Two reasons are persuasive: as a straight proposition, this option would require, for its successful achievement, not only the political intention of Blacks and their allies, but many changes in the racial attitudes and practices of other Americans that, in the first instance, affect the acceptability of a Black politician as a legitimate candidate for president, and secondly, which legitimize the political viability of third parties. The record here is somewhat mixed. While Jesse Jackson was defeated in his bid for the Democratic nomination, Thomas Bradley, mayor of Los Angeles, and Henry Lucas of Michigan were defeated in gubernatorial quests, still Blacks have previously captured the office of lieutenant governor in such states as California, Colorado, and more recently in Virginia. Then, while a May 1984 poll showed Mondale losing to Reagan by 54% to 38%, in a theoretical presidential vote, a comparison between Reagan and Jackson found Jackson losing by only a 13% greater margin.[32]

Although the goal of securing a Black president is not rejected, this writer places *relatively less* emphasis upon this goal than upon securing substantive policy enactments. This choice is made with the understanding that Blacks have often accepted the symbolic rewards of political office rather than substance from the political system, and given the complex functioning of the *institution of the presidency* it is highly questionable that a Black person would either be able or inclined to utilize the office of president to secure ethnic policy benefits in the way it might be more legitimately accomplished through lesser political and administrative offices.

Just as important, the writer takes this same position with respect to political appointments, based partially on the view, discussed elsewhere, that in general every Black leader who achieves a personal position of institutional leadership should not automatically be considered to be primarily an instrument of general Black advancement.[33] It can be demonstrated that in the main Black political leadership is liberal or progressive in its ideological character and that this posture comports well with their constituency. However, such factors as the rise of conservative Black politicians, officials whose basic loyalty is to their chosen institution, or those who have responsibliities falling substantially outside of service to Black constituencies, are all factors which challenge the accuracy and the propriety of imputing *Black community* leadership to such individuals, except in the most symbolic of terms.

Progressive Politics

In most cases it would be far more preferable that such leaders were both Black and committed to the concept of supporting progressive political positions. Such a posture would not only be theoretically consistent with Black and poor constituencies, but would also influence the character of any multi-racial coalition. Such a left-of-center coalition would, then, espouse policies which support governmental assistance for priority human needs and strategies of social change, both domestically and in the international arena. Nevertheless, it should be suggested that this idelogical stance might shape the resource base of the coalition into dependence upon mass-oriented strategies. Because of the capitalist nature of the economic system, left-of-center political coalitions which have a strong social orientation for the role of government and the private sector have been less than successful recently. These same interests, which dominate the leadership of both major parties, have encouraged allied politicians to seek the locus of electability in capitalist-oriented economic policy and safe positions on other difficult political issues. In any case, there is also a reservoir of support in the white community for what may be called "progressive" positions on complex issues of interest to Blacks and other minorities. Some evidence for this assertion may be found in the views of party activists in the Howard University Survey.

At one time, it was most convenient to determine the ideological complexion of whites based substantially on their attitudes toward Blacks. But while data on liberal party activists is difficult to obtain, it is worth noting that what is racially liberal or "progressive" tends to change. Schuman, Steeh, and Bobo have indicated that trends in racial data support the "progressive improvement" concept in the views of whites relative to race relations, suggesting that "what has changed is the normative definition of appropriate relations between blacks and whites" prevailing in society at any given time on a set of issues.[34] So, broad areas of consensus are emerging amid sharpening differences on specific issues, such that it is now possible to rationalize racial liberalism and fiscal conservatism in the same political party. Although the data move in the same direction, they also reflect moderate racial differences on almost every one of these politically loaded issues, with the greatest differences over busing, immigration and the Middle East. Moreover, other analyses by Smith and Seltzer and the Joint Center for Political Studies continue to indicate striking patterns of racial differences over issues related to the status of Blacks in American society.[35]

Whether or not "progressive" whites and Blacks are substantially different in their patterns of support for such issues our data tend to suggest that the proportion of whites who support such issues is small relative to the total white group, although in absolute numbers the

Table 8.5 Ideological Positions of Black and White Democratic Convention Delegates, 1980 (%).

| | Black | | White | |
	Favor	Oppose	Favor	Oppose
Increased Defense Spending	34.2	51.3	45.7	48.6
Business Out of South Africa	70.4	16.1	61.4	21.4
Busing	73.9	16.1	57.1	35.7
Halt Immigration	45.2	40.2	22.0	72.9
Palestinian Home	52.3	19.6	38.6	50.0

white progressive base in the total population may still be larger than a comparable group of Blacks. Thus, the opportunity may exist for an ideologically progressive multi-racial coalition of some consequential size to be formed, although perhaps over a smaller range of issues than those addressed by the Jackson campaign in the 1984 election, since widening the range of issues generally breeds greater opportunities for conflict over specific issues. There is also the residual problem that progressive groups as a whole have only recently come to utilize electoral politics as a primary instrument of social change because of the incremental nature of its reward system. Thus, there is no way of determining to what extent current progressive mobilization within the electoral area will be enduring, or is merely another fad of political behavior.

If an independent course in presidential elections is charted between the two major political parties, it should be remembered that with respect to Black politics there will be many who, for one reason or another, will want to retain a commitment to the major parties. In such a circumstance, there is no *necessary* basis for conflict, except where the interests of each group are clearly allied with different candidates. Otherwise, where it is intended that groups both inside and outside of the major parties desire to support the *same candidate* it would be conceivable to utilize Myrdal's "two-track approach" by mapping out a coordinated division of labor. For example, the group inside the major party might assist the chosen candidate to win the nomination, while the independent party group might allow the victorious nominee to run on its "line," or otherwise provide support of the kinds suggested as voting options in Chapter Five.

Finally, one of the most important corollaries to the use of independent-leverage tactics in a balance of power strategy to affect public policy is their application to congressional elections because of the national policy making implications. The current phenomenon of split-ticket voting, which finds many Americans casting their votes for candidates of different parties for president and congressional elections, presents a strategic problem. Such a problem may be addressed by political organization and strategic voting aimed at Senate and House elections because: (1) single policy-making responsibilities are shared between the president and Congress, the commitment of a president to a course of policy is seldom enough to get it enacted; (2) that, as suggested, the return of complete congressional control to the Democratic party does not in itself insure a return to New Deal liberal policies; (3) that in many congressional elections, Blacks and other minorities will be more directly successful at independent-leverage strategies because of the more direct impact of their votes upon local candidates and thus, there should be more successful bargaining scenarios; (4) and, that the instability of state and national party support for Black and other minority candidates will make independent-leverage strategies a logical electoral alternative in many state elections.

A powerful ingredient which makes such local politics effective is the existence of a connection by local candidates and bargainers to a national political organization that is dedicated to the use of independent-leverage tactics and strategies. In effect, this would constitute a parallel system of political organization rivaling those of the major parties, but most important, it would give local bargainers and candidates the ability to include local political commitments in national bargaining scenarios. Such "packaging" of an agenda of items to be bargained in national elections normally includes a mix of local and national issues at present.

The absence of strong local organization by independent-leverage bargainers and candidates, however, leaves their local issues vulnerable to highly organized major party bargainers who are able to offer considerable incentives in exchange for political support. In turn, the policy impact of independent-leverage bargainers and candidates upon the Congress is weakened in favor of the major party organizations. For example, in situations where a local congressional candidate seeks support from a broad array of interests, including independent-and dependent-leverage bargainers, the candidate is also vulnerable to a "bidding" process, where the acquisition of the greatest political resources from certain groups often determines the candidate's basic political loyalties.

CONCLUSION

I have been keenly aware that some of the tactics and strategies reviewed in this study, together with their preconditions, are unconventional and thus, considered outside the realm of possibility. The worsening policy environment for Blacks and the poor would appear to make it imperative that they expand the range of strategic options, in an attempt to achieve greater political influence leading to more salutary policy results, even though the likelihood of social change is clearly understood as only a probability.

Now at the point of concluding this discourse, I agree substantially with Keech that to the extent the nature of the social change demanded by Blacks in the public arena deals with matters of equity and fairness, something may be accomplished through the use of the ballot, but even then only "when the alternatives to be voted on provide real choice."[36] The implication of this statement should not be missed in our attempt to provide "real" political "choice" to which the voting resources of Blacks are to be applied. Likewise, I agree with his inference that the electoral arena is not amenable to many basic questions and strategies of social change. However, considering the fact that the presidential voting activity of Blacks represents an important political behavior, it should be subject to the most searching examination, to evaluate the basic competence of existing strategies for whatever possibilities of social change they may contain. Then, if the time-honored concept of the "balance of power" may be useful as more than philosophy, considerably more attention must be paid by scholars and practitioners alike to the different ways that power could indeed be balanced by Blacks in order to produce more favorable outcomes. This strategic objective may yield more fruitful interpretations of "winning" in electoral contests.

The concept of winning may appear parochial to some, since this work has been addressed to considerations of increasing the political influence of Blacks, their allies, and other similarly situated Americans, in order to achieve changes in their socio-economic condition. But to the extent that presidential politics is the instrument, the rewards of political participation are ultimately meant to fill out the substance of the American promise to every group in society, for equality of opportunity and social justice.

The philosophical dilemma addressed at the beginning of this work posed the question of how a "permanent minority" such as Blacks might participate fully in the political system, when they are often denied the possibility of a "sincere vote." If this review of strategies reveals practices which might yield satisfactory results, then perhaps they may provide more opportunities for such choice, or at least a potent substitute, both of which might stimulate political participation.

This makes the search for an efficacious basis of participation an urgent undertaking because of the essential truth of Martin Delaney's assertion in 1854. "No people can be free who themselves do not constitute an essential part of the *ruling element* of the country in which they live" (my emphasis).[37] Ultimately, then, evaluating strategies of Black voting amounts to addressing the mechanics through which Blacks become part of a more significant political coalition—the "ruling element" in society. By becoming part of this element which is functional at every level of the political system, Blacks will be able to share in the responsibility for devising those solutions to problems facing their own community and the nation as well.

Appendix

THE HOWARD UNIVERSITY BLACK DELEGATE SURVEY

The Howard University Black Delegate Survey (HUBDS) was initiated in 1976 as a project of the Social Science Research Center (SSRC) in the Institute for Urban Affairs and Research at Howard University to collect original data on the political behavior of Black delegates to the Republican and Democratic Party National Conventions. These studies, conducted every presidential election year between September and December, were initiated by Dr. Ronald Walters, director of the SSRC, who served as principal investigator and project director. The 1980 Survey was administered by a joint team consisting of political scientists and Institute staff, with Dr. Robert Smith of the Political Science Department as principal investigator, Dr. Walter Hill as consultant, and Dr. Diane Brown of the Institute as project director. This joint arrangement has been maintained for the 1984 Survey with Drs. Smith and Walters as co-principal investigators, and Dr. Ashford Baker of the Institute as project director.

The conceptual framework of the study has focused on assessing the effectiveness of the Black Democratic Caucus and the National Black Republican Council within the respective convention processes. In addition, from its inception the study was intended to be a longitudinal data base which might be used to analyze changes in the political behavior of Black party activists within the context of wider political system dynamics over time. Therefore, the following description of HUBDS is intended to provide the reader with a brief sketch of the construction of the original Survey in 1976 with respect to such factors as target population and sampling, data collection, and processing, and the character of the data and its analysis. While we do not discuss interim methodological refinements, the 1980 and 1984 Surveys may be presumed to follow roughly the pattern initiated in 1976, and although a statement regarding the 1980 sample is included here, the 1984 Survey was unavailable, though nearing completion at the time of this writing.

1976 Sampling

The target population consisted of Black delegates and alternates to the Democratic and Republican National Party Conventions in 1976. The sampling strategy in general followed that of the Conyers and Wallace study (James Conyers and Walter Wallace, Black Elected Officials, Russell Sage Foundation, New York, 1976) in that a random sample of Black convention delegates was matched in size with that of white delegates for comparability. Thus the study utilized four data sets: Black Democrats, Black Republicans, white Democrats and white Republicans. The universe of Black Democratic delegates and alternates including 537 listed by the party, but 530 verified by our research staff, and unuseable addresses lowered our total sample to a net of 493 respondents. The net Black Republican sample was 130 out of 135 listed delegates and alternates. The sample populations and the return rate appear below.

Population	Total Sample	Total Return	Percent
Black Democrats	493	126	26
Black Republicans	130	34	26
White Democrats	493	159	34
White Republicans	130	60	46

Instrument Design

The development of the questionnaire involved five areas of focus related to the dependent variable: (1) socio-economic and demographic data, (2) political socialization and recruitment data, (3) specific issues identifying the behavior of delegates within Black caucuses, (4) specific issues identifying the behavior of Black delegates within state delegations, and (5) other conditioning factors such as candidate allegiance, political awareness and ideology. From this matrix, four instruments were developed for each sub-sample to allow for generalizations about delegate behavior. As far as possible, questions have been replicated for each of the three surveys to allow for analyses of changes over time.

Data Collection and Analysis

The questionnaires were mailed and self-administered in three phases: (1) letters of introduction were sent regarding the study; (2) questionnaires were sent together with consent forms, and (3) reminder letters and additional questionnaires were sent to increase the return rate in two waves, for a total of 3,738 mailings.

The collected data were coded and processed using the original IBM version of the Statistical Packages for the Social Sciences (SPSS), with the research team systematically coding and editing all open-ended responses for consistency. The first-stage data analysis plan was to summarize the initial frequencies for a profile of the survey results, and such descriptions were performed for both the 1976 and 1980 studies. The second-stage refined analyses of the data have suffered from lack of adequate funding, however, several studies are planned for three-year data set (1976, 1980 and 1984).

Reliability

In general, the research team was guided by a wide variety of scientific literature on mail surveys, but the greatest reliance in the processing of the survey was on Earl Babbie, *Survey Research Methods* (Wadsworth, Belmont, CA, 1973, pp. 159–169). Thus, the team was familiar with the cautions that exist in the literature concerning acceptable response rates in relationship to survey reliability. Nevertheless, the conclusion of the staff was that high confidence could be placed in the reliability of the study because of three primary indicators: first, there is a significant "fit" between the objective socio-economic and demographic profile of the actual delegates and our respondents. Second, the probable error in the sample is less than + or − 5%. Then, the initial frequencies revealed responses that are consistent with staff participant observation reports on a number of specific items.

In the 1980 study, the desired sample of Black delegates and alternates were stratified by party in the following manner: Black Democrats n = 769, Black Republicans n = 119. A random sampling procedure was used to select the control group of 766 white Democrats and 119 white Republicans. The procedure involved a listing (Black delegates deleted) where the white delegates were chosen randomly, stratified by state delegation. The overall response rate was 27%, in a profile similar to that of the 1976 study.

BLACK DEMOCRATIC DELEGATE QUESTIONNAIRE

1. Education:
A. Grade School: _____ (years)
B. High School: _____ (years)
C. College: _____ (years)
D. Graduate or Professional School: _____ (years)

2. Religious Affiliation: _____

3. Civic Organizations Membership: (Ex. NAACP, Neighborhood Assn. or Community group)
(List) _____
_____
_____

4. Labor Union Membership: Yes _____ No _____ (Check one)
   Do you hold office?   Yes _____ No _____ (Check one)

5. Political Organizations Membership: (District Caucus, Precinct Club, State Political Caucus, National, etc.) (List below)

Organization	Office
_____	_____
_____	_____
_____	_____

6. Are you an elected or public appointed official?
A. Elected _____ Appointed _____ (Check one)
B. List office and Check whether Past or Present.

	Present	Past
Local	_____	_____
State	_____	_____
National	_____	_____

7. Do you attend meetings of your formal Party organization? (Check below)

A.	YES	NO
National	( )	( )
State	( )	( )
County	( )	( )
City	( )	( )
Ward	( )	( )
Precinct	( )	( )

B. How often do you attend meetings? (Check one below)
    NEVER _____   SOMETIMES _____
    OFTEN _____   REGULARLY _____

8. How many previous National Party Conventions have you attended? _____
A. Past Status: Delegate _____ Alternate _____ (Times)
B. Present Status: Delegate _____ Alternate _____

9. How did you get to be a delegate/alternate?
A. Primary election _____
B. Convention (State) _____
C. Caucus _____
D. State Party Central Committee Selection _____
E. Other (Specify) _____

10. Were you committed to any candidate prior to the opening of the Convention?
    YES _____   NO _____ If "YES", to whom _____

11. Were you supported in your efforts to become a delegate by:
A. Any Presidential Candidate _____
B. The Party Organization _____   (Check each which applies)
C. Your Neighborhood Groups and Friends _____
D. Organized Labor _____
E. Other (Specify) _____

12. In your state, do you think the new Party Delegate Selection Rules helped you become a delegate? (Check one below)
A. Helped _____   Not Helped _____
B. If "Not Helped" then, what would you say is the major problem with blacks becoming delegates?
    _____
    _____
    _____

13. What sessions of the Black Caucus were you able to attend at the Convention? (Check each which applies)
A. Monday _____ B. Tuesday _____ C. Wednesday _____
D. Thursday _____

14. Do you have a leadership role in the Black Democratic Caucus?
    YES _____   NO _____
    If "YES", what? _____

15. What do you recall as the most important issues in the Black Caucus sessions?
A. _____
    _____

B. _____

C. _____

16. Did you usually vote in your state delegation according to the decisions reached in the Black Caucus? YES _____ NO _____
A. If "YES", why? IF "NO", why not? Explain.

_____

_____

B. When Delegation's and Caucus's positions conflicted, did you usually vote as decided by the: (Check one)
Delegation _____ Caucus _____ Other (Specify) _____

17. What Convention groups do you see as most effective in coalition efforts with the Black Caucus? (Show order of importance by using 1, 2, 3, 4, etc.)
A. Liberal Caucus   (   ) E. Southerners   (   )
B. Candidate Organizations (   ) F. Labor Caucus   (   )
C. Women's Groups   (   ) G. Other (Specify) _____
D. Combined "minorities"   (   )

18. Did you have access to the chairman of your state delegation? (Check one)
A. Very much (   ) B. Moderately (   ) C. Hardly at all (   )

19. Which one of the following do you think describes your state delegation's general receptivity to your participation?
A. Couldn't stand me   (   )
B. Tolerated my presence   (   )
C. Just one of the gang   (   )
D. Very positive   (   )

20. What do you think was the most important Convention issue?

_____
Why? _____

_____

21. What issues in the Platform would you want to see implemented by a new administration? (Check below)
A. Employment (   ) F. Health   (   )
B. Prices   (   ) G. Welfare   (   )
C. Taxes   (   ) H. Abortion (   )

D. Unions ( ) I. School Aid ( )
E. Campaign ( ) J. Busing ( )
K. Guns ( )

22. What do you think are Carter's:
A. Strongest qualities? _____

_____

_____

B. Weakest qualities? _____

_____

_____

23. If you were not committed to Carter before the Convention, what caused you to change your mind?

_____

_____

_____

24. Do you expect to work for Carter's election?
A. YES _____ NO _____
B. If "YES", in what way? _____

_____

25. Could you envision any circumstances which might make you reconsider voting for the party's presidential candidate?
A. YES _____ NO _____
B. If "YES", what might it be? _____

_____

_____

_____

26. Age: _____

27. Residence: State _____ Congressional District _____

28. Sex: Male _____ Female _____ (Check one)

29. Race: White _____ Non-white _____ (Check one)

30. Marital Status: Married _____ Single _____ (Check one)

31. Occupation: _____

32. Income: (Check one)
A. Under $10,000 ( )
B. $10,000-$19,999 ( )
C. $20,000-$29,999 ( )
D. $30,000-$39,999 ( )
E. $40,000-$49,999 ( )
F. Over $50,000 ( )

33. Is registration and voting, in your city:
A. Increasing (   ) or Decreasing (   )?
B. Why, in your opinion? _____
_____
_____
_____

34. Where do you stand on the following issues? (Quickly check off)

	Favor	Oppose
A. Tough Fire Arms Control	( )	( )
B. U.S. Business out of South Africa	( )	( )
C. School Busing	( )	( )
D. U.S. Military Aid to Israel	( )	( )
E. National Health Insurance	( )	( )

35. Do you think it is time for there to be a Black Democratic Candidate for national office? (Check one)
A. President YES _____   NO _____
     Vice President YES _____   NO _____
B. If "YES", *who* would you suggest?
President _____
_____
Vice President _____
_____

BLACK REPUBLICAN DELEGATE QUESTIONNAIRE

1. Education:
A. Grade School: _____ (years)
B. High School: _____ (years)
C. College: _____ (years)
D. Graduate or Professional School: _____ (years)

2. Religious Affiliation: _____

3. Civic Organizations Membership: (Ex. NAACP, Neighborhood Assn. or Community group)
(List) _____
_____
_____

4. Labor Union Membership: Yes _____ No _____ (Check one)
     Do you hold office?   Yes _____ No _____ (Check one)

5. Political Organizations Membership: (District Caucus, Precinct Club, State Political Caucus, National, etc.) (List below)

Organization   Office

_____   _____
_____   _____
_____   _____

6. Are you an elected or public appointed official?
A. Elected _____ Appointed _____ (Check one)
B. List office and Check whether Past or Present.

            Present   Past
Local   _____   _____
State   _____   _____
National _____   _____

7. Do you attend meetings of your formal Party organization? (Check below)

A.	YES	NO
National	( )	( )
State	( )	( )
County	( )	( )
City	( )	( )
Ward	( )	( )
Precinct	( )	( )

B. How often do you attend meetings? (Check one below)
NEVER _____ SOMETIMES _____
OFTEN _____ REGULARLY _____

8. How many previous National Party Conventions have you attended? _____
A. Past Status: Delegate _____ Alternate _____ (Times)
B. Present Status: Delegate _____ Alternate _____

9. How did you get to be a delegate/alternate?
A. Primary election _____
B. Convention (State) _____
C. Caucus _____
D. State Party Central Committee Selection _____
E. Other (Specify) _____

10. Were you committed to any candidate prior to the opening of the Convention?
YES _____ NO _____ If "YES", to whom _____

11. Were you supported in your efforts to become a delegate by:
A. Any Presidential Candidate _____
B. The Party Organization _____   (Check each which applies)
C. Your Neighborhood Groups and Friends _____
D. Organized Labor _____
E. Other (Specify) _____

12. In your state, do you think the new Party Delegate Selection Rules helped you become a delegate? (Check one below)
A. Helped _____ Not Helped _____
B. If "Not Helped" then, what would you say is the major problem with blacks becoming delegates?

_____
_____
_____

13. Did you attend the National Black Republican Council Caucus for Black Delegates and Alternates? (Check each which applies)
YES _____   NO _____

14. Do you have a leadership role in the Black Republican Caucus?
YES _____   NO _____
If "YES", what? _____

15. What do you recall as the most important issues in the Black Caucus sessions?
A. _____
_____
B. _____
_____
C. _____
_____

16. Did you usually vote in your state delegation according to the decisions reached in the Black Caucus? YES _____   NO _____
A. If "YES", why? IF "NO", why not? Explain.

_____
_____
_____

B. When Delegation's and Caucus's positions conflicted, did you usually vote as decided by the: (Check one)
Delegation _____ Caucus _____ Other (Specify) _____
_____

17. What Convention groups do you see as most effective in coalition efforts with the Black Caucus? (Show order of importance by using 1, 2, 3, 4, etc.)

A. Liberal Caucus   (   )   E. Southerners   (   )
B. Candidate Organizations (   )   F. Labor Caucus   (   )
C. Women's Groups   (   )   G. Other (Specify) _____
D. Combined "minorities"   (   )

18. Did you have access to the chairman of your state delegation? (Check one)

A. Very much (   ) B. Moderately (   ) C. Hardly at all (   )

19. Which one of the following do you think describes your state delegation's general receptivity to your participation?
A. Couldn't stand me   (   )
B. Tolerated my presence   (   )
C. Just one of the gang   (   )
D. Very positive   (   )

20. What do you think was the most important Convention issue?

_____

Why? _____

_____

_____

21. What issues in the Platform would you want to see implemented by a new administration? (Check below)
A. Employment   (   )   F. Health   (   )
B. Prices   (   )   G. Welfare   (   )
C. Taxes   (   )   H. Abortion   (   )
D. Unions   (   )   I. School Aid   (   )
E. Campaign   (   )   J. Busing   (   )
                                       K. Guns   (   )

22. What do you think are Ford's:
A. Strongest qualities? _____

_____

_____

B. Weakest qualities? _____

_____

_____

23. If you were not committed to Ford before the Convention, what caused you to change your mind?

_____

_____

_____

24. Do you expect to work for Ford's election?
A. YES _____ NO _____
B. If "YES", in what way? _____

_____

25. Could you envision any circumstances which might make you re-consider voting for the party's presidential candidate?

A. YES _____   NO _____

B. If "YES", what might it be? _____

_____

_____

_____

26. Age: _____

27. Residence: State _____ Congressional District _____

28. Sex: Male _____   Female _____ (Check one)

29. Race: White _____   Non-white _____ (Check one)

30. Marital Status: Married _____   Single _____ (Check one)

31. Occupation: _____

32. Income: (Check one)

A. Under $10,000   (   )
B. $10,000-$19,999   (   )
C. $20,000-$29,999   (   )
D. $30,000-$39,999   (   )
E. $40,000-$49,999   (   )
F. Over $50,000   (   )

33. Is registration and voting, in your city:

A. Increasing (   ) or Decreasing (   )?

B. Why, in your opinion? _____

_____

_____

_____

34. Where do you stand on the following issues? (Quickly check off)

	Favor	Oppose
A. Tough Fire Arms Control	( )	( )
B. U.S. Business out of South Africa	( )	( )
C. School Busing	( )	( )
D. U.S. Military Aid to Israel	( )	( )
E. National Health Insurance	( )	( )

35. Do you think it is time for there to be a Black Republican Candi-date for national office? (Check one)

A. President YES _____   NO _____

   Vice President YES _____   NO _____

B.   If "YES", *who* would you suggest?

President _____

_____

Vice President _____

_____

Notes

Notes to Chapter 1

1. One uses the term "Black presidential politics," (the author used this term in an article, "Black Presidential Politics: Bargaining or Begging?" *The Black Scholar*, Vol. 11 (March/April, 1980), pp. 22–31) not only as a concept with which to analyze an existing problem of Black leadership, but to indicate the existence of an important sub-area of scholarly focus in the field of Black politics in general. See also other articles in the sparse literature of the field such as: Hanes Walton and Vernon Gray, "Black Politics at the Democratic and Republican Conventions, 1868–1972," *Phylon*, Vol. 36, pp. 269–278; Lenneal Henderson, "Black Politics and American Presidential Elections," in Michael Preston, Lenneal Henderson and Paul Puryear, eds., *The New Black Politics*, (New York: Longman, 1982), pp. 3–27; and several special studies by the Joint Center for Political Studies, such as "The Impact of the Black Electorate," February 1983, and Thomas E. Cavanaugh and Lorn S. Foster, "Jesse Jackson's Campaign: The Primaries and Caucuses, Election '84," Report No. 2, 1984.

2. Joseph Tussman, *Obligation and the Body Politic*, (New York: Oxford University Press, 1960), p. 28.

3. Sir Ernest Barker, *Social Contract*, (New York: Oxford University Press, 1967), p. 273.

4. William Bluhm, *Theories of the Political System*, (Englewood Cliffs: Prentice-Hall, 1965), p. 371.

5. See Robin Farquharson, *Theory of Voting*, (New Haven: Yale University Press, 1969).

6. Cited in Michael Curtiss, *The Great Political Theories*, Vol. II, (New York: Avon Books, 1962), pp. 246–247.

7. Charles Wesley, "The Participation of Negroes in Anti-Slavery Political Parties," *Journal of Negro History* Vol. 29 (January, 1944), p. 35.

8. Robert C. Dick, *Black Protest: Issues and Tactics*, (Westport: Greenwood, 1974), pp. 92–93.

9. Robert P. Turner, *Up To The Front Of The Line*, (Port Washington: Kennikat Press, 1975), pp. 34, 46.

10. Leon F. Litwack, "The Negro Abolitionist," in Martin Duberman, ed., *The Anti-Slavery Vanguard*, (Princeton: Princeton University Press, 1965), p. 150.

11. Charles V. Hamilton, ed., *The Black Experience in American Politics*, (New York: G. P. Putnam and Sons, 1973), p. 250.

12. W. E. B. DuBois, *Black Reconstruction in America*, (Cleveland: Meridian, 1967), p. 371.

13. *Crisis*, Vol. 35 (October, 1928), p. 353.

14. Turner, op. cit., p. 114.

15. John G. Van Deusen, "The Negro In Politics," *Journal of Negro History*, Vol. 21 (July, 1936), pp. 259, 261.

16. W. E. B. DuBois, "The Possibility of Democracy in America," *Crisis*, Vol. 35, (two parts) (September, 1928), p. 295, and (October, 1928), p. 335.

17. Robert H. Terrell, "Theodore Roosevelt," pp. 542–544; H. Latimer, "The Negro and the Democratic Party," pp. 617–618, *The Colored American Magazine*, (October, 1904). Terrell was a member of the group of practical politicans to which I refer during this period, but for a more complete description of their identities, see: William Toll, *The Resurgence of Race*, (Philadelphia: Temple University Press, 1983), pp. 91–98.

18. Louis R. Harlan, Raymond W. Smock, eds., *The Booker T. Washington Papers*, Vol. 8, 1904–6, (Chicago: University of Illinois Press, 1979), p. 29.

19. Turner, op. cit., p. 134.

20. Hamilton, op. cit., pp. 253–256.

21. Douglas C. Strange, "The Making of a President - 1912: The Northern Negroes' View," *The Negro History Bulletin* (November, 1968), p. 21.

22. Ibid, pp. 258–259.

23. James Weldon Johnson, "The Gentlemen's Agreement and The Negro Vote," *Crisis*, Vol. 28 (October 1924), p. 260.

24. Ibid., p. 262.

25. Ibid., p. 264.

26. Herbert Aptheker, ed., *A Documentary History of the Negro People in the United States, 1910–1932*, Vol. 3, (New York: Citadel Press, 1977), p. 303.

27. Hamilton, op. cit., p. 267.

28. W. E. B. DuBois, "Opinion," *Crisis*, Vol. 28 (September, 1924), p. 199.

29. Hamilton, op. cit., p. 271.

30. Ibid., pp. 272–273.

31. "How Shall We Vote?: A Symposium," *Crisis*, Vol. 29, (November, 1924).

32. Aptheker, "An Appeal to America," op. cit., p. 580.

33. W. E. B. DuBois, *Crisis*, Vol. 35 (September, 1928), pp. 368, 386.

34. W. E. B. DuBois, *Crisis*, Vol. 35 (October, 1928), 346.

35. Turner, op. cit., p. 136.

36. J. S. Coague and Rev. John Hawkins, "Vote for Hoover," *Crisis*, Vol. 39 (October, 1932), p. 313.

37. Lester A. Walton, "Vote for Roosevelt," *Crisis*, Vol. 39 (November, 1932), p. 343.

38. Ibid, p. 344.

39. Hamilton, op. cit., p. 287.

40. Ibid, p. 282. I use the term "progressive" in this work to denote politicians with liberal or advanced ideas or policy proposals, not to identify members of the Progressive party which was active at this time. However, as both Strange, op. cit., and Kelly Miller note, the roots of the "progressive movement," itself may be found in this period. See Kelly Miller, "The Political Light of the Negro," *Kelly Miller's Monographic Magazine*, Vol. 1 (1913), p. 3.

41. W. E. B. DuBois, *Dusk of Dawn*, (New York: Schocken, 1968), p. 237.

42. Gunnar Myrdal, *An American Dilemma*, Vol. II, (New York: Harper and Row, 1962), p. 494.

43. Leo Alilunas, "Legal Restrictions on the Negro in Politics," *Journal of Negro History*, Vol. 25 (April, 1940), p. 198.

44. Turner, op. cit., p. 123.

45. Ralph Bunche noted that the process of influencing the Black vote has often involved the "purchase of the Black Press," Dewey Grantham, ed., *Ralph J. Bunche: The Political Status of the Negro in the Age of FDR*, (Chicago: The University of Chicago Press, 1973), p. 92.

46. Paul Lewinson, *Race, Class & Party*, (New York: Grosset and Dunlap, 1965), pp. 165–166.

47. W. E. B. DuBois, "Opinion," *Crisis*, Vol. 28 (September, 1924), p. 199.

48. August Meier, *Negro Thought in America, 1880–1915*, (Ann Arbor: The University of Michigan Press, 1966), p. 31.

49. "A Declaration by Negro Voters," *Crisis*, Vol. 51 (January, 1944), pp. 16–17.

50. Bunche, op. cit., p. 88.

51. Ibid.

52. Meier, op. cit., p. 187.

53. Lewinson, op. cit., p. 88.

54. Bunche, op. cit., p. 93.

55. Parker Moon, *Balance of Power: The Negro Vote*, (New York: Kraus Reprint, 1969), p. 198.

56. J. Erroll Miller, "The Negro in Present Day Politics," *Journal of Negro History*, Vol. 33 (July, 1948), p. 321.

57. Ibid., p. 35.

58. Ibid., p. 10.

59. Ibid., p. 11.

60. Turner, op. cit., p. 145.

Notes to Chapter 2

1. Robert P. Turner, *Up To The Front Of The Line*, (Port Washington: Kennikat Press, 1975), p. 146.

2. David L. Lewis, *King*, (Chicago: University of Illinois Press, 1978), pp. 123–128.

3. Martin Luther King, Jr., *Why We Can't Wait*, (New York: Mentor, 1964), p. 147.

4. Ibid., p. 148.

5. Ibid., p. 149.

6. Bayard Rustin, *Down the Line*, (Chicago: Quadrangle, 1971), p. 112.

7. Ibid., p. 119.

8. James Forman, *The Making of Black Revolutionaries*, (New York: Macmillan, 1972), pp. 386–406; August Meier and Elliott Rudwick, *CORE: A Study in the Civil Rights Movement*, (Chicago: University of Illinois Press, 1975), p. 281.

9. Ibid., pp. 320–321; Clayborne Carson, *In Struggle: SNCC and the Black Awakening of the 1960s*, (Cambridge: Harvard University Press, 1981), pp. 223–229; Roy Wilkins, *Standing Fast*, (New York: Viking Press, 1982), pp. 304–306.

10. Lewis, op. cit., pp. 250–252.

11. Richard Scammon and Ben Wattenberg, *The Real Majority*, (New York: Coward, McCann and Goeghegan, Inc., 1971), p. 56.

12. John Dean, "A Survey of Black Political Attitudes in the Aftermath of the Florida Presidential Primary," Joint Center for Political Studies, Washington, D. C., September, 1972.

13. R. W. Apple, "Impact of the Florida Vote," *The New York Times*, March 10, 1976, p. 1.

14. Christopher Lyndon, "Carter's Backers are Reassessing Him," *New York Times*, March 14, 1976, p. 44.

15. Candidate Reports, Jimmy Carter Presidential Campaign, Federal Election Commission, 1976. These records clearly indicate the sums provided to various Black political operatives in the various states for expenditures in connection with the campaign.

16. "Blacks Support Carter 94% Against Ford," *The Washington Post*,

November 11, 1976, p. A22.

17. "Black Voters Provided Carter with Winning Margin in Key States," *News*, Joint Center for Political Studies, Washington, D. C. (November 5, 1976).

18. Ibid.

19. "Joint Center President Calls on Carter Administration to Include Blacks in Policy Making Process," *News*, Joint Center for Political Studies, Washington, D. C. (November 9, 1976).

20. Ibid.

21. "A Debt That Must Be Paid," *Ebony Magazine*, Vol. 32 (January, 1977), p. 110.

22. "Jimmy's Debt to Blacks—and Others," *Time*, Vol. 108 (November 22, 1976), p. 6.

23. J. K. Obatala, "Black Constituency: How Carter Should Pay His Debt," *The Nation*, Vol. 223 (November 27, 1976), p. 16.

24. Vernon Jordan, "Blacks Have a Claim on Carter," *Newsweek*, Vol. 88 (November 22, 1976), p. 13.

25. Chuck Stone, "Black Political Power in the Carter Era," *The Black Scholar*, Vol. 8 (January/February, 1977), p. 6.

26. Stuart Eizenstat, *Newsweek*, Vol. 88 (November 22, 1976), p. 27.

27. "Minority Report: U.S. Blacks Show Little Urge to Vote This Year," *The Wall Street Journal*, October 3, 1980, p. 22.

28. *Focus*, Joint Center for Political Studies, Washington, D. C. (February, 1976), p. 2.

29. Michael Barone, Grant Ujifusa, Douglas Matthews, *The Almanac of American Politics*, (Boston: Gambit, 1972), p. 340.

30. Speech, Senator Edward Brooke, Third National Institute for Black Elected Public Officials, Joint Center For Political Studies, Washington, D. C., December 11, 1975.

31. "Ford Talks to Black Delegates Pushing Brooke a Veep Choice," *The Kansas City Times*, August 18, 1976, p. 26.

32. Speech, Edward Brooke, op. cit.

33. Charles Rangel, "The President and the Black Caucus," *Focus*, Vol. 2 Joint Center for Political Studies, Washington, D. C. (September, 1974), p. 5.

34. Ellis Cose, "Representative Jordan Halts Drive to Make Her Veep Possibility," *Chicago Sun-Times*, July 13, 1976, p. 1.

35. *Focus*, Vol. 1, (December, 1972).

36. "Minority Report: U.S. Blacks Show Little Urge to Vote This Year," *The Wall Street Journal*, op. cit.

37. *News*, Joint Center for Political Studies, Washington, D. C. (April 7, 1980).

38. Voting and Registration in the Election of November 1984, Advance Report, Bureau of the Census, Dept. of Commerce, January , 1985.

228   BLACK PRESIDENTIAL POLITICS IN AMERICA

Notes to Chapter 3

1. *When the Marching Stopped*, (New York: National Urban League, November, 1973), p. 88.

2. Martin Luther King, Jr., *Where Do We Go From Here: Chaos or Community?* (Boston: Beacon Press, 1968), p. 147.

3. James Forman, *The Making of Black Revolutionaries*, (New York: Macmillan, 1972), p. 395.

4. John Neary says that 50% of the delegates at this convention were Black. See John Neary, *Julian Bond: Black Rebel*, (New York: Morrow, 1971), p. 195.

5. Ibid, p. 200.

6. F. Rhodes Cook, "National Conventions and Delegates Selection," in Jeff Fishel, ed., *Parties and Elections in an Anti-Party Age*, (Bloomington: Indiana University Press, 1978), pp. 190–191.

7. Ibid, p. 191.

8. Ibid, p. 192.

9. John Stewart, *One Last Chance: The Democratic Party 1974–76*, (New York: Praeger, 1975), p. 54.

10. "The Call," Democratic National Convention of 1972, Democratic National Committee, Washington, D. C., November 1971, p. 5.

11. Ibid., p. 9.

12. Guide to Black Politics 1972, Joint Center for Political Studies, Washington, D. C., June 26, 1972, p. 21.

13. Stewart, op. cit., p. 170.

14. The Charter Commission's 160 members contained fifteen Blacks, who were: Congresswoman Yvonne Burke Braithwaite, Vice-Chairman; Arthur Shores of Alabama, Jerry Jewell of Arkansas, Willie Brown of California, Barbara Morgan of D. C., Janet Watlington of the Virgin Islands, Mary Singleton of Florida, Ben Brown of Georgia, Evelyn Jamison of Illinois, Francis Blake of Kansas, Zeline Richard of Michigan, Charles Hughes of New York, Lucille King of New York, Joseph Jordan, Jr. of Virginia, Cecil Ward of New York. The Black members of the Delegate Selection Commission were: Dr. E. Lavonia Allison of North Carolina, Hannah Atkins of Oklahoma, William Clay of Missouri, James Clayburn of South Carolina, Gwendolyn Cherry of Florida, Esther Harrison of Mississippi, William Hart of New Jersey, Richard Hatcher of Indiana, Mildred Nichols of Rhode Island, Arie Taylor of Colorado. Commission Final Reports, Democratic National Committee.

15. Christopher Lyndon, "Democrats have Panel on Delegates," *The New York Times*, September 22, 1973, p. 14.

16. Ibid.

17. Stewart, op. cit., p. 173. See also Memorandum, Kansas City Mid-Term Conference, Caucus of Black Democrats, November 11, 1974.

The following statement is excerpted:

"In the interest of Party unity . . . following much debate, negotiation, and many compromises, Black members of the Mikulski Commission and their allies—women, youth, Latinos, and reformers—agree to a compromise which would ban the use of quotas in the delegate selection process while at the same time adding two extremely important new features to the Party's delegate selection rules."

(These were: the promise of participation in "all party affairs," and the establishment of the Compliance Review Commission to monitor Affirmative Action plans).

18. Ibid.

19. Report of the Commission on Delegate Selection and Party Structure, (adopted unanimously), Democratic National Committee, Washington, D. C., October 27, 1973, p. 8.

20. Draft Charter of the Democratic Party, Democratic National Committee, Washington, D. C., December 15, 1973.

21. Christopher Lyndon, "Democrats Face New Split on Policing Convention Rules," *The New York Times*, November 2, 1973, p. 8.

22. The writer was a consultant to some Black Democratic leaders in the Article 10 drafting process.

23. Michael Malbin, "Political Report/Controversy over Charter Reflects Democratic Party Division," *National Journal Reports*, September 21, 1974, p. 1410.

24. Ibid., p. 1413.

25. Press Release, the Black Democratic Caucus, Black Affairs Office, Democratic National Committee, Washington, D. C., September 28, 1974.

26. Ibid. The Steering Committee consisted of: Willie Brown, member of the Charter Commission; Yvonne Burke, vice chairperson of the Charter Commission; Ruth Charity, member of the DNC Executive Committee; Earl Craig, Jr., chair, DNC Black Caucus; Richard Hatcher, vice chair, Commission on Delegate Selection and Party Structure, and the CRC; Aaron Henry, chair, Mississippi State Democratic Executive Committee; William Lucy, secretary/treasurer, AFSCME; Basil Patterson, vice chair, DNC; Charles Rangel, chair, Congressional Black Caucus; Mark Stepp, vice president, UAW; Coleman Young, member, DNC, Mid-West coordinator, Democratic Caucus of Mayors.

27. "Black Delegates and Alternates to the 1975 Democratic Conference on Party Organization and Policy," The Black Affairs Office, Democratic National Committee, Washington, D. C., 1975.

28. Memorandum, Frank Cowan, Democratic National Committee; data sheet, Coalition for a Democratic Majority, Washington, D. C., January 17, 1975.

29. Writer's notes.

30. Ibid.

31. Ibid.

32. See R. M. Koster, "Suprise Party," *Harpers*, Vol. 250 (March, 1975), p. 31.

33. Writer's notes. Draft language.

34. Koster, "Surprise Party," *Harpers*, op. cit.

35. "Black Democrats Score Stunning Rules Victories, Floor Fight Set on Minority Participation," Press Release, Democratic National Committee, Washington, D. C., June 24, 1976.

36. Rules Committee Transcript, Democratic National Committee, Washington, D. C., June, 1976.

37. Interviews and discussions: Martin, Cowan, and Harrison.

38. Richard Hatcher, Open Letter, Democratic National Committee, Washington, D. C., September 27, 1984.

39. *The New York Times*, March 24, 1976, p. 1.

40. John Britton, "Operation Big Vote to the Rescue," *Focus*, Joint Center for Political Studies, Washington, D. C. (August, 1976), p. 4.

41. "Black Voter Turnout Low in Primaries: Carter and Ford Big in Black Wards," *News*, Joint Center for Political Studies, Washington, D. C. (March 19, 1976).

42. John Britton, "Operation Big Vote," *Focus*, Joint Center for Political Studies, Washington, D. C. (August, 1976), p. 4.

43. William K. Stevens, "Detroit Mayor Telling Blacks Carter Will End Neglect," *The New York Times*, May 13, 1976, p. 11.

44. James Wooten, "Carter Tired But Happy," *The New York Times*, June 16, 1976, p. 1.

45. Ken Bode, "Why Carter's Big with Blacks," *The New Republic*, Vol. 174 (April 10, 1976), p. 14.

46. Ibid.

47. Roger Williams, "Toward a Politics of Trust: the Making of Andrew Young," *Saturday Review*, Vol. 4 (October 16, 1976), p. 6.

48. Ibid, p. 10.

49. Christopher Lyndon, "Carter Issues an Apology on 'Ethnic Purity' Phrases," *The New York Times*, April 9, 1976, p. 1.

50. "Why Carter Wins the Black Vote," *Time*, Vol. 107 (April 5, 1976), p. 17.

51. "Blacks Need More Social Programs — Not Fewer," Interview, *U.S. News and World Report*, Vol. 88 (April 7, 1980), pp. 69–70.

52. Sheila Rule, "Third of Blacks in Poll Support the President for Job Performance," *The New York Times*, January 18, 1980, p. 1.

53. "Black Leaders Out of Step with Their People?" *U.S. News and World Report*, Vol. 88 (April 7, 1980), p. 68.

54. *The New York Times*, January 23, 1980, p. 16.

55. Edward Walsh, "Miami Blacks Boo, Throw Bottles at Carter Motorcade," *The Washington Post*, June 10, 1980, p. A1.

56. *Encore Magazine*, Vol. 8 (October 1, 1979).

57. *The Voice*, Springfield, Ill., December 27, 1979; "Caucus Split," *San Francisco Observer*, January 10–16, 1979; Chuck Stone, "Our Leaders Are in Trouble," *African-American News and World Report*, Baltimore, July 20, 1980; Warren Brown, "Young Counsels Blacks to Stick by the President," *The Washington Post*, September 23, 1979.

58. *News*, Joint Center for Political Studies, Washington, D. C. (April 7, 1980).

59. See Appendix.

60. Statement by Congresswoman Barbara Jordan, Democratic National Convention, New York, N.Y., July 13, 1976.

61. Ellis Cose, "Black Delegates Readying Fight for Bigger Minority Role," *Chicago Sun-Times*, July 11, 1976 p. 31.

62. *The Amsterdam News*, July 10, 1976, pp. A1, A9.

63. Ellis Cose, "Leader's Era Ending," *Chicago Sun-Times*, July 26, 1976; "Upset by Carter By-Pass, Black Leaders Want Meeting," *Chicago Sun-Times*, July 18, 1976, p. 72.

64. Ellis Cose, "Black Closest to Carter: Trust is Cement," *Chicago Sun-Times*, July 18, 1976, p. 11.

65. Austin Scott, "Women, Black Leaders are with Carter on Goals," *The Washington Post*, July 13, 1976, p. A15.

66. Ibid.

67. "Meet the Press," July 11, 1976.

68. "Rev. Jesse Jackson Seeking to have South Africa Resolution Accepted," *The Washington Post*, July 2, 1976, p. A3.

69. "Black Politics in 1980: A Guide to the 1980 Convention," Joint Center for Political Studies, Washington, D. C., August, 1980.

70. "Delegate Selection Rules for the 1980 Democratic National Convention," Democratic Natonal Committee, Washington, D. C., June 9, 1976, Section 6.

71. Memorandum, Carl Green, Legislative Director, Congressional Black Caucus, Washington, D. C., undated.

72. Writer's convention notes.

73. Ethel L. Payne, "Carter's High Risk Re-evaluation Gamble," *Dollars and Sense*, (October/November, 1980), p. 20.

74. Writer's convention notes.

Notes to Chapter 4

1. The "Black and Tans" were the Black faction of the Republican party, organized in opposition to the attempt of "lily-white" Republicans in the South to remove them from the party. For a discussion, see: Hanes Walton, *Black Politics: A Theoretical and Structural Approach*, (New York: Lippincott, 1972), pp. 91–94. See also, Rayford Logan, *The Negro in American Life and Thought: The Nadir, 1877-1901*, (New York: Dial Press, 1954).

2. Gabriel Almond and Bingham Powell, *Comparative Politics: A Developmental Approach*, (Boston: Little Brown, 1966), p. 102.

3. Writer's notes. Writer served as a member of the Planning Committee and Platform Committee staff of the convention.

4. Draft Resolution, South Carolina Delegation, National Black Political Convention, March 11, 1972.

5. *The New York Times*, March 21, 1972, p. A18.

6. The National Black Political Agenda, *Draft Document*, 1972, p. 13B.

7. Ibid.

8. Ibid., p. 38B.

9. Writer's press conference notes, June 1, 1972.

10. Imamu Amiri Baraka, "Black and Angry," *Newsweek*, Vol. 80 (July 10, 1972), p. 35.

11. Ibid.

12. Alex Pointsett, "Black Politics at the Crossroads," *Ebony*, Vol. 27 (December, 1972), p. 38.

13. Poinsett says that at one point, a Black Caucus meeting was cleverly coopted by the appearance of Julie Nixon Eisenhower, who again made the standard pitch concerning the record of the Nixon administration toward Blacks. Poinsett, op. cit., p. 42.

14. Letter, Ad Hoc Committee, February 9, 1976.

15. Ibid.

16. Position Paper, Caucus of Black Democrats, Charlotte, N. C., May 1, 1976, p. 23.

17. Ibid., p. 30.

18. Writer's convention notes.

19. Ibid. For a summary of the press conference and opening speeches, see also, Jerry Lazarus and Dan Moreau, "Young Supports Role for PLO, Scores Boycott," *Richmond Times-Dispatch*, March 1, 1980, pp. 1, A6.

20. Ibid.

21. Ibid.

22. Ibid.

23. Ibid.

24. Ibid.

25. Ibid.

26. The National Black Agenda for the '80s, Richmond Conference Recommendations, Joint Center for Political Studies, Washington, D. C., Item no. 4.

27. Ibid.

28. Almond and Powell, op. cit., p. 73.

29. Ibid., p. 88.

30. Roger W. Cobb and Charles D. Elder, "The Politics of Agenda-Building: An Alternative Perspective for Modern Democratic Theory," *The Journal of Politics*, Vol. 33, No. 4, p. 902.

31. Ibid., p. 903.

32. Ibid., p. 909.

33. Lenneal Henderson, "Black Politics and American Presidential Elections," in Michael Preston, Paul Puryear, and Lenneal Henderson, Jr., *The New Black Politics*, (New York: Longman, 1982), p. 20.

34. "For the People," Congressional Black Caucus, Washington, D. C., April-May 1976.

35. "For the People," Congressional Black Caucus, Washington, D. C., June-July 1976,

36. *The Washington Post*, March 31, 1976, p. A13.

37. Almond and Powell, op. cit., pp. 100–108.

Notes to Chapter 5

1. Lawrence Guyot and Mike Thelwell, "Toward Independent Political Power," *Freedomways*, Vol. 6, (Summer 1966), p. 253.

2. Ibid. pp. 253–254.

3. *The Nation*, Vol. 212 (September 27, 1971), p. 265.

4. Ibid.

5. Ibid, p. 266.

6. John Conyers, "A Black Political Strategy for 1972," in Nathan Wright, ed., *What Black Politicians Are Saying*, (New York: Hawthorn Books, 1972).

7. "How the Black Vote Can Elect a President," *Sepia*, (January, 1972), p. 26.

8. *The New York Times*, June 14, 1972, p. 36.

9. "Black Representation Doubles at Democratic National Convention," Press Release, Joint Center for Political Studies, Washington, D. C., June 29, 1972.

10. Michael Preston, Paul Puryear and Lenneal Henderson, Jr., *The New Black Politics*, (New York: Longman, 1982), p. xviii.

11. Ibid, xix.

12. Ibid, p. 21.

13. See also John Kessel, *Presidential Campaign Politics*, Homewood: Dorsey Press, 1980), pp. 8–10.

14. Undated fragment. This article was discovered by Ms. Evelyn Barnett, Moorland Springarn Research Center, Howard University, 1976.

15. *Crisis*, Editorial (October, 1916), pp. 268–269.

16. Chuck Stone, "Black Politics: Third Force, Third Party, or Third-Class Influence?" *The Black Scholar*, Vol. 1 (December, 1969).

17. Chuck Stone, "Black Politics: Participate or Perish," *The Black Collegian*, Vol. 5 (March/April, 1975), p. 41.

18. Hanes Walton, *Black Political Parties*, (New York: Free Press, 1972), p. 204.

19. Matthew Holden, *The Politics of the Black Nation*, (New York: Chandler, 1973), p. 196.

20. Ibid.

21. Milton Morris, *The Politics of Black America* (New York: Harper and Row, 1975), p. 206.

22. Mark Levy and Michael Kramer, *The Ethnic Factor: How America's Minorities Decide Elections*, (New York: Simon and Schuster, 1972), p. 191.

23. Ibid, p. 193.

24. Ibid.

25. Ronald Walters, "Black Presidential Politics in 1980: Bargaining or Begging?" *The Black Scholar*, Vol. 11 (March-April, 1980), pp. 22–31.

26. Kessel, op. cit., p. 63–66.

27. Chuck Stone, op. cit., p. 43.

28. Seymour Martin Lipset, "The American Party System: Concluding Observations," in Lipset, ed., *Party Coalitions in the 1980s*, (San Francisco: Institute for Contemporary Studies, 1981), pp. 427–429.

29. For the voter-candidate issue consistency research, see Herbert Asher, *Presidential Elections and American Politics*, (Homewood: The Dorsey Press, 1980), p. 124; and for Democrat coalition-candidate relationships, see Kessel, op. cit., p. 83.

30. Dina Zinnes, "Coalition Theories and the Balance of Power," in Sven Groennings, E. W. Kekkey, and Michael Lieserson, eds., *The Study of Coalition Behavior*, (New York: Holt Rinehart and Winston, 1970), p. 352.

31. Erving Goffman, *Strategic Interaction*, (Philadelphia: University of Pennsylvania Press, 1969), pp. 100–101.

32. Paul T. Hill, "A Theory of Political Coalitions in Simple and Policy-Making Situations," Sage Professional Paper No. 04–008, (Beverly Hills: Sage Publications, 1973), p. 19.

33. Walters, "Black Presidential Politics in 1980," op. cit., p. 28.

34. Phil Gailey, "Panel of Teachers Union Recommends Endorsement of Mondale," *The New York Times*, September 30, 1983, Sec. I, p. 18.

35. Walter Mondale, Meet the Press, April 7, 1985, Vol. 85, p. 6.

36. Ibid, p. 7. My emphasis.

37. William Keech, "Some Conditions of Negro Influence Over Public Policy Through Voting," in William Crotty, Donald Freeman, and Douglas Gatlin, eds., *Political Parties and Political Behavior*, (Boston: Allyn and Bacon, 1971), p. 542.

Notes to Chapter 6

1. *Malcolm X Speaks*, (Collected Speeches) New York: Grove Press, 1965.

2. Ibid, p. 25.

3. Ibid, p. 38.

4. Ibid, p. 57.

5. Stokeley Carmichael, "Power and Racism: What We Want," Pamphlet, (Boston: New England Free Press, 1966).

6. James Forman, *The Making of Black Revolutionaries*, (New York: Macmillan, 1972), p. 522.

7. Ibid., p. 479.

8. Chuck Stone, *Black Political Power in America*, (New York: Bobbs-Merrill, 1968), pp. 20–21.

9. Imamu Amiri Baraka, ed., *African Congress*, (New York: William Morrow, 1972), p. 139.

10. Ibid, p. 167.

11. Chuck Stone, "Black Politics: Third Force, Third Party, or Third-Class Influence?" *The Black Scholar*, Vol. 1 (December, 1969), p. 11.

12. The writer conducted a workshop on "Launching a Candidacy."

13. Draft Recommendations, writer's notes.

14. Paul Delaney, "Black Political Group Is Facing Problems on Unity and Leaders," *The New York Times*, March 13, 1974, p. 39.

15. Writer's notes.

16. Ibid.

17. Ibid.

18. *Arkansas Democrat*, March 14, 1974, p. 7A.

19. *Arkansas Gazette*, March 18, 1974, p. 1.

20. Ronald Walters, paper, "The '76 Political Strategy," January 1976, unpublished.

21. Pre-convention Memoranda, Press Release, January 9, 1976; Press Release, January 21, 1976, National Black Political Assembly.

22. Amendments to the Charter, NBA - National Black Assembly; NBPC - National Black Political Convention.

23. Press Release, National Black Political Assembly, January 21, 1976, p. A5.

24. "NBPA Effort to Find Nominee," *The Washington Post*, March 20, 1976, p. A5.

25. Speech, Julian Bond, National Black Political Convention, Cincinnati, Ohio, March 20, 1976, writer's notes.

26. Speech, Ronald Dellums, writer's notes. See also, "Dellums Won't Be Candidate," *The Washington Post*, March 21, 1976, p. A13; "Dellums Declines," *The Washington Post*, March 22, 1976, p. A12.

27. "Blacks to Form a Party," *The Times-Picayune*, August 24, 1980, p. 1.

28. "New Political Party Formed As Voice For Minorities," *The New York Times*, August 25, 1980, p. A18.

29. Press Release, National Black Political Assembly, Philadelphia, Pennsylvania, September 4, 1980.

30. Manning Marable, "The Road Toward Effective Black Power," unpublished paper, April 4, 1980; Also, the party Congress eliminated the draft section compromise on electoral politics altogether.

31. *Black Enterprise*, Vol. 16 (August, 1985), p. 100.

236 Black Presidential Politics in America

32. The National Black Election Study, Institute for Social Research, University of Michigan, Ann Arbor, Michigan, 1984.

33. Press Release, Joint Center for Political Studies, Washington, D.C., August 1984.

34. See, for example, James Q. Wilson, *Negro Politics*, (New York: The Free Press, 1965), pp. 221–230, 238. This supposed dichotomy is not static since, apparently, the views of a generation of Black elected officials in the early 1970s were strongly independence-oriented. See, James Conyers and Walter Wallace, *Black Elected Officials*, (New York: The Russell Sage Foundation, 1976), pp. 29–43.

35. Letter, Harold Cruse to Ronald Walters, March 23, 1981, p. 2.

36. "New Politics for Black People," Policy Statement of The National Black Political Assembly, 1979.

37. Ibid, p. 4.

38. Ron Daniels, "The National Black Political Assembly: Building Independent Black Politics in the 1980s," *The Black Scholar*, Vol. 11 (March-April, 1980), pp. 32–33.

39. Frank Smallwood, *The Other Candidates*, (Hanover: University Press of New England, 1983), p. 25. Daniel Mazmanian also suggests that among the four factors which cause the emergence of "significant third parties" is the "rejection or avoidance of the position of the minority by both major parties, causing alienation of the minority." See Daniel Mazmanian, "Third Parties in Presidential Elections," in Jeff Fishel, ed., *Parties and Elections in an Anti-Party Age*, (Bloomington: Indiana University Press, 1978), p. 312.

40. Letter, Harold Cruse to Ronald Walters, op. cit.

Notes to Chapter 7

1. Abdul Alkalimat (Gerald McWorter) and Doug Gillis, "Black Power vs. Racism: Harold Washington Becomes Mayor," in Rod Bush, ed., *The New Black Vote*, (San Francisco: Synthesis Publications, 1984), pp. 53–180.

2. Ronald Walters, "The Emergent Mobilizaton of the Black Community in the Jackson Campaign," in Ronald Walters and Lucius Barker, eds., *The Jesse Jackson Campaign for President of 1984*, University of Illinois Press, Forthcoming.

3. Milton Coleman, "Black Leaders Hear Plan for Key role in Democratic Convention," *The Washington Post*, March 13, 1983, p. A9a.

4. Ron Walters, "Why Blacks Can't Wait," *The Washington Post*, March 25, 1983, p. 22.

5. Milton Coleman, "Black Leaders Hear Plan for Key Role . . . ," op. cit.; Also, "Jackson Has No Chance, Says Coretta King," *The Washington Afro-American*, November 26, 1983.

6. Howell Raines, "Group of Black Leaders Supports Idea of Bid by Blacks for Presidency," *New York Times*, June 21, 1983, Sec. I, p. 1.

7. Victoria Bassetti, "Urban Leaguers Disagree on Black in Race for President," *Times-Picayune*, August 2, 1983, p. 1.

8. Ibid. Vernon Jarrett, a Black Chicago journalist, made this statement.

9. "Should a Black Man Run for President," *Ebony Magazine*, Vol. 38 (October 9, 1983), p. 125.

10. David Garth Poll, *The New York Times*, October 13, 1983, Sec. II. p. 13.

11. Ibid.

12. Ibid.

13. Ibid.

14. Howell Raines, "Pressure on Jesse Jackson," *The New York Times*, June 22, 1983, Sec. I, p. 21.

15. *The New York Times*, October 31, 1983, Sec. I, p. 1.

16. Bill Peterson, "Jackson Woos Black Leaders," *The Washington Post*, November 11, 1983, p. A2.

17. Howell Raines, "Jackson Gets Support Apparently Without Poll of Group," *The New York Times*, December 2, 1983, Sec. II, p. 8.

18. "C.O.G.I.C. Praises Jackson: Hints at Support," *The Challenger*, Buffalo, January 18, 1984.

19. Report of Receipts and Disbursements by an Authorized Committee of a Candidate for the Office of President, FEC Form 3P, Federal Election Commission, Washington, D. C.

20. "State Religious Leaders Endorse Jesse Jackson," Press Release, Jackson for President 1984 Campaign, undated.

21. Mark Skoneki, "South's Churches Preach Politics," *USA Today*, March 12, 1984, p. 3A.

22. David Broder, "Jesse Jackson's Leverage," *The Washington Post*, March 21, 1984, p. A23.

23. *National Leader*, October 6, 1983, p. 5.

24. Bill Peterson, "Jackson Woos Black Leaders," op. cit.

25. *National Leader*, October 6, 1983.

26. "The Quest for a Just Society and a Peaceful World," Speech, the Presidential Announcement of the Reverend Jesse L. Jackson, November 3, 1983.

27. Campaign Policy Papers. As Deputy Campaign Manager for Issues, the writer participated in the development of these issues.

28. James Jackson, Shirley Hatchett, and Ronald Brown, "Attitudes of the Black Electorate Toward the Candidates and Issues in Election 1984," National Black Election Study, Institute for Social Research, University of Michigan, Ann Arbor, Michigan, April 30, 1985.

29. *Congressional Quarterly*, June 16, 1984, p. 1443. See also Eric Pianin, "Jesse Jackson's Rainbow Coalition Displays a Wider Spectrum," *The Washington Post*, May 19, 1984, p. A7a.

30. "Mondale's Primary Weakness Bodes Ill for November Hopes," *Congressional Quarterly*, op. cit., p. 1441.

238   BLACK PRESIDENTIAL POLITICS IN AMERICA

31. Letter, Jesse Jackson to Charles Manatt, December 3, 1983.

32. Ronald Walters, "Unfair Reflection of Minority Participation in Presidential Nominating Process of the Democratic Party," January 1984, unpublished.

33. "Jackson Asks Manatt for Return of Stolen Delegates," *The Washington Post*, April 24, 1984, p. A3a.

34. "Hispanic Leaders Attack Mondale for Skipping Their Conference," *The Washington Post*, April 19, 1984.

35. Gerald Boyd, "Jackson Bids for Black and Hispanic Cooperation," *The New York Times*, April 17, 1984, Sec. I, p. 16.

36. Juan Williams, "Jackson Sees His Backers Holding Victory Margin in November," *The Washington Post*, May 9, 1984, p. A14a.

37. ABC/Washington Post Poll, Study No. 8401, May, 1984.

38. "Aide Says Jackson Influences 6 Million," *Boston Globe*, June 8, 1984.

39. Jackson, Hatchett, and Brown, The National Black Election Study, op. cit.

40. Speech, Jesse Jackson, Operation PUSH Convention, Washington, D. C., May 7, 1984.

41. "Jackson Seeks Talks with Rivals," *Boston Globe*, June 7, 1984.

42. Juan Williams, "Jackson Won't Pledge to Support Mondale," *The Washington Post*, June 7, 1984, p. A15a.

43. Writer's notes, July 10, 1984.

44. Writer's notes, July 19, 1984.

45. (Rainbow Coalition was waiting for the Party), *The New York Times*, July 26, 1984 Sec. I, p. 21; (Rangel's appointment not sufficient), *The New York Times*, July 31, 1984 Sec. I, p. 14; (Jackson reserved the right to criticize Mondale.), *The New York Times*, August 2, 1984 Sec. I, p. 16; (Mondale needed to appoint more minorities.), *The New York Times*, August 10, 1984 Sec. II, p. 5; (Jackson was not aboard the Mondale campaign.), *The New York Times*, August 17, 1984 Sec. I, p. 10.

46. Draft Statement, Joint Center for Political Studies, *Americana Annual Encyclopedia Yearbook*, 1984.

47. "Pride and Prejudice," *Time*, Vol. 123 (May 7, 1984), p. 30.

48. ABC/Washington Post Poll, Study No. 8401, op. cit.

49. Jackson, Hatchett, and Brown, National Black Election Study, op. cit, Post-election Survey, Table 2, unweighted marginals.

50. Draft Statement, *Americana Annual Encyclopedia Yearbook*, Joint Center for Political Studies, Washington, D. C., op. cit.

51. "Black Elected Officials in 1985," *Focus*, Vol. 13, Joint Center for Political Studies, Washington, D. C. 1985 (May 1985), p. 5.

52. Survey, National Rainbow Coalition, Washington, D. C., January, 1985.

53. Raised in Robert Smith and Joseph McCormick, "The Style and Issue Substance of the Jackson Campaign Movement," in Walters and Barker, op. cit.

54. Ronald Walters, "Emergent Mobilization of the Black Community in the Jesse Jackson Campaign for President," in Walters and Barker, op. cit.

Notes to Chapter 8

1. Pearl Robinson, "Whither the Future of Blacks in the Republican Party," *Political Science Quarterly*, Vol. 97 (Summer, 1982), p. 228.

2. Ibid. p. 221.

3. Ernest Hosendolph, Bob Maynard, and Grayson Mitchell, "Blacks and the Grand Old Party," *Black Enterprise*, Vol. 9 (August, 1978), p. 19.

4. Robinson, op. cit., p. 222.

5. Howell Raines, "Conference at the Cabinet Level on the Black Vote," *The New York Times*, November 19, 1982, p. 22.

6. Speech, John E. Jacobs, "Working Together to Make a Difference," National Urban League Convention, San Francisco, California, July 20, 1986.

7. "Falling Behind," Report of the Center on Budget and Policy Priorities, Washington, D. C., 1984.

8. Adam Herbert, "Blacks, Reagan and the Republican Party: Prospects for the 1984 Election," *Election Politics*, Vol. 1 (Summer, 1984), pp. 6–7.

9. J. Clay Smith, Jr., "Blacks and the Right," *The Washington Afro-American*, April 20, 1985, p. 27.

10. Clarence McKee, "Time To Call Time-Out," *The Washington Afro-American*, April 20, 1985, p. 27

11. "Reagan's Handling of Civil Rights," (January 27–30, 1985), *The Gallup Report*, May 1984, No. 224, p. 30. The Washington Post/ABC Poll, raw data, June 1985. These sensational reports neglected to indicate that in 1981 Gallup polls shows Blacks rating Reagan at the 50% approval level "as a person."

12. Warren Miller, Arthur Miller, and Edward Schneider, *American National Election Studies Data Sourcebook, 1952*–1978, (Cambridge: Harvard University Press, 1980). Table 2.68, "Feeling Thermometer for Republicans by Social Group." This data indicates a relatively stable "feeling thermometer" rating by Blacks at a low level for the period indicated above.

13. *The New York Times*, August 16, 1980, p. 2.

14. Jeff Fishel, ed., *Parties and Elections in an Anti-Party Age*, (Bloomington: Indiana University Press, 1978). Also, Walter Dean Burnham, *The Current Crisis in American Politics*, (New York: Oxford University Press, 1982), p. 114.

15. Seymour Martin Lipset, "Party Coalitions and the 1980 Elections," in Seymour Martin Lipset, ed., *Party Coalitions in the 1980s*, (San Francisco: Institute for Contemporary Studies, 1981), pp. 15–46.

16. Wilson Carey McWilliams, "The Meaning of the Election," in

Gerald Pomper, ed., *The Election of 1984*, (Chatham: Chatham House, 1985), pp. 166–171.

17. In the spring of 1985, the Democratic National Committee elected its own Black vice chair, Roland Burris, attorney general of the state of Illinois, in opposition to the choice of the Black Democratic Caucus, Mayor Richard Hatcher.

18. Dom Bonafede, "Kirk at the DNC's Helm," *National Journal*, Vol. 18 (March 2, 1986), p. 705.

19. Ronald Walters, "Racial Polarization in the Election of 1984," *Baltimore Sun*, January 6, 1985, p. 5J. Also, "The Racial Voting Gap Widens," *The Washington Post National Weekly Edition*, November 26, 1984, p. 38.

20. Symposium, "Political Parties and the Nomination Process," Institute of Politics, Kennedy School of Government, Cambridge, Mass., March 1, 1986.

21. *The Washington Post*, March 3, 1986 p. A5a and March 5, p. A16a; also David Broder, Editorial, *The Washington Post*, March 12, 1986, p. A23b.

22. Diane Pinderhughes, "Political Choices: A Realignment in Partisanship Among Black Voters?" *The State of Black America*, (New York: National Black Urban League, January 1984), p. 97.

23. Ibid.

24. Ibid, p. 98.

25. See the comment by Vernon Jarrett in Chapter Seven.

26. Benjamin Hooks said: "There was a supposition that Jesse Jackson couldn't make a viable and serious run. And Jesse Jackson is making a very viable and dynamic bid." "A Conversation with Ben Hooks," *National Scene*, Vol. 53 (July, 1984), p. 20.

27. Samuel Eldersveld, "A Theory of the Political Party," in William J. Crotty, Donald M. Freeman, and Douglas S. Gatlin, eds., *Political Parties and Political Behavior*, 2nd ed. (Boston: Allyn and Bacon, 1971), pp. 36–39.

28. *The New York Times*, July 10, 1984, p. 23.

29. "Voting and Registration in the Election of November 1984," Advance Report, Bureau of the Census, U. S. Department of Commerce, Washington, D. C., January 1985.

30. Spencer Rich, "Number of Elected Hispanic Officials Doubled in a Decade, Study Shows," *The Washington Post*, September 19, 1986, p. A6.

31. CBS/New York Times exit poll, November 1984, raw data.

32. ABC/Washington Post poll, Chilton Research Service, Radnor, Pennsylvania, Study 8401, May 1984.

33. Ronald Walters and Robert Smith, ed., "Reflections on Black Leadership," Special issue, *National Urban League Review*, Vol. 9 (Summer, 1985), (entire).

34. Howard Schuman, Charlotte Steeh, and Lawrence Bobo, *Racial Attitudes in America*, (Cambridge: Harvard University Press, 1985), Table 3.1, p. 74.

35. Robert Smith and Richard Seltzer, "Race and Ideology: Patterns of Issue Differentiation," Paper delivered at the annual meeting of the National Conference of Black Political Scientists, April 1984. (National Opinion Research Center Data base). See also, Thomas Cavanaugh, *Inside Black America: The Message of the Black Vote in the 1984 Election*, (Washington: Joint Center for Political Studies, 1985), pp. 3–10.

36. William Keech, "Some Conditions of Negro Influence Over Public Policy Through Voting," in Crotty, Freeman, and Gatlin, op. cit., p. 538.

37. Martin Delaney was a Harvard-trained Black physician, who was a strong advocate of Black self-determination. Vincent Harding, *There Is A River: The Black Struggle For Freedom In America*, (New York: Harcourt Brace Jovanovich, 1981), p. 186.

Bibliography

Almond, Gabriel, and Bingham Powell. *Comparative Politics: A Developmental Approach.* Boston: Little Brown, 1966.

Asher, Herbert. *Presidential Elections and American Politics.* Homewood: The Dorsey Press, 1980.

Aptheker, Herbert, ed. *A Documentary History of the Negro Peoples in the United States,* 3 vols. New York: Citadel Press, 1977.

Baraka, Imamu. *African Congress.* New York: William Morrow, 1972.

Bluhm, William. *Theories of the Political System.* Englewood Cliffs: Prentice-Hall, 1965.

Bush, Rod, ed. *The New Black Vote.* San Francisco: Synthesis Publications, 1984.

Burham, Walter Dean. *The Current Crisis in American Politics.* New York: Oxford University Press, 1982.

Carson, Clay. *In Struggle: SNCC and the Black Awakening of the 1960s.* Cambridge: Harvard University Press, 1981.

Clotfelter, James, and Charles L. Prysby. *Political Choices: A Study of Elections and Voters.* New York: Holt Rinehart and Winston, 1980.

Crotty, William J., and Gary C. Jacobson. *American Parties in Decline.* Boston: Little Brown, 1980.

DuBois, William Edward Bughardt. *Black Reconstruction in America.* Cleveland: Meridian, 1967.

———. *Dusk of Dawn: An Autobiogrpahy of a Race Concept.* New York: Schoecken, 1968.

Dick, Robert C. *Black Protest: Issues and Tactics.* Westport: Greenwood Press, 1974.

Fishel, Jeff, ed. *Parties and Elections in an Anti-Party Age.* Bloomington: Indiana University Press, 1978.

Forman, James. *The Making of Black Revolutionaries.* New York: Macmillan, 1972.

Goffman, Erving. *Strategic Interaction*. Philadelphia: University of Pennsylvania Press, 1969.

Grantham, Dewey, ed. *Ralph Bunche: The Political Status of the Negro in the Age of FDR*. Chicago: The University of Chicago Press, 1973.

Hamilton, Charles V., ed. *The Black Experience in American Politics*. New York: G. P. Putnam, 1973.

Holden, Matthew, Jr. *The Politics of the Black Nation*. New York: Chandler, 1973.

Farquharson, Robin. *Theory of Voting*. New Haven: Yale University Press, 1969.

Kessel, John. *Presidential Campaign Politics*. Homewood: The Dorsey Press, 1980.

King, Martin Luther, Jr. *Why We Can't Wait*. New York: Mentor, 1964.
——. *Where Do We Go From Here: Chaos or Community?* Boston: Beacon Press, 1968.

Lewis, David L. *King*. Chicago: University of Illinois Press, 1978.

Lewinson, Paul. *Race, Class & Party*. New York: Grosset and Dunlap, 1965.

Levy, Mark, and Michael Kramer. *The Ethnic Factor: How America's Minorities Decide Elections*. New York: Simon and Schuster, 1972.

Lipset, Semour Martin, ed. *Party Coalitions in the 1980s*. San Francisco: Institute for Contemporary Studies, 1981.

Malcolm X Speaks. New York: Grove Press, 1965.

Meier, August, *Negro Thought in America 1880–1915*, The University of Michigan Press, Ann Arbor, 1966.

Moon, Parker Lee, *Balance of Power: The Negro Vote*, Doubleday, New York, 1948.

Morris, Milton, *The Politics of Black America*, Harper and Row, New York, 1975.

Myrdal, Gunnar, *An American Dilemma*, Harper and Row, New York, 1962, 2 Vols.

Neary, John, *Julian Bond: Black Rebel*, Morrow, New York, 1971.

Page, Benjamin, *Choices and Echos in Presidential Elections*, The University of Chicago Press, Chicago, 1978.

Pompers, Gerald, *Voters Choice: Varieties of American Electoral Behavior*, Dodd, Mead and Co., New York, 1972.

Preston, Michael, Paul Puryear, Lenneal Henderson, eds., *The New Black Politics*, Longman, New York, 1982.

Stewart, John, *One Last Chance: The Democratic Party 1974–1976*, Praeger, New York, 1975.

Stone, Chuck, *Black Political Power in America*, Bobbs-Merrill, Indianapolis, 1968.

Sullivan, Dennis, Jeffrey Pressman, Benjamin Page and John Lyons, *The Politics of Representation: The Democratic Convention of 1972*, St. Martins Press, New York, 1974.

Sullivan, Dennis, Jeffrey Pressman, and F. Christopher Arterton, *Explorations in Convention Decision Making: The Democratic Party in the 1970s*, W. H. Freeman and Co., San Francisco, 1976.

Turner, Robert P., *Up To The Front of The Line*, Kennikat, Port Washington, 1975.

Walton, Hanes, Jr., *Black Political Parties*, Free Press, New York, 1972.

——. *Black Politics: A Theoretical and Structural Analysis*. Philadelphia: J. B. Lippincott, 1972.

Wattenberg, Ben, and Richard Scammon. *The Real Majority*. New York: Coward, McCann and Goeghegan, Inc., 1971.

Wright, Nathan. *What Black Politicians Are Saying*. New York: Hawthorn Books, 1972.

Index